Women in Russia and the Soviet Union

An Annotated Bibliography

Women in Russia and the Soviet Union

An Annotated Bibliography

Rochelle Goldberg Ruthchild

G.K. Hall & Co.
An Imprint of Macmillan Publishing Company
New York

Maxwell Macmillan Canada
Toronto

Maxwell Macmillan International
New York   Oxford   Singapore   Sydney

G.K. Hall & Co.
An Imprint of Macmillan Publishing Company
866 Third Avenue
New York, NY 10022

Maxwell Macmillan Canada, Inc.
1200 Eglinton Avenue East
Suite 200
Don Mills, Ontario M3C 3N1

Macmillan Publishing Company is part of the Maxwell Communication Group of Companies

Library of Congress Catalog Card Number: 92-4516

Printed in the United States of America

Printing Number
1   2   3   4   5   6   7   8   9   10

Library of Congress Cataloging-in-Publication Data

Ruthchild, Rochelle Goldberg.
  Women in Russia and the Soviet Union : an annotated
bibliography / Rochelle Ruthchild.
    p.   cm.
  Includes bibliographical references and indexes.
  ISBN 0-8161-8989-7 (alk. paper)
  1. Women—Soviet Union—History—Bibliography.   I. Title.
Z7964.S68R88 1992
  [HQ1662]   92-4516
  016.3054'0947—dc20   CIP

The paper used in this publication meets the minimum requirements of American National Standard for Information Sciences—Permanence of Paper for Printed Library Materials. ANSI Z39.48-1984. ∞ ™

To my parents, Ruth and the late Samuel A. Goldberg

Scientia Potentia Est
Knowledge Is Power

Contents

The Author

Rochelle Goldberg Ruthchild, Professor of Graduate Studies and Director of the Russian School at Norwich University, is a specialist in Russian/Soviet studies. She studied in the Soviet Union for two years on grants from the International Research and Exchanges Board (IREX) and is a Fellow at the Russian Research Center at Harvard University. She is also a founder and served as the first president of the Association for Women in Slavic Studies. Her next project is a book about the feminist movement in prerevolutionary Russia.

Introduction

In terms of women's studies, the Russian/Soviet field is in the early stages of development. Gender-neutral language is rarely used; books on social history and literature routinely omit specific discussion of women or at best provide a few token pages.

Scope

I began by researching works in history, but it soon became clear that the entries could not be restricted to history in the narrow sense. Accordingly, this annotated bibliography comprises a very eclectic group of sources, primarily historical but including anthropology, art, mathematics, literature, and linguistics. No attempt has been made to select certain sources; my aim has been to be inclusive, to show the range of what has been done. The reader will find listings of works with brief but significant information about gender as well as those specifically focused on women.

Categories

The question of periodization has been raised by women's studies scholars in other fields.[1] So far there has been no serious challenge to traditional periodization from women's studies scholars in Russian/Soviet studies. As much as possible, I have kept to traditional demarcations of historical periods. I have limited the categories to a consistent few in the time periods (1855–1917,

1. See Joan Kelly's pathbreaking essay "Did Women Have a Renaissance?" in her *Women, History, and Theory* (Chicago: University of Chicago Press, 1984), pp. 19–50. Reprinted from *Becoming Visible: Women in European History* (Boston: Houghton Mifflin, 1977).

1918–1991) for which there are the most entries. The author, title, and subject indexes are meant to aid in the location of listed sources. In a number of cases, particularly in the twentieth century, the life and work of political and literary figures stretch over two of the time periods. Generally, I have placed autobiographies and collections of their work in the first time period in which they gained prominence. For example, all collections of Anna Akhmatova's poetry are listed in the Reform, Reaction, and Revolutions section. Only those memoirs and biographies that discuss Akhmatova's activities during the Soviet period are listed in the section on that period. An exception is made in the case of Aleksandra Kollontai, to whom a separate section is devoted.

The word *index* appears at the end of each entry for a work that contains an index.

Transliteration

No attempt has been made to standardize transliteration in listings. To do so would invite confusion, as transliterations in book and journal article titles cannot be changed. However, each author and subject name is indexed according to one spelling; where necessary, alternate spellings are cross-listed.

Dissertations

A special effort has been made to include dissertations, as too many valuable studies in this field have never been published. Given the limited number of monographs about significant subjects or historical figures in our field, dissertations are an important source of information, especially for those doing their research primarily or solely in English.

Uses

This bibliography is intended to aid students, teachers, and scholars in the field of Russian/Soviet studies. A quick perusal of this book will show that there has been an increase in the number of articles and books about women in Russia and the Soviet Union published in recent years. It is my hope that the current work will help identify areas for further study and stimulate research, teaching, and learning about this subject.

Acknowledgments

I am very grateful to G. K. Hall, specifically to Borgna Brunner, Lee Ripley, and Henriette Campagne, for giving me the opportunity and challenge to embark on this project, and to Catherine Carter and Michael Sander for being patient about its completion.

No bibliography like this is completed without the help and support of many people. Thanks go to Esther Kingston-Mann, Deborah Pearlman, Elizabeth Wood, and Heather Hogan for their faith in me and this project, and to Ruth Dudgeon, Brenda Meehan, Roberta Manning, Tim Mixter, Charlotte Rosenthal, and Lynne Viola for bibliographic suggestions and general support. Barbara Heldt, Martha Bohachevsky-Chomiak, Barbara Norton, and Norma Noonan provided helpful advice at different stages of this project. Mary Zirin, with her pioneering bibliographic work in the field provided inspiration and important critical feedback in the final stages. This help and support not withstanding, I am responsible for any errors of fact and interpretation that remain in this bibliography.

A Dana Faculty Research grant and a Research and Publication grant, both from Norwich University, supported parts of my work. I am grateful to the Russian Research Center of Harvard University for granting me the affiliation as Fellow that made more accessible the rich and varied Harvard collections at the Widener, Schlesinger, and Russian Research Center libraries. Susan Gardos, Russian Research Center librarian, was as always very helpful. Norwich University librarian Paula Arnold aided in computer searches and especially in locating dissertations in this field. Norwich's chief librarian, Paul Heller, gave critical support. The staff at the Library of Congress were unfailingly courteous and professional.

The Norwich University Graduate Program Core Faculty continues to provide a very special colleagueship. Special thanks to Loriann Lajeunesse and Ted Smith of the Russian School for their unfailingly positive attitudes and support in thousands of ways. Without De Larson's efficient typing and general assistance this project would not have been possible. Carl Hooker aided in early printing efforts. My brother Steve's wisecracks kept things in perspective. Judy

Fisch and Ann Crisafulli helped. Vicki Gabriner gave valuable support in the later stages. Stan Kaplan is now critically responsible for the birth of two creations in my life; in this case his vast computer mavenry was indispensable to the successful completion of this project. Last but not least, my son Rafael patiently endured the countless hours devoted to the never-ending bibliography with grace and good humor.

References and General Bibliographies

1 *American Bibliography of Slavic and East European Studies*. Edited by J.T. Shaw (1956–1958); J.T. Shaw and David Djaparidze (1959); J.T. Shaw, Albert C. Todd, and Stephen Viederman (1960); Albert C. Todd and Stephen Viederman (1961–1962); Fritz T. Epstein, Albert C. Todd, and Stephen Viederman (1963); Fritz T. Epstein (1964–1966); Kenneth E. Naylor (1967–1969; published in 1972); James P. Scanlan (1970–1972; published in 1974); David H. Kraus (1973–1979); Zenon E. Kohut (1980–1981); Roberta W. Goldblatt (1982–1985); Barbara L. Dash (1986–1988). Bloomington: Indiana University Press, 1957–1966; Columbus: Ohio State University Press, 1972–1976; Chicago: American Association for the Advancement of Slavic Studies, 1977; Stanford, Calif.: American Association for the Advancement of Slavic Studies, 1978 to present. Published annually from 1956–1967; one volume each for 1968–1969 and 1970–1972; and annually from 1973 to present. Author and subject indexes.

Comprehensive listing, including books, book reviews, articles/sections in books, journal articles, review articles, and dissertations. From 1989, includes a Women's Studies category (in Sociology section). Very useful bibliography.

2 DOSSICK, JESSE JOHN. *Doctoral Research on Russia and the Soviet Union*. New York: New York University Press, 1960. 248 pp. Index.

List of dissertations divided into subject-matter categories.

3 ———. *Doctoral Research on Russia and the Soviet Union, 1960–1975: A Classified List of 3,150 American, Canadian Dissertations and Statistical Analysis*. Garland Reference Library of Social Science, vol. 7. New York: Garland, 1976, 345 pp.

Continues Dossick's earlier work (entry 2).

4 *Great Soviet Encyclopedia: A Translation of the Third Edition*. 31 vols. New York: Macmillan, 1975–1983. Index.

Entries on the women's movement in Russia and the Soviet Union, the woman

1

question, the journals *Rabotnitsa* (Woman worker) and *Soviet Woman*, and the *Zhenotdely* (Women's Sections of the Party), *Zhensovety* (Women's Councils), and Krupskaia (Lenin's wife and an important educational theorist) are the chief ones relating to women. Contributions by Soviet scholars assert that the "emancipation of women in socialist countries has, on the whole, been achieved." Highly critical of "bourgeois feminism."

   5   GRIERSON, PHILIP. *Books on Soviet Russia, 1917–1942*. London: Methuen, 1943. 354 pp. Index.
Pages 265–67 list books under the heading "Woman in the USSR," with succinct comments about each.

   6   HORAK, STEPHAN M. *Russia, the USSR, and Eastern Europe: A Bibliographic Guide to English Language Publications, 1964–1974*. Edited by Rosemary Neiswender. Littleton, Colo.: Libraries Unlimited, 1978. 488 pp.
The category "Women, Family, Youth" contains two entries on women and one on the family. Several entries on women in literature are listed. In all, meager pickings in a list of 1,611 publications. Annotations written by various scholars.

   7   ———. *Russia, the USSR, and Eastern Europe: A Bibliographic Guide to English Language Publications, 1975–1980*. Littleton, Colo.: Libraries Unlimited, 1982. 279 pp. Index.
Eleven entries are listed in the index under "Women in Russia and the Soviet Union," reflecting a bit more writing about women in this period. Total of 1,027 works listed, including monographs. Annotations culled mostly from book reviews.

   8   ———. *Russia, the USSR, and Eastern Europe: A Bibliographic Guide to English Language Publications, 1981–1985*. Edited by Rosemary Neiswender. Littleton, Colo.: Libraries Unlimited, 1987. 273 pp.
Six entries on women in a total of 1,035 listings.

   9   HORECKY, PAUL L. *Russia and the Soviet Union: A Bibliographic Guide to Western-Language Publications*. Chicago: University of Chicago Press, 1965. 473 pp. Index.
Entries on women and family, education and research, demography, labor, and folklore. Annotations written by different scholars on a wide variety of subjects. Total of 1,950 listings.

   10   HYER, JANET. *Women in Russia and the Soviet Union*. Institute of Soviet and East European Studies. Bibliography no. 3, suppl. 1. Ottawa: Carleton University, 1988. 40 pp. Subject and name indexes.
Supplement to the Yedlin/Wilman bibliography (entry 14).

11   IGNASHEV, DIANE M. NEMEC, and SARAH KRIVE. *Women and Writing in Russia and the USSR: A Bibliography of English-Language Sources.* New York and London: Garland, 1992. 328 pp. Index.
A massive listing of sources by and about women writers, but also including shorter sections on "Women's Art in Overview," "Images of Women," "Education," "Health and Medicine," "Law," "Military," "Mothering: Childbearing, Childrearing, Family, and Marriage," "National Identity and Ethnic Identification," "Politics," "Prison and Labor Camps," "Religion and Spirituality," "Rural Communities," "Work," "Interviews, Journals, and First-Hand Accounts," "Status of Women: Overviews," and "Yearbooks and Statistical Reports." Listings not annotated.

12   MANNING, ROBERTA T. "Bibliography of Works in English on Women in Russia and the Soviet Union: A Guide for Students and Teachers." *Slavic and East European Education Review* 1 (1979): 31–62.
The first annotated bibliography on this subject to appear in English. Though much has been written since 1979, still useful. Wide-ranging choice of sources.

13   WIECZYNSKI, JOSEPH L., ed. *The Modern Encyclopedia of Russian and Soviet History*, vols. 1–54. Gulf Breeze, Fl.: Academic International Press, 1976–1990. Title index at the end of each volume.
Excellent resource. Articles on women's movements, status of women, women's organizations, and individual women activists and writers by American and Soviet scholars.

14   YEDLIN, TOVA, and J. WILMAN. *Women in Russia and the Soviet Union.* Institute of Soviet and East European Studies. Bibliography no. 3. Ottawa: Carleton University, 1985. 80 pp. Author index.
Massive alphabetical listing of books, pamphlets, and articles in Russian, English, and French. Some with brief annotations.

15   ZIRIN, MARY, ed. *Women East-West.* Newsletter of the Association for Women in Slavic Studies. Published five times a year.
Each issue contains current bibliographic listings. A very informative source.

16   ———. *Women, Gender and Family in the Soviet Union and Central/East Europe: Preliminary Bibliography.* Altadena, Calif.: Mary Zirin. Continuously updated.
Far-ranging bibliography by the editor of *Women East-West.* The November 1990 edition (67 pages) is divided into sections on the following topics: bibliographies and reviews of the literature, prerevolutionary history and culture; Soviet society, 1917–1985; contemporary society; Russian and Soviet literature; and arts in Russia and the USSR. Also contains sections on Central and Eastern Europe. Some entries annotated; most unannotated.

General Works

17 ATKINSON, DOROTHY, ALEXANDER DALLIN, and GAIL WARSHOFSKY LAPIDUS. *Women in Russia*. Stanford, Calif.: Stanford University Press, 1977. 410 pp. Index.

One of several excellent books published toward the end of the seventies, marking a great leap forward in the study of women in Russia and the USSR. The papers included in this volume, mostly about the Soviet period, were initially presented at the Women in Russia conference at Stanford in 1975. Contributions include the following: Dorothy Atkinson on a historical overview from the Amazons to the Soviets, Richard Stites on women and the intelligentsia, Rose Glickman on factory women from 1880 to 1914, Alfred Meyer on Marxism and the women's movement, Gail Warshofsky Lapidus on sexual equality and Soviet policy, Beatrice Farnsworth on the 1926 Marriage Law debate, Ethel Dunn on rural women, Michael Paul Sacks on female industrial workers, Norton Dodge on professional women, Janet Chapman on wage equality, Peter Juviler on sex, women, and Soviet law, Richard Dobson on educational policy, Mollie Schwartz Rosenhan on images of the sexes in Soviet children's readers, Bernice Madison on social services for women, Joel Moses on women's political participation, Jerry Hough on women's participation and women's issues in Soviet policy debates, and Colette Shulman on the conflict between the individual and the collective for women.

18 ELNETT, ELAINE PASVOLSKY. *Historic Origin and Social Development of Family Life in Russia*. Preface by Franklin Giddings. New York: Columbia University Press, 1926. 151 pp. (2d ed., 1927.) Bibliography.

The only treatment of this topic in English. Anecdotal survey relying on peasant proverbs. Includes excerpts from the *Domostroi* (the proscriptive manual for patriarchal family relations) and discussion of Ivan the Terrible's brutality toward women. Relies heavily on Shashkov's *History of Russian Women*, a key work that needs an English translator.

19   ENGEL, BARBARA ALPERN. "Engendering Russia's History." *Slavic Review* 51, no. 2 (Summer 1992): 309–21.

Engel reviews "major themes" in recently published scholarship about women in Russia and the Soviet Union. She traces the evolution from "contribution" history to a more multi-faceted, diverse approach, challenging notions about the universality of male experience. While a gender perspective is still new for Russian and Soviet historians in the West and even more so in the former Soviet Union, it provides the opportunity for exploring new approaches to historical research and the question of historical change.

20   FIENE, DONALD M. "What is the Appearance of Divine Sophia?" *Slavic Review* 48, no. 3 (Fall 1989): 449–76.

Fiene discusses, describes, and categorizes "all the known types of Sophia icons." Claims for the divinity of Sophia, pressed by such thinkers as Vladimir Solov'ev and Sergei Bulgakov, have been rejected by the Orthodox church. The church's position is that Jesus Christ is the true Sophia. In practice, iconographic images of Sophia show a variety of representations of her place in the Orthodox pantheon.

21   GRAY, FRANCINE DU PLESSIX. "The Russian Heroine: Gender, Sexuality and Freedom." "Perestroika and Soviet Culture" issue, edited by Jane Burbank and William G. Rosenberg. *Michigan Quarterly Review* 27, no. 4 (Fall 1989): 699–718.

Gray argues that "Russian fiction is the only one that has not been profoundly marked by the female imagination." She cites comparative differences in the status of Russian women, the influence of Russian Orthodoxy, and the *Domostroi* as possible factors. Images of women in nineteenth-century Russian and twentieth-century Soviet prose fiction are briefly surveyed. Gray concludes by acknowledging the contributions of contemporary Soviet women writers who, she argues, "have greatly feminized Russian letters." Many of the themes of her book *Soviet Women* (entry 539) are previewed here. Like that book, this essay is marred by problems of inaccuracy and superficiality (e.g., Gray incorrectly identifies Karolina Pavlova as Alexandra Pavlova).

22   HELDT, BARBARA. "Russian Literature." In *Women in Print I: Opportunities for Women's Studies in Language and Literature*, edited by Joan E. Hartman and Ellen Messer-Davidow, pp. 149–54. New York: MLA Publications, 1982. Bibliography by Sandra Thomson, pp. 155–57.

Brief overview of the state of the field, including a critique of theories of "strong woman" as a type. Bibliography includes works in Russian and English.

23 HUBBS, JOANNA. *Mother Russia: The Feminine Myth in Russian Culture*. Bloomington: Indiana University Press, 1988. 302 pp. Index. Bibliography.

An ambitious and wide-ranging work, tracing the symbolism of Mother Russia in folk tradition and religion, both pagan and Christian. Argues for the staying power and strength of female images in Russian language, literature, and culture. This provocative and controversial book has been criticized for errors in scholarship and interpretation. Nevertheless, Hubbs's thesis is compelling and deserves more study.

24 KARLINSKY, SIMON. "Russia's Gay Literature and History (11th–20th centuries)." *Gay Sunshine: A Journal of Gay Liberation*, no. 29/30 (Summer/Fall 1976): 1–7.

The only survey of this subject yet published. Discusses male homosexuality for the most part, but includes some information about lesbians, most notably the poet Sophia Parnok, for a time the lover of Marina Tsvetaeva. Two of Parnok's poems are translated here.

25 LINCOLN, W. BRUCE. *The Romanovs: Autocrats of all the Russias*. New York: Dial, 1981. 852 pp. Index. Bibliography.

This massive work is the product of extensive research, including some conducted in the Soviet archives. Good but brief summaries of the reigns of Anna, Elizabeth, and Catherine. Touches on many of the key historiographic debates about eighteenth-century Russia. Next to nothing about women's status or gender issues. One-fifth of the book devoted to the reign of Nicholas II. Accepts notion that Nicholas was dominated by his wife ("it was submission, not equality, that she demanded").

26 MADISON, BERNICE. "Russia's Illegitimate Children before and after the Revolution." *Slavic Review* 22, no. 1 (March 1963): 82–95.

Covers state policies toward "shameful" children, from the reign of Peter the Great to the Soviet period. Early examination of this subject and the system of foundling homes first established by Catherine II to address this problem. Discusses radical shift in policy after the Revolution, with abolition of status of illegitimacy (reinstated in 1944); wartime losses of men; growth in number of single mothers.

27 MOSELEY, PHILIP. "The Russian Family: Old Style and New." In *Essays by Philip E. Moseley and Essays in His Honor*, edited by Robert Byrnes, pp. 70–84. Notre Dame, Ind.: University of Notre Dame Press.

Basic survey of the subject. General framework.

28 RAEFF, MARK, ed. *Plans for Political Reform in Imperial Russia, 1730–1905*. Englewood Cliffs, N.J.: Prentice-Hall, 1966. 159 pp. Bibliography.

Plans and projects ranging from the resolution of the 1730 succession crisis that led to Empress Anna's accession to the throne, to Panin's proposals to Catherine the Great, to the project for the Bulygin duma in 1905.

29 ROSENTHAL, CHARLOTTE, and MARY ZIRIN. "Russian Women Writers." In *Bloomsbury Guide to Women Writers*, edited by Kate Newman. London: Bloomsbury, 1992.
Survey of the major themes and trends in Russian women's writing. One hundred seventy-five entries on individual writers, works, and topics. Bibliographies at the end of each entry. A significant aid to research and to the recognition of the work of these women writers.

30 SELIVANOVA, NINA NIKOLAEVNA. *Russia's Women*. New York: E. P. Dutton, 1923. Reprint. Westport, Conn.: Hyperion, 1975. 226 pp.
The history of Russian women from ancient times to the first years of Soviet rule. Information about many now-forgotten women writers and political activists.

31 SENYK, SOPHIA. *Women's Monasteries in Ukraine and Belorussia to the Period of Suppressions*. Rome: Pontificium Institutum Studiorum Orientalium, 1983. 235 pp. Index. Bibliography.
Seeks to remedy the complete lack of attention by scholars of Ukrainian church history to women's monasteries. Covers Ukraine and Belorussia, primarily during the seventeenth and eighteenth centuries. Includes a list of all the women's monasteries in the region studied, with a brief history of each.

32 TERRAS, VICTOR, ed. *Handbook of Russian Literature*. New Haven, Conn.: Yale University Press, 1985. Index.
Useful reference work. Entries for individual women writers and section on women and Russian literature. Many important omissions.

33 WEBER, HARRY B., ed. *Modern Encyclopedia of Russian and Soviet Literatures*. Gulf Breeze, Fla.: Academic International Press, 1977–present. Index at end of each volume. Bibliographical References.
Volumes one to nine (last entry Holovko) are in print and include information about many Russian and Soviet women writers.

34 WEINER, LEO. *Anthology of Russian Literature from the Earliest Period to the Present Time*. 2 vols. New York: G. P. Putnam's Sons, 1902–1903. Vol. 1, 447 pp.; vol. 2, 500 pp. Index in each volume.
Volume 1 covers the period from the tenth to the end of the eighteenth century; volume 2 covers the nineteenth century. Volume 1 contains excerpts from the *Domostroi* (such as, "The Wife is always and in all Things to Take Counsel with her Husband").

35   *The Woman Question: Selections from the Writings of Karl Marx, V. I.
     Lenin, Friedrich Engels and Joseph Stalin*. New York: International
     Publishers, 1951. 96 pp. Bibliography.

Excerpts from the writings of the forefathers of the Bolshevik Revolution and
of Stalin. Tellingly, only a very thin volume about women could be culled from
the voluminous writings and speeches of these men. Besides the more familiar
passages from Marx and Engels, excerpts include two letters from Lenin to
Inessa Armand on free love, Lenin on the right to divorce, and Stalin on
women collective farmers.

Folk and Peasant Culture

36 AFANAS'EV, ALEXANDER. *Russian Fairy Tales*. Translated by Norbert Guterman. Commentary by Roman Jakobson. New York: Pantheon, 1945 (2d ed., 1973). 662 pp. Index.
Classic compilation by the Russian Grimm. Afanas'ev (1826–71) began publishing collected tales in 1866. The tales contain many standard characters and themes, including fair princess, pretty maiden, unfaithful wife, clever girl, wise woman, warrior maiden, Baba Yaga, woman as evil, man saves beautiful maiden, and man beats wife. By far the most complete source in English.

37 ALEXANDER, ALEX E. *Bylina and Fairy Tale: The Origins of Russian Heroic Poetry*. The Hague: Mouton, 1973. 162 pp. Index.
Argues that the *bylina*—the Russian oral epic—evolved from the fairy tale. In general, describes the role of women only in relation to male heroes.

38 ———. *Russian Folklore: An Anthology in English Translation*. Belmont, Mass: Nordland, 1975. 400 pp.
Contains ceremonial poetry, wedding ceremonials and chants, funeral laments, charms, proverbs, folktales, *byliny*, historical songs, ballads, religious verses, songs of serfdom, love lyrics, and *chastushki*.

39 ARANT, PATRICIA. *Compositional Techniques of the Russian Oral Epic, the Bylina*. New York: Garland, 1990. 192 pp.
Reprint of Arant's dissertation, with a new preface. Argues for the formulaic nature of the composition and performance of the *bylina*. Some linguistic analysis, some analysis of sample byliny.

40 BALZER, MARJORIE MANDELSTAM. "Rituals of Gender Identity: Markers of Siberian Khanty Ethnicity, Status and Belief." *American Anthropologist* 83, no. 4 (December 1981): 855–58.
Description of menstrual taboos and of rituals pertaining to birth, naming, and marriage among the Khanty, who believe female power to grow with age.

Explores interaction between male dominance and female independence. Good discussion of roots of female conservatism in traditional societies.

41 BENET, SULA, ed. and trans. *The Village of Viriatino*. Garden City, N.Y.: Anchor Books, 1970. 300 pp. Index.

Translation of this pioneering work on one of the first community studies done in the USSR, under the direction of P. I. Kushner. Contains chapters written by nine specialists. Discusses economic life, family life, culture, education, social life, dress, and architecture of a village in Tambov Province before and after the Revolution. A very valuable source of information about Russian village life and its continuities and changes. Shows changes in standard of living and expectations after the Revolution, and ways in which women's roles were altered legally and economically.

42 CAREY, BONNIE, trans. and adapt., *Baba Yaga's Geese and Other Russian Stories*. Bloomington: Indiana University Press, 1973. 128 pp.

Russian folktales; some riddles also included. Brief but helpful introduction. Aimed at young readers.

43 ———. "Typological Models of the Heroine in the Russian Fairy Tale." Ph.D. diss., University of North Carolina at Chapel Hill, 1983. 217 pp.

Carey has done pioneering work in applying gender analysis to Russian fairy tales, folk tales, and oral traditions. Her most extensive discussion of the subject.

44 CHADWICK, NORA KERSHAW. *Russian Heroic Poetry*. Cambridge: Cambridge University Press, 1932. 294 pp.

Epic songs and poetry dating from ancient times in Kiev and Novgorod to the mid-nineteenth century.

45 COXWELL, C. FILLINGHAM, ed. and trans. *Siberian Folktales: Primitive Literature of the Empire of the Tsars*. London: C. W. Daniel, 1925. 1,056 pp. Index. Reprint. New York: AMS Press, 1983.

Folktales of various ethnic groups and tribes of the Russian Empire, including the Chukchis, Yukaghirs, Gilyaks, Tungus, Buryats, Kalmucks, Yakuts, Altaians, Tarantchi-Tatars, Yellow Ugurs, Kirghiz, Turkomans, Chuvash, Kumuks, Gagauzy, Bashkirs, Georgians, Samoyeds, Ostyaks, Cheremisses, Mordovians, Votyaks, Lapps, Finns, Estonians, Letts, Lithuanians, Poles, Ossetians, Armenians, Darvash, Russians, White Russians, and Ukrainians (or, as they are called in this book, Little Russians).

46 DUNN, STEPHEN PORTER, and ETHEL DUNN. *The Peasants of Central Russia*. New York: Holt, Rinehart & Winston, 1967. 139 pp. Glossary. Bibliography.

See entry 47.

47 ———. *The Peasants of Central Russia*. Prospect Heights, Ill.: Waveland
    Press, 1988. 147 pp.
Reissue, with an introduction by the authors assessing the changes wrought by
Gorbachev, critiquing Sula Benet's *Village of Viriatino*, and responding to critiques by Soviet and Western scholars. Sections on the family and the position
of women especially useful.

48 FARNSWORTH, BEATRICE. "The Soldatka: Folklore and Court
    Record." *Slavic Review* 49, no. 1 (Spring 1990): 58–73.
Explores the role of the *soldatka* (soldier's wife), "the most vulnerable member
of the peasant household," comparing a variety of sources, such as folk laments
and postemancipation court records. Shows the marginalization of these
women once their husbands had left for twenty-five years of military service.
Imaginative use of sources to show how *soldatki* lamented and resisted their
place in the peasant household.

49 HAPGOOD, ISABEL FLORENCE. *The Epic Songs of Russia*.
    Introductory note by Professor Francis J. Child. New York: Charles
    Scribner's Sons, 1886. 358 pp. 2d ed. Introductory note by J. W.
    Mackail. New York: Charles Scribner's Sons, 1916. Reprint. New York:
    Kraus Reprint Co., 1969. 281 pp.
The first collection of *byliny* in English.

50 IVANITS, LINDA. *Russian Folk Belief*. Armonk, N.Y.: M. E. Sharpe,
    1989. 257 pp. Index.
Helpful survey of the subject, influenced by the work of Felix J. Oinas.
Although the author provides information about peasant women, she makes no
attempt at gender analysis of the material presented.

51 KELLY, CATRIONA. Petrushka: The Russian carnival Puppet
    Theatre. Cambridge: Cambridge University Press, 1990. 292 pp. Index.
    Bibliography.
Bakhtin-influenced examination of the traditional puppet play *Petrushka*, with
its stereotyped sex roles.

52 LESHCHENKO, V. IU. "The Position of Women in the Light of
    Religious-Domestic Taboos among the East Slavic Peoples in the
    Nineteenth and Early Twentieth Centuries." *Soviet Anthropology and
    Archaeology* 17, no. 3 (Winter 1978–79): 22–40.
This translated article enumerates taboos such as those about spinning, weaving, agriculture, pregnancy, and birth, as reflected in church rituals and everyday life.

53   MATOSSIAN, MARY KILBOURNE. "The Peasant Way of Life." In
     The Peasant in Nineteenth Century Russia, edited by Wayne Vucinich,
     pp. 1–40. Stanford: Stanford University Press, 1968. Index.
     Bibliography.
Very informative about the specifics of Russian village life around 1860, right
before the emancipation of the serfs. Describes basic plan of peasant houses,
food, dress, family structure, everyday life, play, wedding customs, holidays,
and the peasant economy.

54   ——. "In the Beginning, God Was a Woman." *Journal of Social History*
     6 (Spring 1973): 325–43.
In Russian folk culture, sexist proverbs coexist side by side with strong rem-
nants of goddess worship, as in the cult of Paraskeva Piatnitsa. Matossian
argues that the mother goddess was the original model for the "strong woman"
motif in Russian literature.

55   OINAS, FELIX J. *Essays on Russian Folklore and Mythology*. Columbus,
     Ohio: Slavica, 1984. 183 pp. Index.
Although no essay explicitly focuses on women or gender in folktales, useful
bits of information are scattered throughout.

56   OINAS, FELIX J., and STEPHEN SOUDAKOFF, eds. and trans. *The
     Study of Russian Folklore*. The Hague: Mouton, 1975. 341 pp. Index.
Translations of key essays by Russian and Soviet scholars.

57   POTAPOV, LEONID PAVLOVICH. *The Peoples of Siberia*. Translated
     by Scripta Technica. Translation edited by Stephen P. Dunn. Chicago:
     University of Chicago Press, 1964. 948 pp. Bibliography.
Translation of an encyclopedic work published in 1956 by the Russian
Academy of Science. Includes historical background, documentation of oral
tradition, and descriptions of everyday life and the incredible variety of peoples
and traditions of this vast region.

58   RALSTON, WILLIAM RALSTON SHEDDEN. *The Songs of the
     Russian People, as Illustrative of Slavonic Mythology and Russian Social Life*.
     London: Ellis and Green, 1872. Reprint. New York: Haskell House,
     1970. 447 pp. Index.
Covers mythology, folktales (including the Baba Yaga tales), mythic and ritual
songs, marriage and funeral songs, sorcery, and witchcraft.

59   ——. *Russian Folktales*. London: Smith, Elder, 1873. Reprint. New
     York: Arno, 1977. 382 pp. Index.
Translated tales taken from the collections published by Afanas'ev, Khudiakov,
ErlenVein, Chudinsky, and Rudchenko. Includes a discussion of the character
Baba Yaga.

60 REEDER, ROBERTA, ed. and trans. *Down along the Mother Volga: An Anthology of Russian Folk Lyrics*. Introductory essay by V. Ja. Propp. Philadelphia: University of Pennsylvania Press, 1975. 246 pp. Index.

Translation of Propp's *The Russian Folk Lyric* (1961), as well as selected lyrics from Propp's anthology *Lyric Folk Songs*, supplemented by selections from I. I. Zemcovskii's *The Poetry of Peasant Festivals* and N. P. Kolpakova's *Lyrics of the Russian Wedding*. A useful addition to the literature on a subject that deserves much further study.

61 SHELLEY, GERARD, trans. *Folktales of the Peoples of the Soviet Union*. London: Herbert Jenkins, 1945. 139 pp.

Contains "Vassilissa the Wise" (Russian) and "The Three Daughters" (Tatar), among other tales.

62 SOKOLOV, IURII M. *Russian Folklore*. Translated by Catherine Ruth Smith. New York: Macmillan, 1950. Reprints. Hatboro, Pa.: Folklore Associates, 1966; Detroit, Mich.: Folklore Associates, 1971. 760 pp. Index.

An excellent source of information about all kinds of prerevolutionary folklore, including wedding and funeral ceremonies, divinations, charms, proverbs, *byliny*, folktales, religious verses, historical songs, plays, lyric songs, *chastushki*, popular songs, and folklore of the factory. Also discusses Soviet folklore, including that of non-Russian peoples.

63 WARNER, ELIZABETH. *The Russian Folk Theatre*. The Hague: Mouton, 1977. 257 pp. Index.

Discussion of various aspects of the topic, including the marriage ritual, non-ritual drama, puppet theaters, and folk actors.

64 WOROBEC, CHRISTINE. "Victims or Actors? Russian Peasant Women and Patriarchy." In *Peasant Economy, Culture and Politics in European Russia, 1800–1921*, edited by Esther Kingston-Mann and Timothy Mixter, pp. 177–206. Princeton, N.J.: Princeton University Press, 1991.

Marriage and the Russian peasant woman in the central agricultural and industrial provinces of European Russia. Examination of a variety of sources, from economic, demographic, and court records to folklore. Argues that peasant women did not openly rebel against the patriarchal system, because of their commitment to the preservation of the peasant family and community.

The Ancient and
Medieval Periods to 1682

65 BARON, SAMUEL. *The Travels of Olearius in Seventeenth-Century Russia*. Translated and edited by Samuel H. Baron. Stanford, Calif.: University Press, 1967. 349 pp. Index.

Describes life in the terem (separate women's quarters in wealthy medieval Russian homes), marriage ceremonies, divorce, and social and dress customs.

66 CHALLIS, NATALIA. "Glorification of Saints in the Orthodox Church." *Russian History* 7, pts. 1–2 (1980): 239–46.

Describes the process for selection and glorification of female and male saints in the Orthodox church.

67 CONYBEARE, FREDERICK C. *Russian Dissenters*. Cambridge: Harvard University Press, 1921. 370 pp. Bibliography.

Discusses the position of women in the religious sects, attitudes toward marriage, and relations between the sexes in radical groups such as the Molokanye, Dukhobors, and Bezpopovtsy.

68 CROSS, SAMUEL, and OLGERD P. SHERBOWITZ-WETZOR, eds. and trans. *The Russian Primary Chronicle*. Laurentian text. Cambridge, Mass.: Medieval Academy of America, 1953. 313 pp. Index.

Contains descriptions of the status of women in Slavic tribes, the exploits of Princess Olga, and women in early Russia.

69 DEWEY, HORACE W., ed. and trans. *Muscovite Judicial Texts, 1488–1556*. Michigan Slavic Materials no. 7. Ann Arbor: Dept. of Slavic Languages and Literatures, University of Michigan, 1966. 94 pp. Glossary.

Laws affecting women of all classes.

70   DEWEY, HORACE W., and ANN M. KLEIMOLA, eds. and trans. *Russian Private Law, XIV–XVII Centuries: An Anthology of Documents*. Michigan Slavic Materials, no. 9. Ann Arbor: Dept. of Slavic Languages and Literatures, University of Michigan, 1973. 260 pp. Index.
Documents from old Russian lawsuits, including information about wife beating, widows, and slave and peasant women.

71   FLETCHER, GILES. *Of the Russe Commonwealth*. Introduction by Richard Pipes. Cambridge, Mass.: Harvard University Press, 1966. 212 pp. Glossary. Index.
Queen Elizabeth sent Giles Fletcher to Russia in 1588 to reestablish trade relations. His impressions include descriptions of the dress, wedding celebrations, and customs of the Tatar, Siberian, and Russian peoples.

72   GROSSMAN, JOAN DELANEY. "Feminine Images in Old Russian Literature and Art." *California Slavic Studies* 11 (1980): 33–70.
Portrayal of women in medieval art (which almost always had a religious theme), including embroidery, and in written and oral literature, including *byliny* and *skazki* (fairy tales). Argues for recognition of a Russian tradition distinct from that of the West.

73   HALPERIN, CHARLES J., ed. "Women in Medieval Russia" (special issue). Introduction by Charles J. Halperin. *Russian History* 10, pt. 2 (1983): 139–242.
Excellent issue; brings together research by top scholars in the field. The lead article, by Gail Lenhoff, discusses the "Tale of Moses the Hungarian" and its representation of the wayward woman. Eve Levin analyzes the actual (not perceived) status of women in Novgorod, arguing that women had extensive property rights but little political power. Nancy Shields Kollmann studies the ramifications of the seclusion of elite Muscovite women and argues for their social significance. Horace Dewey and Ann Kleimola write about Russian heroines—women who inspired Muscovite men. Sandry Levy reviews women's property rights in Muscovy. Richard Hellie discusses female slavery in Muscovy, and Marie Thomas reveals that the lives of nuns in seventeenth-century Muscovite convents reflected the general condition of upper-class women in many ways.

74   HELLIE, RICHARD. *Slavery in Russia, 1450–1725*. Chicago: University of Chicago Press, 1982. 776 pp. Index. Bibliography.
This encyclopedic work contains information about female slaves and slaveholders, as well as female infanticide.

75   KAISER, DANIEL. *The Growth of the Law in Medieval Russia*. Princeton, N.J.: Princeton University Press, 1980. 308 pp. Index.
The subject of women and the law is not directly addressed, but bits and pieces of useful information can be gleaned.

76 LEVIN, EVE REBECCA. "The Role and Status of Women in Medieval Novgorod." Ph.D. diss., Indiana University, 1983. 413 pp.
Challenges the traditional historical view of the status of women in medieval Novgorod, arguing that women had substantial power and legal rights. The family was the center of economic and political power; this was an advantage for women, although they could not exercise power directly. Emphasizes the role of the church in strengthening the position of "good" women while condemning "evil" women. Differs from other accounts in stressing that women were no more drawn to pagan practices than men.

77 ———. "Infanticide in Pre-Petrine Russia." *Jahrbücher für Geschichte Osteuropas* 34, no. 2 (1986): 215–24.
Supports Richard Hellie's assertion that infanticide existed in medieval Russia by reference to previously untapped ecclesiastical literature. Girl babies were more likely to be victims than boys, but both were subject to the practice.

78 ———. *Sex and Society in the World of the Orthodox Slavs, 900–1700.* Ithaca, N.Y.: Cornell University Press, 1989. 326 pp. Index. Bibliography.
Impressive survey utilizing a wide variety of sources and reflecting wide-ranging scholarship, including pathbreaking archival research. Explores Orthodox concepts of sexuality, church attitudes toward marriage, incest, rape, extramarital sex, and homosexuality, and sexual norms for the clergy. Levin concludes that the church was "eminently practical" in its sexual politics and that ecclesiastical and community standards were not that far apart. Introduction surveys the range of approaches to the study of sexuality. Soft on the church, hard on feminist theories of Christian misogyny.

79 McNALLY, SUSANNE. "From Public Person to Private Prisoner: The Changing Place of Women in Medieval Russia." Ph.D. diss., State University of New York at Binghamton, 1976. 298 pp.
The only survey of this topic. Criticized by Eve Levin for confusing "perceived role and reality."

80 POUNCY, CAROLYN JOHNSTON. "The Origins of the *Domostroi*: A Study in Manuscript History." *Russian Review* 46, no. 4 (October 1987): 357–73.
Challenges prevailing views about the *Domostroi*, about its authorship by Sil'vestr, and about its audience. Argues that its primary readers were lay Muscovites and that it originated in Moscow.

81 SOFFER-BOBYSHEV, OLGA, ed., "Female Imagery in the Paleolithic: An Introduction to the Work of M. D. Gvozdover." *Soviet Anthropology and Archaeology* 27, no. 4 (Spring 1989). 94 pp.
The Soviet Union is the site of much Paleolithic research and a particularly rich

source of female figurines. Two articles by the archaeologist M. D. Gvozdover are translated here. In the first, "Ornamental Decoration on Artifacts of the Kostenki Culture," she finds "an identity and inter-changeability of the image of woman and animal." In the second article, "The Typology of Female Figurines of the Kostenki Paleolithic Culture," Gvozdover develops a typology of the figurines so far discovered and argues for more study of the differences between them. She notes that too often archaeologists fit their evidence into their preexisting theories about the role of women and female representation.

82   THOMAS, MARIE. "Managerial roles in the Suzdal'skii Pokrovskii Convent during the Seventeenth Century." *Russian History* 7, pts. 1–2 (1980): 92–112.
Comparison between male monasteries and convents. Conflict between domestic and political areas of convent management. Growing amount of time spent on relations with the central government. Relations of the nuns and the tsar with the convent managers (*striapchie*), who were always men.

83   VERNADSKY, GEORGE, ed. and trans. *Medieval Russian Laws*. Introduction by George Vernadsky. New York: Columbia University Press, 1947. 106 pp. Index.
Laws about inheritance, women's property. Helpful introduction.

84   ZENKOVSKY, SERGE A. ed. and trans. *Medieval Russia's Epics, Chronicles and Tales*. New York: E. P. Dutton, 1963. 436 pp. 2d. ed., rev. and enl. New York: E. P. Dutton, 1974. 526 pp.
Stories from the *Primary Chronicle, Lives of Saints and Monks*, and other homiletic and didactic works, from the Time of Troubles to the reign of Peter the Great.

85   ZGUTA, RUSSELL. "Was There a Witch Craze in Muscovite Russia?" *Southern Folklore Quarterly* 41 (1977): 119–27.
The answer is yes. Zguta argues that during the period of the "witch craze" in Western Europe and the American colonies, "the Muscovite authorities . . . managed quite handily to bring to trial, torture, convict, and, on occasion, to burn a goodly number of male and female witches, particularly during the seventeenth century." He points out that witchcraft was never viewed as heresy in Russia. No examination of gender issues in relation to witch persecution.

86   ———. "The Ordeal by Water (Swimming of Witches) in the East Slavic World." *Slavic Review* 36, no. 2 (June 1977): 220–30.
Asserts that the ordeal by water for alleged witches was used much earlier in the East Slavic areas (mid-twelfth century) than in the West (sixteenth and seventeenth centuries). Explores origins of this practice.

87   ZGUTA, RUSSELL. *Russian Minstrels: A History of the Skomorokhi*. Philadelphia: University of Pennsylvania Press, 1978. 160 pp. Index. Bibliography.

Tantalizing but brief accounts of female *skomorokhi* and the role of women in minstrels' songs. Zguta seeks to flesh out the history of this group. He argues that the *Skomorokhi*, or minstrels, were "originally priests of the pagan religion of the Eastern Slavs."

Sophia, Peter the Great, and the Era of the Empresses, 1682–1796

88 AKSAKOV, SERGEI TIMOFEEVICH. *Chronicles of a Russian Family*. Translated by Prince Mirsky. London: G. Routledge & Sons; New York: E. P. Dutton, 1924. 398 pp. Reprint, abridged and with introduction by Ralph Matlaw. New York: E. P. Dutton, 1961. 227 pp.
See entry 89.

89 ———. *Years of Childhood*. Translated by J. D. Duff. New York: Longmans Green; London: E. Arnold, 1916. 340 pp. Reprint. London: Oxford University Press, 1923. 446 pp. Reprint. Westport, Conn.: Hyperion, 1977. 340 pp. Reprint, with introduction by Edward Crankshaw. London: Oxford University Press, 1982.
This book, a work of autobiographical fiction that has appeared in numerous editions, gives a vivid description of Aksakov's childhood on a large estate near Ufa in the Orenburg district from 1791 to 1799, when he left for school in Kazan. Good material about gentry family life.

90 ———. *A Family Chronicle: Childhood Years of Bagrov Grandson Sergei Aksakov*. Translated by Olga Shartse. Moscow: Raduga, 1984. 540 pp.
See entry 89.

91 ANDREW, JOE. "Radical Sentimentalism or Sentimental Radicalism: A Feminist Approach to Eighteenth-Century Russian Literature." In *Discontinuous Discourses in Modern Russian Literature*, edited by Catriona Kelly, Michael Makin, and David Sheperd, pp. 136–56. Houndmills, Basingstoke, Hampshire, England: Macmillan, 1989.
The only attempt so far to apply feminist and gender insights to the literature of this period.

92   BAIN, R. NISBET. *Daughter of Peter the Great*. Westminster, England:
     Archibald Constable, 1899; New York: Dutton, 1900. 328 pp. Index.
     Bibliography. Reprint. New York: AMS Press. 328 pp. Index.
     Bibliography.
Rare English-language biography of Elizabeth.

93   ———. *The Pupils of Peter the Great: A History of the Russian Court and
     Empire from 1697 to 1740*. Westminster, England: Archibald Constable,
     1897. Reprint. Folcroft Library Editions, 1976. 318 pp.
Chapters on Peter and Catherine, Catherine's accession to the throne and her
brief rule, Peter II, and Empress Anne. Narrative style; has utilized some
Russian sources, such as Solovyev.

94   BLACK, J. L. "Educating Women in Eighteenth-Century Russia:
     Myths and Realities." *Canadian Slavonic Papers* 20 (March 1978):
     23–43.
Petrine reforms, rule by women, influence of European educational theories as
factors in opening education to females. Most attention given to the Smol'ny
Institute and its program, but mention also made of other educational opportunities for girls.

95   BRENNAN, JAMES F. *Enlightened Despotism in Russia: The Reign of
     Elizabeth, 1741–1762*. New York: Peter Lang, 1987. 295 pp.
     Bibliography. Notes.
Argues for continuity in policies between Elizabeth and Catherine. Scholarly
biography using many Russian sources.

96   CONSETT, THOMAS. *For God and Peter the Great. The Works of
     Thomas Consett, 1723–1729*. Edited by James Cracraft. Boulder, Colo.:
     East European Monographs, No. 96, 1982. 461 pp. Index.
Consett, an Episcopal priest hired to minister to resident British merchants,
lived in Russia from 1717 to 1727. In this volume are documents related to
Catherine I. One is Peter's proclamation of Catherine's coronation; the other is
a funeral oration about Catherine by Feofan Prokopovich. This book is reprinted from the original 1729 London edition, with the text printed horizontally
rather than vertically on the page. Awkward to read.

97   COUGHLAN, ROBERT. *Elizabeth and Catherine*. Edited by Jay Gold.
     New York: G. P. Putnam's Sons, 1974. 347 pp. Index. Bibliography.
Views Elizabeth as precursor of Catherine. Attempts to provide Elizabeth with
her proper place in history.

98   CRACRAFT, JAMES, ed. "'The Doldrums?': Russian History from
     1725–1762." *Canadian American Slavic Studies* 12, no. 1 (Spring 1978).
Contains the following articles: "The Drama of the Time of Troubles,

1725–30" by Alexander Yanov, "The Succession Crisis of 1730: A View from the Inside" by James Cracraft, "The Evolution of the Governor's Office, 1727–64" by John Le Donne, "Medical Professionals and Public Health in 'Doldrums' Russia" by John T. Alexander, "Great Power Politics in Eastern Europe and the Ukrainian Emigres" by Orest Subtelny, and "Communicable Disease, Anti-Epidemic Policies and the Role of Medical Professionals in Russia, 1725–62" by John T. Alexander. Also contains James Keith's memoir of the succession crisis which brought Anna Ivanovna, the second of four female rulers in eighteenth-century Russia, to the throne. Helpful background information about Keith's work by Paul Dukes and Brenda Meehan-Waters.

99   CURTISS, MINA. *A Forgotten Empress: Anna Ivanovna and Her Era*. New York: Frederick Ungar, 1974. 335 pp. Index.

Attempt at a more balanced portrait of Anna. Uses French, English, German, and Russian sources. Cites Anna's positive accomplishments (support for the performing arts, including the founding of the Russian ballet) but cannot ignore the repressive aspects of her rule. Some coverage of the accusations of Regent Anna Leopoldovna's lesbianism.

100   DOLGORUKAJA, NATALIA BORISOVNA. *Memoirs of Princess Natal'ja Borisovna Dolgorukaja*. Edited and translated by Charles E. Townsend. Columbus, Ohio: Slavica, 1977. 146 pp.

Dolgorukaja's memoirs are reprinted here in Russian with the English translation on the facing page. They are short, altogether about 9,000 words, but they provide a valuable eyewitness account of life in the post-Petrine period, particularly the years 1729–1730, during which the Dolgorukii clan's ill-fated plot to marry Ekaterina Dolgorukaia to Emperor Peter II failed and Natalia Sheremeteva, newly married to Ivan Dolgorukii, found herself accompanying her husband to Siberian exile after the accession of Empress Anne. The memoirs end in Siberia. Ivan was executed in 1739 in Novgorod. Ekaterina raised their two sons, entered a Kiev convent in 1758, lost her youngest son in 1769 and died two years later.

101   DONNERT, ERICH. *Russia in the Age of Enlightenment*. Leipzig: Edition Leipzig, 1986. 219 pp. Index. Bibliography.

Survey, with many pictures, of Russian cultural life of this period and the role of the Empresses in its development.

102   HUGHES, LINDSEY. *Sophia, Regent of Russia*. New Haven, Conn.: Yale University Press, 1990. 345 pp. Index. Bibliography.

The definitive work on Sophia, who as regent became the first de facto female ruler of Russia. Does much to illuminate Sophia's accomplishments and move her out of the shadow of Peter the Great. Postscript reviews earlier portraits of Sophia, many of which were blatantly sexist.

103   LONGWORTH, PHILIP. *The Three Empresses: Catherine I, Anne and Elizabeth of Russia*. London: Constable, 1972. 242 pp. Index. Bibliography.
Some discussion of changes for women under these rulers. A decent survey using the standard Russian, French, German, and English sources.

104   MANSTEIN, GENERAL CHRISTOPHER HERMANN V. *Contemporary Memoirs of Russia*. Edited by David Hume. London: Longman, Brown, Green & Longmans, 1856. 416 pp. Index.
Memoirs of a Russian-born Prussian who served in the Russian army from 1736 to 1744. With the accession of Elizabeth he fell out of favor, left the country, and joined the Prussian army. Covers the period 1727–44.

105   MASSON, CHARLES FRANÇOIS PHILIBERT. *Secret Memoirs of the Court of St. Petersburg*. Translated from the French. London: H. S. Nichols, 1895. 390 pp.
Chapter 9, "On Female Government," views eighteenth-century Russia as a strong argument against women rulers.

106   MEEHAN-WATERS, BRENDA. "Popular Piety, Local Initiative and the Founding of Women's Religious Communities in Russia, 1764–1807." *St. Vladimir's Theological Quarterly* 30, no. 2 (1986): 117–42.
Factors involved in the emergence and growth of women's religious communities. Comparison between women's and men's monasteries. Influence of the religious revival of the mid-eighteenth to early nineteenth centuries. Functional role of the *zhenskie obshchiny* (women's religious communities) and their connection with shelters for abused and abandoned women.

107   MOLLOY, V. FITZGERALD. *The Russian Court in the Eighteenth Century*. 2 vols. London: Hutchinson, 1906. Vol. 1, 318 pp.; vol. 2, 597 pp.
Popular account of the period.

108   O'BRIEN, C. BICKFORD. *Russia under Two Tsars, 1682–1689: The Regency of Sophia Alekseevna*. Berkeley: University of California Press, 1952. 178 pp. Index. Bibliographic essay. Bibliography.
Reevaluation of this period, and the first English-language biography of Sophia. Argues that Sophia's was "a government of unusual distinction and promise"; many of her policies were precursors of the Petrine reforms. Sophia, the first female to rule since Olga, challenged prevailing customs related to women's roles and refused to be confined to the Terem.

109   PUTNAM, PETER, ed. *Seven Britons in Imperial Russia*. Princeton, N.J.: Princeton University Press, 1952. 424 pp. Index. Bibliography.

Excerpts from the writings of John Perry, Jonas Hanway, William Richardson, Sir James Harris, William Coxe, Robert Ker Porter, and Sir Robert Thomas Wilson about their service in Russia. Covers the period 1698–1812. Bibliography lists all the published works of British travelers during that time. Descriptions of the impact of Petrine reforms on women.

110   RICE, TAMARA TALBOT. *Elizabeth, Empress of Russia*. London: Weidenfeld & Nicolson, 1970. 231 pp. Index. Bibliography. Biographical notes. Endnotes.

The best English biography of Elizabeth. Uses Russian, French, German, and English sources. Well-written and literate.

111   SEGEL, HAROLD B., ed. and trans. *The Literature of Eighteenth-Century Russia: A History and Anthology*. 2 vols. New York: E. P. Dutton, 1967. Vol. 1, 472 pp.; vol. 2, 448 pp. Bibliography.

Volume 1 contains writings from 1725 to 1762, during the reigns of the empresses Catherine I, Anna, and Elizabeth. It also contains selections from the polemics exchanged by Catherine the Great and Novikov, as well as from the writings of Fonvizin, Radishchev, and Karamzin during Catherine's reign. Volume 2 contains Chulkov's *The Comely Cook; or, the Adventures of a Debauched Woman*, a "fallen woman" novel somewhat akin to Defoe's *Moll Flanders*. Also contains excerpts from Karamzin's novel *Poor Liza*.

112   SOLOVIEV, SERGEI M. *History of Russia*. Vol. 35, *The Rule of Empress Anna*. Edited and translated by Richard Hantula. Gulf Breeze, Fla.: Academic International Press, 1982. 217 pp. Index.

Does not include three of Soloviev's five chapters on Anna (reason not given). Nevertheless, the translation of this basic historical work contributes to the scarce material in English about Anna's reign.

113   STONG, PHIL. *Marta of Muscovy: The Fabulous Life of Russia's First Empress*. Garden City, N.Y.: Doubleday, Doran, 1945. 274 pp. Index. Bibliography.

Mediocre biography of Catherine I, dubbed "truly great" by Stong, who describes Catherine II (the Great) as a "vain German nymphomaniac."

Catherine the Great, 1762–1796

Called by G. P. Gooch, one of her biographers, "the first and last intellectual to occupy the Russian throne," Catherine the Great has been the subject of countless biographies. Unfortunately, most of the authors have devoted the bulk of their attention to her love life. Those who have paid attention to her policies have often ascribed them to the influence of one or more male advisors. Catherine's intellectual interests and accomplishments have been the least studied. She not only corresponded with Enlightenment intellectuals such as Voltaire and Diderot but also commissioned the first Russian dictionary, encouraged translations of foreign works, established the first girls' school, and initiated the compilation of the first comparative study of world languages. The definitive study of this woman remains to be written. The following is a list of books and articles in English about Catherine, her life, and her rule.

114 ALEXANDER, JOHN T. *Autocratic Politics in a National Crisis: The Imperial Russian Government and Pugachev's Revolt, 1771–75.* Bloomington: Indiana University Press, 1969. 346 pp. Index.
The best study in English of the Pugachev revolt and Catherine's reaction to it.

115 ———. *Emperor of the Cossacks: Pugachev and the Frontier Jacquerie of 1773–1775.* Lawrence, Kans.: Coronado Press, 1973. 245 pp. Index.
Pugachev's revolt and Catherine's policies.

116 ———. "Politics, Passions, Patronage: Catherine II and Petr Zavadovskii." In *Russia and the World of the Eighteenth Century*, edited by R. P. Bartlett, A. G. Cross, and Karen Rasmussen, pp. 616–30. Columbus, Ohio: Slavica, 1988.
A revealing glimpse into the reality of one of Catherine's love affairs, using her love letters—a source that was not tapped for earlier writings about Catherine's affairs. Shows her as an independent-minded woman who worked and loved intensely, not simply as the tool of her male advisors and lovers.

117 ——. *Catherine the Great: Life and Legend*. New York: Oxford
     University Press, 1989. 418 pp. Index.
Well-researched, balanced account. Unique among biographies of Catherine in
its use of Soviet archival sources and the court ceremonial journals. Solid narrative, but lacks a strong introduction and conclusion to articulate the author's
perspective on the life of one of the great female rulers. Minimal gender analysis would have been helped by reference to Meehan-Waters's article "Catherine
the Great and the Problem of Female Rule" (see entry 167). Interesting epilogue on the Catherine legend, focusing on her sexuality.

118 ALMEDINGEN, E. M. *Catherine the Great: A Portrait*. London:
     Hutchinson, 1963. 240 pp. Index. Bibliography.
Derivative; offers nothing new. Bibliography lists nine books, none in Russian.

119 ANTHONY, KATHERINE SUSAN. *Catherine the Great*. Garden
     City, N.Y.: Garden City Publishing Co., 1927. 331 pp.
Biography by the niece of feminist Susan B. Anthony. A sympathetic but not
especially feminist presentation. Numerous printings.

120 BAIN, R. NISBET. *Peter III: Emperor of Russia*. Westminster, England:
     Archibald Constable; New York: E. P. Dutton, 1902. 208 pp. Index.
     Bibliography. Appendixes.
Contains information on Catherine before she became empress.

121 BARTLETT, R. P. "Russia in the Eighteenth-Century European
     Adoption of Inoculation for Smallpox." In *Russia and the World of the
     Eighteenth Century*, edited by R. P. Bartlett, A. G. Cross, and Karen
     Rasmussen, pp. 193–213. Columbus, Ohio: Slavica, 1988.
Discusses Russian participation in the advances in smallpox treatment. Shows
how the Russian government and learned elite were part of "the international
interchange of the learned European world." Describes Catherine's decision to
get inoculated and its effect.

122 BARTLETT, R. P., A. G. CROSS, and KAREN RASMUSSEN, eds.
     Russia and the World of the Eighteenth Century. Columbus, Ohio: Slavica,
     1988. 680 pp. Bibliographies.
Many of the essays included in this book are listed separately here. Discussants'
comments and concluding lecture by Marc Raeff, "On the Heterogeneity of the
Eighteenth Century in Russia," also worth attention.

123 CATHERINE II, EMPRESS OF RUSSIA. *Memoirs of Empress
     Catherine II*. Translated from the French. Preface by A. Herzen.
     London: Trubner, 1859. 352 pp. Appendix.
The first English edition of the Empress's autobiography known to the author.
Introduction by Herzen, a well-known émigré critic of Tsarist rule.

124   ———. *Memoirs of Catherine the Great*. Translated and introduced by
        Katharine Anthony. New York: Alfred A. Knopf, 1927. 337 pp. Index.
The best edition of the *Memoirs*, with explanatory notes.

125   ———. *Correspondence of Catherine When Grand Duchess with Sir Charles
        H. Williams and Letters from Count Poniatowski*. Edited and translated by
        the Earl of Ilchester and Mrs. Langford-Brooke. Introduction by Serge
        Goriainov. London: Thornton Butterworth, 1928. Index.
Correspondence with the British ambassador and with Catherine's lover,
Stanislas Poniatowski, for the years 1755–57. In his introduction, Goriainov
claims that the letters to Poniatowski, in French, "are written as if the correspondence was carried on between people of the masculine sex."

126   ———. *The Correspondence with Voltaire and the Instruction of 1767 in the
        English Text of 1768*. Edited by W. F. Reddaway. Cambridge:
        Cambridge University Press, 1931. 349 pp. Index.
The letters are in French, untranslated, and date from October 1763 to
December 1777. The Instruction is, as the title indicates, in English. Includes
explanatory notes to both texts and a helpful chronology of events from 1762
to 1777 in the field of philosophy in Britain, the Continent, and Russia.

127   ———. *The Memoirs of Catherine the Great*. Translated, with foreword
        and epilogue, by Lowell Bair. With the preface to the first edition by
        Alexander Herzen. New York: Bantam, 1957. 305 pp.
A new translation of the Herzen edition (paperback).

128   COUGHLAN, ROBERT. *Elizabeth and Catherine*. Edited by Jay Gold.
        New York: G. P. Putnam's Sons, 1974. 347 pp. Index. Bibliography.
See entry 97.

129   CRONIN, VINCENT. *Catherine, Empress of all the Russias*. New York:
        William Morrow, 1978. 349 pp. Index. Appendixes.
Yet another popular history. Notable chiefly for Appendix B, which lists
Catherine's children.

130   CROSS, A. G. "The Philanthropist, the Travelling Tutor and the
        Empress: British Visitors and Catherine II's Plans for Penal and Medical
        Reform." In *Russia and the World of the Eighteenth Century*, edited by R.
        P. Bartlett, A. G. Cross, and Karen Rasmussen, pp. 214–28. Columbus,
        Ohio: Slavica, 1988.
Discusses the visits of John Howard and the Reverend William Coxe and their
descriptions of prison and hospital conditions. Argues that they were among
those who influenced Catherine to continue penal reforms started in the 1770s
and 1780s. Further reforms were unrealized.

131   DASHKOVA, EKATERINA ROMANOVA. *Memoirs of the Princess Dashkova*. 2 vols. Edited by Mrs. W. Bradford. London: Henry Colburn, 1840. Vol. 1, 397 pp.; vol. 2, 439 pp.
Memoirs of Catherine's close friend and confidante, president of the Russian Academy of Arts & Sciences and publisher of the first Russian dictionary. Certain controversial passages expunged. See pages 291–308 on Dashkova's appointment to the presidency of the Academy. Initially, she had refused, telling Catherine that "nature herself, in making me a woman, had disqualified me for the direction of an academy of science."

132   ———. *The Memoirs of Princess Dashkova*. Translated and edited by Kyril Fitzlyon. London: John Calder, 1958. 322 pp. Index. Biographical notes.
Note the differences between Fitzlyon's translation of the section on Dashkova's appointment and the version in entry 131. In Fitzlyon the passage quoted in entry 131 reads, "God himself, by creating me a woman, had exempted me from accepting the employment of a Director of an Academy of Sciences." See p. 232 for an account of Dashkova's correspondence with Benjamin Franklin. Through Franklin's efforts, Dashkova became a member of the Philosophic Society of Philadelphia.

133   De MADARIAGA, ISABEL. "Catherine II and the Serfs: A Reconsideration of Some Problems." *Slavonic and East European Review* 52, no. 126 (January 1974): 34–62.
Challenges the V. I. Semevsky argument that the reign of Catherine II represented the "high point of serfdom." Questions the notion that the empress's policies represented a change from previous policies. Argues for more study of the actual impact of Catherine's land grants and other policies.

134   ———. *Russia in the Age of Catherine the Great*. New Haven, Conn.: Yale University Press, 1981. 698 pp. Index.
The first attempt by a contemporary scholar to write a history of the reign of Catherine the Great (as opposed to a biography of Catherine) of the breadth of Bruckner's 1883 work *Katharina die Zweite*. Based on prodigious research and examination of source materials outside the Soviet Union. Much information in a narrative format. Impressive list of sources.

135   ———. "Autocracy and Sovereignty." *Canadian-American Slavic Studies* 16, nos. 3–4 (Fall–Winter 1982): 369–87.
The tsars' use of specific terms to describe their power; Catherine the Great's introduction of the concept of sovereignty. Nothing about gender and concepts of power.

136 De RUHLIERE, CLAUDE C. *A History of Anecdotes of the Revolution in Russia*. New York: Arno Press and the *New York Times*, 1970. 200 pp.
Memoirs of a Frenchman in St. Petersburg during Catherine's successful coup d'état against her husband.

137 DREIFUSS, JEROME. *Catherine and Potemkin: An Imperial Romance*. New York: Covici Friede, 1937. 343 pp. Bibliography.
Based on newly discovered correspondence from Catherine to Potemkin. Novelistic approach; makes all sorts of assumptions about the thoughts and preoccupations of the main characters.

138 DUKES, PAUL. *Catherine the Great and the Russian Nobility: A Study Based on the Materials of the Legislative Commission of 1767*. Cambridge: Cambridge University Press, 1967. 269 pp. Index.
A thorough scholarly study of the legislative policies of Catherine and how they were influenced by the nobility.

139 ——, ed. and trans. *Russia under Catherine the Great*. 2 vols. *Vol. 1: Select Documents on Government and Society. Vol. 2: Catherine the Great's Instruction (Nakaz) to the Legislative Commission, 1767*. Newtonville, Mass.: Oriental Research Partners, 1977. Vol. 1, 176 pp.; vol. 2, 129 pp. Bibliography.
Very useful collection, with a thirty-seven-page introduction in volume 2, surveying the historiography of the Nakaz. Volume 1 begins with the 1722 Table of Ranks. Documents include Peter III's Manifesto freeing the nobility, Catherine's Directions to Prince Viazemski on his appointment as procurator-general, S. E. Desnitskii's 1768 "Proposal for the Establishment of Legislative, Judicial and Executive Power in the Russian Empire," A. Ia. Polenov's essay "On the Serf Condition of the Peasants," P. I. Rychkov's "Instruction for a Steward or Bailiff, 1770," and several documents from the Pugachev Revolt, Catherine's administrative reform of 1774, and the 1785 Charter to the Rights of the Nobility. Each document is preceded by a helpful introduction. Additional readings for each document or set of documents are suggested.

140 DURAN, JAMES A. "Catherine the Great and the Origin of the Russian State Debt." In *Russia and the World of the Eighteenth Century*, edited by R. P. Bartlett, A. G. Cross, and Karen Rasmussen, pp. 469–80. Columbus, Ohio: Slavica, 1988.
Calls Catherine the "Mother of the Russian State Debt." Explores the rationale behind her resort to deficit financing; sees it as result of "solid administrative reform."

141 FISHER, ALAN. "Enlightened Despotism and Islam under Catherine II." *Slavic Review* 37, no. 4 (December 1968): 542–53.
Argues that Catherine's application of policies toward Russian Moslems was significant and deserves more attention.

142   GIVENS, ROBERT. "To Measure and to Encroach: The Nobility and the Land Survey." In *Russia and the World of the Eighteenth Century*, edited by R. P. Bartlett, A. G. Cross, and Karen Rasmussen, pp. 533–47. Columbus, Ohio: Slavica, 1988.
History of land surveys as means of extending and rationalizing state control and the obstacles in its path. Describes Catherine's approach to the problem.

143   GLEASON, WALTER J. *Moral Idealists, Bureaucracy and Catherine the Great*. New Brunswick, N.J.: Rutgers University Press, 1981. 252 pp. Index. Bibliography. Footnotes.
Focuses on the activities of three men—the journalist Nikolai Novikov, the poet Ippolit Bogdanovich, and the playwright Denis Fonvizin—all of whom held posts within Catherine's bureaucracy. First chapter devoted to Lomonosov and Sumarokov and their notion of the ideal ruler in relation to Anna, Elizabeth, and Catherine. Sections on Catherine's correspondence with Voltaire and the impact of the French Revolution better than most.

144   GOLOVINA, V. N. *Memoirs of Countess Golovine*. Translated from the French by G. M. Fox-Davies. London: David Nutt, 1910. 390 pp. Index.
Memoirs begin in 1777 and continue through the rest of Catherine's reign and through that of her son Paul and her grandson Alexander I, ending in 1817.

145   GOOCH, G. P. *Catherine the Great and Other Studies*. London: Longmans Green, 1954. 292 pp. Index.
Consists of four essays, the first (pp. 1–108) about Catherine, the rest about non-Russian subjects. Very positive about Catherine as a ruler who Europeanized Russia and who personified the concept of Enlightened Autocracy. Dispassionate, informative analysis of the key elements of Catherine's rule.

146   GREY, IAN. *Catherine the Great, Autocrat and Empress of All Russia*. London: Hodder & Stoughton, 1961; Philadelphia: J. B. Lippincott, 1962. 254 pp. Index. Bibliography.
Critical biography. Places Catherine in the context of the enlightened autocrats of the eighteenth century. Uses some Russian sources.

147   GRIBBLE, FRANCIS. *The Comedy of Catherine the Great*. London: Eveleigh Nash, 1912. 368 pp. Index.
By the author of *George Sand and Her Lovers*, *Madame de Staël and Her Lovers*, and other such books.

148   GRIFFITHS, DAVID. "Catherine II: The Republican Empress." *Jahrbücher für Geschichte Osteuropas* 21, no. 3 (1973): 323–44.
Catherine and her policies and pronouncements in the context of eighteenth-century absolutism. A balanced appraisal.

149   ———, ed. "Russia and the West in the Eighteenth Century."
      Canadian-American Slavic Studies 13, no. 4 (Winter 1979): 391–554.
Includes two articles about Catherine the Great: "Eighteenth-Century
Perceptions of Backwardness: Projects for the Creation of a Third Estate in
Catherinian Russia" by David Griffiths, and "Catherine II's *Nakaz*, State
Finances and the Encyclopedie" by Victor Kamendrowsky. Georg von Rauch's
"Political Preconditions for East-West Cultural Relations in the Eighteenth
Century" discusses Catherine II and Peter I almost exclusively.

150   ———. "In Search of Enlightenment: Recent Soviet Interpretations of
      Eighteenth-Century Russian Intellectual History." *Canadian-American
      Slavic Studies* 16, nos. 3–4 (Fall–Winter 1982): 317–56.
Soviet scholarship on the Russian Enlightenment and Catherine the Great's
role in it.

151   ———. "To Live Forever: Catherine II, Voltaire and the Pursuit of
      Immortality." In *Russia and the World of the Eighteenth Century*, edited
      by R. P. Bartlett, A. G. Cross, and Karen Rasmussen, pp. 446–68.
      Columbus, Ohio: Slavica, 1988.
Examines the relationship between Catherine and Voltaire. Considers the prevailing interpretations and argues that Catherine was "obsessed with obtaining
[Voltaire's] approval." Connects this obsession with the desire to achieve
immortality. Mentions the eighteenth-century belief that immortality was for
men only.

152   HASLIP, JOAN. *Catherine the Great: A Biography*. New York: G. P.
      Putnam's Sons, 1977. 382 pp. Index. Bibliography.
Another narrative about Catherine, based on French and English sources only.

153   HODGETTS, E. A. BRAYLEY. *The Life of Catherine the Great of
      Russia*. London: Methuen, 1914. 335 pp. Index.
Typical popular biography.

154   HYDE, H. MONTGOMERY. *The Empress Catherine and Princess
      Dashkov*. London: Chapman & Hall, 1935. 282 pp. Index.
      Bibliographical note.
On the friendship between these two exceptional women. Also touches on
Dashkova's close friendships with other women, particularly Martha and
Catherine Wilmot and Catherine Hamilton. Brief mention of Regent Anna
Leopoldovna's lesbian affair with Julia Mengden, a factor in Empress
Elizabeth's successful coup.

155   JONES, R. E. "Ukrainian Grain and the St. Petersburg Market." In
      Russia and the World of the Eighteenth Century, edited by R. P. Bartlett,
      A. G. Cross, and Karen Rasmussen, pp. 565–76. Columbus, Ohio:
      Slavica, 1988.

Discusses Catherine's failure to build canals to transport Ukrainian grain to the Russian capital, in the context of her southern policy.

156   KAMENDROWSKY, V. "State and Enterprise in the Thought of N. I. Panin." In *Russia and the World of the Eighteenth-Century*, edited by R. P. Bartlett, A. G. Cross, and Karen Rasmussen, pp. 481–92. Columbus, Ohio: Slavica, 1988.
Argues that Panin's 1763 memorandum to Catherine shows "eighteenth-century Russian economic thought at its best" and that this document is unfairly neglected by historians.

157   KAUS, GINA. *Catherine, the Portrait of an Empress*. Translated from the German by June Head. New York: Viking, 1935. 384 pp.
Popular history. No bibliography or footnotes. Head writes of eighteenth-century Russia after Peter as "fifty years of petticoat government."

158   KEY, MARY RITCHIE. *Catherine the Great's Linguistic Contribution*. Carbondale, Ill.: Linguistic Research, 1980. 200 pp. Index.
Catherine the Great initiated and compiled the first comparative study and classification of world languages. This is the only book in English that devotes any attention to Catherine's pioneering achievement, and she rarely gets credit for influencing others. Her achievements in this area include the first comparative linguistic study of American Indian languages. Unfortunately, Catherine's linguistic study was published in Cyrillic script, rendering it inaccessible to many Western scholars. Key also discusses Catherine's gender as an impediment to recognition of her accomplishments.

159   KLIER, JOHN. "The Ambiguous Legal Status of Russian Jewry in the Reign of Catherine II." *Slavic Review* 35, no. 3 (September 1976): 504–17.
Argues that Catherine's policy toward the large Jewish population inherited in the first partition of Poland in 1772 was relatively benevolent.

160   KOCHAN, MIRIAM. *Life in Russia under Catherine the Great*. London: B. T. Batsford; New York: G. P. Putnam's Sons, 1969. 182 pp. Index. Bibliography.
Good information on everyday life of the nobility, serfs, merchants, and workers, as well as an outline of the political history of the period. Includes a paragraph from Radishchev on the sexual abuse of serf women; mentions some women writers. No other specific attention to women. Many illustrations.

161   KRIEGER, LEONARD. *Kings and Philosophers, 1689–1789*. New York: W. W. Norton, 1970. 369 pp. Index.
Catherine the Great and her policies, considered in the context of the enlightened despots of this period.

162   LANG, DAVID M. *The First Russian Radical: Alexander Radishchev,
      1749–1802*. London: George Allen & Unwin, 1959. Reprint. Westport,
      Conn.: Greenwood, 1977. 298 pp. Index.
Radishchev's publication of *A Journey From St. Petersburg to Moscow* in 1790,
with its blistering attack on serfdom and autocracy, aroused the ire of Catherine
the Great. For his work he was arrested, tried for treason, and ultimately exiled
to Siberia. Lang places Radishchev within the context of a long line of Russian
writers "who have fallen victim to Russian official intolerance."

163   MAROGER, DOMINIQUE, ed. *The Memoirs of Catherine the Great*.
      Translated by Moura Budberg. Introduction by G. P. Gooch. New
      York: Macmillan, 1955. 400 pp. Index.
Paperback edition by Collier Books published in 1961.

164   McARTHUR, GILBERT H. "Novikov and Catherine II: Some
      Observations." In *Russia and the World of the Eighteenth Century*, edited
      by R. P. Bartlett, A. G. Cross, and Karen Rasmussen, pp. 411–18.
      Columbus, Ohio: Slavica, 1988.
Weighs the traditional interpretation that Catherine persecuted Novikov
against Isabel de Madariaga's claim that such assertions are not supported by
the evidence. Argues that "some troublesome questions remain" before the latter interpretation can be accepted.

165   McCONNELL, ALLEN. "Catherine the Great and the Fine Arts." In
      *Imperial Russia, 1700–1917: State, Society, Opposition (Essays in Honor of
      Marc Raeff)*, edited by Ezra Mendelsohn and Marshall Shatz, pp. 37–57.
      DeKalb, Ill.: Northern Illinois University Press, 1988.
Addresses the lack of attention to, and appreciation for, Catherine as a patron
of the fine arts. Argues that Catherine took an active interest in the arts, architecture, and the building of monuments, most notably *The Bronze Horseman*.

166   ———. *A Russian Philosophe: Alexander Radishchev, 1749–1802*. The
      Hague: Martinus Nijhoff, 1964. Reprint. Westport, Conn.: Hyperion,
      1981. 228 pp. Index.
Radishchev's publication of *A Journey from St. Petersburg to Moscow* in 1790,
with its blistering attack on serfdom and autocracy, aroused the ire of Catherine
the Great. For his work he was arrested, tried for treason and ultimately exiled
to Siberia. McConnell places Radishchev in the tradition of the Enlightenment
philosophes, a tradition to which Catherine also professed allegiance.

167   MEEHAN-WATERS, BRENDA. "Catherine the Great and the
      Problem of Female Rule." *Russian Review* 34, no. 3 (July 1975):
      293–307.
Germinal article, pinpointing comparative attitudes toward women in power
(positive traits viewed as masculine, negative ones as feminine). Comparison

with Catherine's contemporary Maria Theresa. Russians were far more accepting of a female ruler than were western Europeans; the "problem" lay in the eyes of the beholder.

168 ————. "Russian Convents and the Secularization of Monastic Property." In *Russia and the World of the Eighteenth Century*, edited by R. P. Bartlett, A. G. Cross, and Karen Rasmussen, pp. 112–24. Columbus, Ohio: Slavica, 1988.
Discusses the background and effects of Catherine the Great's 1764 order transferring control of church property to the state. One function of local convents was to be "dignified retirement homes for female relatives." With the state's move to greater consolidation and limitation of the church and monastics, women formed unofficial religious communities. Support of leaders of monastic revival for these communities and significance of peasant support described. Eventually, many of these communities attained official monastic status.

169 MOTTLEY, JOHN. *The History of the Life and Reign of the Empress Catharine*. 2 vols. London: William Meadows, 1844. Vol. 1, 410 pp. Index. Vol. 2., 323 pp. Index.
The life of Catherine by a contemporary. Hard-to-read old-style English print.

170 MURAT, PRINCESSE LUCIEN. *The Private Life of Catherine the Great of Russia*. Translated by Garnett Saffery. New York: Louis Carrier, 1928. 212 pp. Index.
From the series Love Lives of the Great. As the title indicates, the focus is on Catherine's love affairs. Story told much better elsewhere.

171 NASH, CAROL. "The Education of Women in Russia, 1762–1796." Ph.D. diss., New York University, 1978. 316 pp.
Catherine the Great established the first school for girls in Russia, the Smol'nyi Institute. Discusses attitudes toward female education, the operation of Smol'nyi, and the educational experience of its students.

172 ————. "Students and Rubles: The Society for the Education of Noble Girls as a Charitable Institution." In *Russia and the World of the Eighteenth Century*, edited by R. P. Bartlett, A. G. Cross, and Karen Rasmussen, pp. 258–72. Columbus, Ohio: Slavica, 1988.
An examination of the composition of the student body and the finances of the Smol'nyi Institute at the time of Catherine the Great. Describes the deliberate policy of recruiting and subsidizing needy gentry students. Many examples.

173 NIKOLAEV, VSEVELOD, and ALBERT PARRY. *The Loves of Catherine the Great*. New York: Coward, McCann and Geoghegan, 1982. 287 pp.
Superficial treatment. Does not use all of Catherine's love letters.

174   OLDENBOURG, ZOE. *Catherine the Great*. Translated from the
      French by Anne Carter. New York: Random House, 1965. 378 pp.
      Index. Chronological table. Notes.
More about Catherine's early years, accession to the throne, and attempts to
rehabilitate Peter. Better than most, but still falls into sexist stereotypes (e.g.,
portrays Catherine as simply a passive vehicle for Potemkin).

175   OLIVA, L. JAY, ed. *Catherine the Great*. Englewood Cliffs, N.J.:
      Prentice-Hall, 1971. 184 pp. Index. Chronology.
 Covers Catherine's instructions to the Commission recodifying Russian laws,
her reaction to the French Revolution, her accession manifesto, a serf decree,
her manifesto against Pugachev, and her Charter to the Gentry. Includes
excerpts from her memoirs and correspondence, parts of Dashkova and
Golovine's memoirs, observations by the French and British ambassadors,
Radishchev and Karamzine's essays, Herzen's introduction to *The Memoirs of
Catherine the Great* (entry 119), and Klivchevsky, Pokrovsky, and Billington's
interpretations. Useful bibliographic essay.

176   PETSCHAUER, PETER. "Catherine the Great's Conversion of 1744."
      Jahrbücher für Geschichte Osteuropas 20, no. 2 (1972): 179–93.
Catherine's conversion portrayed as based on more than solely political expe-
diency.

177   PIPES, RICHARD. "Catherine II and the Jews." *Soviet Jewish Affairs* 5,
      no. 2 (1975): 3–20.
Argues that Catherine's policies in relation to Jews were more progressive than
those in western Europe at the time. These policies failed because of the resistance of the Poles and Muscovite merchants.

178   POLOVTSOFF, ALEXANDER. *The Favourites of Catherine the Great*.
      London: Herbert Jenkins, 1940. 288 pp. Index.
The lives of Catherine's twelve principal lovers. Disputes notion of Catherine's
"promiscuous looseness."

179   PUSHKIN, ALEXANDER. *The History of Pugachev*. Translated by Earl
      Sampson. Ann Arbor, Mich.: Ardis, 1983. 154 pp.
Translation of Pushkin's 1833 work about this massive peasant uprising during
Catherine's reign.

180   RAEFF, MARC, ed. *Catherine the Great: A Profile*. New York: Hill and
      Wang, 1972. 331 pp. Chronology. Bibliography.
A collection of articles, including a number translated from the Russian for the
first time. Raeff emphasizes in his introduction that this work examines
Catherine's rule, not her romances. Scholars and their essays include Aleksandr
Kizevetter ("Portrait of an Enlightened Autocrat" and "The Legislator in Her

Debut"), Vasilii Bil'bassov ("The Intellectual Formation of Catherine II"), Ivan Luppol ("The Empress and the Philosophe"), Grigorii Gukovskii ("The Empress as Writer"), Paul Miliukov ("Educational Reforms" and "Voices of the Land and the Autocrat"), Allen McConnell ("The Autocrat and the Open Critic"), Sergei Bakhrushin and Sergei Skazkin ("Diplomacy"), Marc Raeff ("In the Imperial Manner"), Aleksandr Lappo-Danilevskii ("The Serf Question in an Age of Enlightenment"), and A.M. Ammann ("Church Affairs"). A gem in the wasteland of Catheriniana.

181 ——. *The Well-Ordered Police State: Social and Institutional Change through Law in the Germanies and Russia, 1600–1800.* New Haven, Conn.: Yale University Press, 1983. 284 pp. Index.
Discusses Catherine's role in the development of the Russian state.

182 RAGSDALE, HUGH. "New Light on the Greek Project: A Preliminary Report." In *Russia and the World of the Eighteenth Century,* edited by R. P. Bartlett, A. G. Cross, and Karen Rasmussen, pp. 493–501. Columbus, Ohio: Slavica, 1988.
Argues for more serious attention to this proposal to expel the Turks from Greece. Also notes that Catherine and her chief advisors were aware of their lack of the military wherewithal to carry it out.

183 RANSEL, DAVID L. *The Politics of Catherinian Russia: The Panin Party.* New Haven, Conn.: Yale University Press, 1975. 327 pp. Index. Bibliography.
Argues for the importance of family parties as patronage networks in eighteenth-century Russia. Explores the role of Panin and his party. Critiques the prevailing view that Panin was part of a gentry opposition to Catherine II. Offers more useful information about Catherine and her policies than almost all the biographies of her.

184 ——. "Undervaluation of Females: Evidence from the Foundling Homes." In *Russia and the World of the Eighteenth Century,* edited by R. P. Bartlett, A. G. Cross, and Karen Rasmussen, pp. 247–57. Columbus, Ohio: Slavica, 1988.
Correlates the sex ratio of children delivered to foundling homes with the social value of boys and girls, from the establishment of these homes in Moscow and St. Petersburg in the 1760s and 1770s to the 1880s. Finds a shift toward equalization in the sex ratios of abandoned children and attributes this in part to the growing influence of western European values.

185 RICHARDSON, WILLIAM. *Anecdotes of the Russian Empire.* London: W. Strahan and T. Cadell, 1784. New York: Arno Press and the *New York Times,* 1970. 478 pp.
An Englishman's account of his stay in St. Petersburg from 1768 to 1772.

186　SCHMUCKER, SAMUEL M. *Memoirs of the Court and Reign of Catherine the Second, Empress of Russia*. Philadelphia: Porter & Coates, 1886. 338 pp. Appendix.

Favorable survey of Catherine's rule. In Schmucker's view, Catherine ruled a country not worthy of her talents: "being placed over a community by no means remarkable for the genial gifts of nature, but rather deficient in intellectual resources, she deserves great praise for what she did accomplish under such very unfavorable circumstances."

187　SERGEANT, PHILIP W. *The Courtships of Catherine the Great*. Philadelphia: J. B. Lippincott; London: T. Werner Laurie, 1905. 337 pp. Index.

Derivative.

188　THOMSON, GLADYS SCOTT. *Catherine the Great and the Expansion of Russia*. Introduction by A. L. Rowse. London: English Universities Press, 1955. Reprint. Westport, Conn.: Greenwood, 1985. 294 pp. Index.

Part of the Teach Yourself History series for the general reading public. Narrative format.

189　TOOKE, WILLIAM. *Life of Catherine II, Empress of All the Russias*. London, 1802.

190　TROYAT, HENRI. *Catherine the Great*. Translated by Emily Read. Henley on Thames, England: Aidan Ellis, 1979. 385 pp. Index. Bibliography. Chronology.

Based on French and English sources. Views Catherine as manipulated by Potemkin.

191　———. *Catherine the Great*. Translated by Joan Pinkham. New York: E. P. Dutton, 1980. 377 pp. Index. Bibliography. Chronology.

More comprehensive than most, but offers no new interpretations.

192　VOLTAIRE and CATHERINE THE GREAT. *Voltaire and Catherine the Great: Selected Correspondence*. Edited, annotated, and introduced by Anthony Lentin. Foreword by Elizabeth Hill. Cambridge, England: Oriental Research Partners, 1974. 186 pp. Bibliography.

Another edition of this correspondence.

193　WALISZEWSKI, KASIMIR. *The Romance of an Empress*. New York: D. Appleton & Co., 1894. Reprint. Hamden, Conn.: Archon Books, 1968.

The source of much of the information used in later popular biographies.

Return of the Emperors, 1796–1855

194   ANDREW, JOE. *Women in Russian Literature*, 1780–1863. New York: St. Martin's, 1988. 210 pp. Index. Bibliography.
The title is misleading, as this book is about women as portrayed by male writers—specifically Pushkin, Lermontov, Gogol, Turgenev, and Chernyshevsky. Nevertheless, this is a rare attempt to critique the writing of these authors from a feminist perspective. Andrew has read the feminist classics by Millett, Firestone, and de Beauvoir, among others. He argues that the "real day" for women is represented in the work of Chernyshevsky, in contrast to the "generally negative representation of women" found in the works of Pushkin, Lermontov, Gogol, and Turgenev, and in Russian literature as a whole.

195   APLIN, HUGH ANTHONY. "M. S. Zhukova and E. A. Gan: Women Writers and Female Protagonists, 1837–1843." Ph.D. diss., University of East Anglia, 1988. 436 pp.
Argues that these women won "unprecedented recognition and acceptance" from their peers. Describes the creative process and problems of these major early Russian female writers, and how they participated in early discussions of the woman question.

196   BINGHAM, MADELEINE. *Princess Lieven, Russian Intriguer*. London: Hamish Hamilton, 1982. 261 pp. Index.
Biography of the German-born wife of the Russian ambassador to Prussia and then Britain. From 1810 to 1834 she was a leading society figure, intimate with major British and continental political figures, including Metternich, and served as a spy for the tsars through her brother, the head of the Russian secret police.

197   CLAY, CATHERINE BLACK. "Ethos and Empire: The Ethnographic Expedition of the Imperial Russian Naval Ministry, 1855–1862." Ph.D. diss., University of Oregon, 1989. 353 pp.
Survey of reports of this expedition. Chapter 7 analyzes the Naval Ministry's treatment of the woman question.

198   DUROVA, NADEZHDA. *The Cavalry Maid: The Memoirs of a Woman Soldier of 1812*. Translated by John Mersereau, Jr., and David Lapeza. Ann Arbor, Mich.: Ardis, 1988. 222 pp.

Two translations of Durova's memoirs appeared in 1988. Unfortunately for Merserau and Lapeza, theirs suffers by comparison with the other (entry 199). Their work contains a short autobiography of Durova, but no index or annotations. In the *Slavic Review* (Fall 1989, pp. 490–92) reviewer Ron LeBlanc criticized the translators for making "a large number of egregious errors that mar the translation and often render it highly confusing," such as "*chasa na dva* as two, *temno* as hot and *zhelaiu* as I regret."

199   ———. *The Cavalry Maiden: Journals of a Russian Officer in the Napoleonic War*. Translated, introduced and annotated by Mary Fleming Zirin. Bloomington: Indiana University Press, 1989. 243 pp. Index. Bibliography. Notes.

Excellent, authoritative translation of the fascinating autobiography of Durova. Translator's introduction is very helpful in placing Durova's journal and other works in context. More comprehensive and accurate than the version by Mersereau and Lapeza (entry 198).

200   EIDELMAN, DAWN DIANE. "George Sandism and the Woman Question in Nineteenth Century Russia: Desire and Culpability in the Love Triangle in Ten Russian Selections." Ph.D. diss., Emory University, 1990. 315 pp.

Discusses the success of George Sand's novels in Russia, particularly *Jacques* (1834), *Mauprat* (1837), and *Horace* (1842), and their influence on prominent Russian male writers, including Turgenev, Chernyshevsky, Goncharov, and Dostoyevsky. Concludes by seeking to ascertain reasons "for the incapacity of women writers to address the woman question." No mention of early Russian women writers, such as E. A. Gan, or her many successors, who did address these issues.

201   HERZEN, ALEXANDER. *My Past and Thoughts: The Memoirs of Alexander Herzen*. 5 vols. Translated by Constance Garnett. Revised by Humphrey Higgens. Introduction by Isaiah Berlin. London: Chatto & Windus, 1968. 1,908 pp. Index.

Autobiography of the great revolutionary thinker, including his thoughts on love, marriage, and the status of women. Description of the ménage à trois with Natalya Herzen and Nikolai Ogarev.

202   ———. *My Past and Thoughts*. Translated by Constance Garnett. Revised by Humphrey Higgens. Introduction by Isaiah Berlin. Abridged, with preface and notes by Dwight MacDonald. Berkeley: University of California Press, 1982. 684 pp. Index.

Abridged version of the 1968 edition (entry 201).

203 ———. *Childhood, Youth and Exile. Parts I and II of My Past and Thoughts*. Translated by J. D. Duff. Introduction by Isaiah Berlin. Oxford: Oxford University Press, 1980. 271 pp. Bibliography.

Herzen's life from early childhood (he was born in 1812) until 1838, when he returned from exile in Vyatka. As the illegitimate child of a nobleman, Herzen provides a different portrait of gentry family life.

204 LAYTON, SUSAN. "Eros and Empire in Russian Literature about Georgia." *Slavic Review* 51, no. 2 (Summer 1992): 195–213.

Gender relations in the literature of the mid 1820s–1850, specifically the works of Pushkin, Griboedov, Lermontov, Marlinskii, Iakov Polonskii, and Odoevskii, as symbolic of Russian male power over an orientalized and eroticized female Georgia.

205 MAZOUR, ANATOLE G. *Women in Exile: Wives of the Decembrists*. Tallahassee, Fla: Diplomatic Press, 1975. 134 pp.

This book focuses primarily on Ekaterina Trubetskaya, Maria Volkonskaya, and two French women, Camilla Ledantu Ivasheva (mother of the Russian feminist leader Maria Trubnikova) and Pauline Gueble Annenkova. Criticized by Richard Stites for superficiality (see entry 314).

206 MEEHAN-WATERS, BRENDA. "The Authority of Holiness: Women Ascetics and Spiritual Elders in Nineteenth-Century Russia." In *God's Servants: Church, Nation and State in Russia and Ukraine*, edited by Geoffrey A. Hosking, pp. 38–51. London: Macmillan, 1990.

Seeks to bring proper attention to the role of the *staritsa*, or holy woman, in nineteenth-century Russian Orthodoxy by examining the lives of two women— the hermit Anastasia Semenovna Logacheva and the Abbess Evgeniia, founder of the Boriso-Glebo-Anosino women's communal monastery. Provocative comparison of religious and radical women's ideals ("hard work, renunciation of luxury and a spartan life").

207 ———. "Metropolitan Filaret (Drozdov) and the Reform of Russian Women's Monastic Communities." *Russian Review* 50 (July 1991): 310–23.

Discusses Filaret's role in reforming the communal and spiritual life of existing women's monastic communities and encouraging the development of semiofficial women's religious communities (*zhenskie obshchiny*). Meehan-Waters is almost alone in researching and writing about women and religion in prerevolutionary Russia.

208 ———. *Holy Women of Russia: The Lives of Five Orthodox Women Offer Spiritual Guidance and Insight for Today*. San Francisco: Harper San Francisco, 1993. 222 pp. Index. Bibliography. Notes.

As the title indicates, this book presents positive portraits of five Russian

Orthodox religious women: Margarita Tuchkova (1781–1852), founder of a religious community at Borodino; Anastasia Logacheva (1809–1875), famed ascetic and holy woman; Matrona Naumovna Popova (1769–1851), pilgram and founder of the Tikhon Zadonsk religious community at Tvorozhko; and the Abbess Taisiia (1840–1915), educator and visionary. Meehan's presentation makes visible the lives and contributions of these remarkable women, part of a history and tradition suppressed during the Soviet period.

209   PAVLOVA, KAROLINA. *A Double Life*. Translated and introduced by
       Barbara Heldt Monter. Ann Arbor, Mich.: Ardis, 1978. 111 pp.
Translation of the 1848 novel about Cecily von Lindenborn, a young gentry-woman, as she is guided/manipulated into marriage to a young nobleman. Dmitri is interested in Cecily mainly for her money. The "double life" of the title consists of Cecily's life in society and her very different and vivid interior life. The novel points up the largely sex-segregated worlds inhabited by the two main characters. The introduction puts Pavlova's work in context and explores issues of gender as well as the obstacles to creativity in Pavlova's life.

210   SANDLER, STEPHANIE. "The Two Women of Bakhchisarai."
       Canadian Slavonic Papers 29, no. 2/3 (June/September 1987): 255–65.
Addresses underlying themes in Pushkin's tale. Disputes the notion that a "secret love" inspired its writing. Argues instead that underneath multiple layers lies "an ideology of democratic equality more revolutionary than one finds in Pushkin's better known political lyrics."

211   SEACOLE, MARY. *Wonderful Adventures of Mrs. Seacole in Many*
       Lands. London: J. Blackwood, 1857. Reprint. Introduction by William
       Andrews. New York: Oxford University Press, 1988. 200 pp.
The travels of a Jamaican black woman take her to Balaclava during the Crimean War, where she builds a hotel and infirmary, witnesses the battle of Sebastopol, and travels to Simferopol and Baktchiserai.

212   SUTHERLAND, CHRISTINE. *The Princess of Siberia: The Story of*
       Maria Volkonsky and the Decembrist Exiles. New York: Farrar, Straus &
       Giroux; London: Methuen, 1984. 340 pp. Index.
Popular biography of Maria Volkonsky, one of the Decembrist wives who followed their husbands into exile after the abortive uprising.

213   SWARTZ, ANNE. "Maria Szymanowska to Adam Mickiewicz:
       Unpublished Letters from 1827." *Australian Slavonic and East European*
       Studies 5, no. 1 (1991): 25–43.
Maria Szymanowska (1789–31) moved from Warsaw to Moscow and then St. Petersburg to become First Pianist to the Empress of Russia, from 1827–1829. There, apparently influenced by Mickiewicz, she composed art songs set to vernacular texts, paralleling Chopin's early work in this same vein.

214 TOVROV, JESSICA. "Action and Affect in the Russian Noble Family from the Late Eighteenth Century through the Reform Period." Ph.D. diss., University of Chicago, 1980.

Covers the period between the late eighteenth and early nineteenth centuries. Discusses the significance of three basic organizing principles of the family: role-related activity, authority and hierarchy, and sexual division. Analyzes the ideology of childhood and childrearing practices. Last three chapters describe typical life patterns. Concludes that the ideology of the modern family was discernible by the mid-nineteenth century.

215 WAN, NING. "Female Characters in A. Ostrovskii's 'The Storm' and Cao Yu's 'The Thunderstorm.'" Ph.D. diss., University of Pittsburgh, 1985. 248 pp.

Comparison between Ostrovskii (1823–86) and Cao Yu (1910–), a leading contemporary Chinese playwright.

216 ZETLIN, MIKHAIL. *The Decembrists*. Translated by George Panin. Preface by Michael Karpovich. New York: International Universities Press, 1958. 349 pp. Appendix.

Some information about the Decembrist wives. Recommended by Stites as more accurate and insightful than Mazour (entry 205).

Reform, Reaction, and Revolutions, 1855–1917

HISTORIES AND GENERAL WORKS

217 ALLWORTH, EDWARD. *Central Asia: A Century of Russian Rule*.
New York: Columbia University Press, 1967. 552 pp. Index. Glossary.
Discusses women only in terms of their portrayal in literature and song by male authors. Judging by the amount of space devoted to women, the reader would never guess that the changing role of women was "central Asia's most persistent modern literary theme." Tantalizing mention of women poets and musicians in one paragraph.

218 ALSTON, PATRICK. *Education and the State in Tsarist Russia*.
Stanford, Calif.: Stanford University Press, 1969. 322 pp. Index.
Pages 15, 69–70, 202–4, and 230 contain the only information about women's education.

219 ANDERSON, BARBARA A. *Internal Migration During Modernization in Late Nineteenth-Century Russia*. Princeton, N.J.: Princeton University Press, 1980. 222 pp. Index.
Revision of Anderson's dissertation. Good but limited information on female literacy, working patterns, migration, and nonworker migration. The author disputes the notion that population pressures caused much outmigration.

220 ATKINSON, DOROTHY. *The End of the Russian Land Commune, 1905–1930*. Stanford, Calif.: Stanford University Press, 1983. 457 pp. Index.
Contains a few references to women. Particularly useful is the information on

women's participation in the electoral process, reasons for their low attendance at commune assemblies, and women's attitudes toward collectivization.

221 BERNSTEIN, LAURIE ANNABELLE. "Sonia's Daughters: Prostitution and Society in Russia." Ph.D. diss., University of California at Berkeley, 1987. 445 pp.
Examines the development of the regulation of prostitution, the system's effect on urban prostitutes and society's responses to the existence of prostitutes and the medical-police system of regulation. Provides comparative data. Discusses ways in which the movement against legalized prostitution reflected larger social and political questions in the last years of tsarism.

222 BOBROFF, ANNE LOUISE. "Working Women, Bonding Patterns, and the Politics of Daily Life: Russia at the End of the Old Regime." 2 vols. Ph.D. diss., University of Michigan, 1982. 778 pp.
Examines whether women's daily-life bonding networks have helped or hindered their political activity. Interdisciplinary approach utilizing insights and information from psychology, anthropology, and ethnography. Comparison of female and male life cycles in part 1, concluding that women were culturally bound to put husband and children first, whereas men often gave priority to male bonding groups. Part 2 describes women's participation in food riots and organized activities in 1917. Study limited to the four central industrial provinces, with Moscow as the center.

223 BOHACHEVSKY-CHOMIAK, MARTHA. *Feminists Despite Themselves: Women in Ukrainian Community Life, 1884–1939.* Edmonton: Canadian Institute of Ukrainian Studies, University of Alberta, 1988. 460 pp. Index.
The first serious study of this subject in any language. Bohachevksy-Chomiak combines important archival research, interviews with former activists in the Ukrainian women's movement (including her mother), a love for her subject, and an intimate knowledge of Ukrainian culture. A great deal of information is provided about Ukrainian women in the Austrian and Russian empires; nationalism and feminism; relations among Ukrainians, Poles, Jews, and Russians; and the impact of Bolshevik pro-woman policies. A number of the major themes and conflicts covered echo those examined by students of women's political movements in other countries (e.g., articulating women's political priorities in male-dominated movements, establishing autonomous women's organizations, national conflicts within women's organizations, chauvinism, use of the term feminist). This pioneering work provides an important and heretofore lacking comparative perspective.

224 BONNELL, VICTORIA E., ed. *The Russian Worker: Life and Labor under the Tsarist Regime.* Berkeley: University of California Press, 1983. 240 pp. Index.
Contains a translation of excerpts from E. A. Olivnina's *The Tailoring Trade in*

Moscow and the Villages of Moscow and Riazan Provinces: Material on the History of the Domestic Industry in Russia. Olivnina's work describes conditions for female and male tailors. The needle trades were one of the major areas of female employment. Also contains the section on female labor from A. M. Gudvan's *Essays on the History of the Movement of Sales-Clerical Workers in Russia.* Sporadic information about women provided in translations of the memoirs of S. I. Kanatchnikov, P. Timofeev and F. P. Pavlov.

225   BROIDO, VERA. *Apostles into Terrorists: Women and the Revolutionary Movement in the Russia of Alexander II.* London: Maurice Temple Smith, 1978. 238 pp. Index. Bibliography.
Eva Broido's daughter writes about the comparatively large number of women revolutionary activists in Russia. From the outset her sympathies are clear. She explicitly denies that her book is feminist, writing that "to assign to revolutionary women the narrow partisan role of feminists is to distort their position in the revolutionary movement and to diminish their contribution to Russian history." Includes discussion of both women and men revolutionary activists in this period. Selective bibliography does not include work by Engel (entry 276) available at the time this book was written.

226   BRYANT, LOUISE. *Six Red Months in Russia.* New York: George Doran, 1918. 299 pp.
As soon as she heard about the February 1917 Russian Revolution, American Louise Bryant left for Petrograd. Her impressions of her visit, including portraits of Kollontai, Spiridonova, and the Women's "Death Battalion."

227   CIORAN, SAMUEL. *Vladimir Solov'ev and the Knighthood of the Divine Sophia.* Waterloo, Ontario: Wilfred Laurier University Press, 1977. 280 pp. Index.
The rise and fall of the concept of the Divine Feminine and its apostasy, the Demonic Feminine, in the works of Solov'ev, Blok, Belyi, Briusov, and Sergei Bulgakov.

228   DORR, RHETA CHILDE. *Inside the Russian Revolution.* New York: Macmillan, 1917. 243 pp.
Describes the disillusionment of an American feminist socialist after a three-month trip to Russia, beginning in May 1917. Very critical of the Bolsheviks and the July uprising ("I saw the dream of the socialists suddenly come true, and the dream turned out to be a nightmare"). Dorr describes time spent with the Women's Battalion, her encounters with Breshko-Breshkovskaia, Spiridonova, Virubova, and Yusupov, and the visit of the suffragist Emmeline Pankhurst to Russia.

229   DRUMM, ROBERT ELMER. "The Bolshevik Party and the Organization and Emancipation of Working Women, 1914 to 1921; or,

A History of the Petrograd Experiment." Ph.D. diss., Columbia University, 1977. 743 pp.

A richly detailed examination of the twists and turns of Bolshevik policy in relation to women workers. Still the only in-depth scholarship in English on the subject.

230 DUDGEON, RUTH ARLENE FLUCK. "Women and Higher Education in Russia, 1855–1905." Ph.D. diss., George Washington University, 1975. 439 pp.

Still the best survey of the subject. A thoughtful, well-researched study arguing that the struggle for women's higher education was "the training ground for Russian feminists." Wide-ranging discussion of the close connection between the development and growth of the female intelligentsia and a variety of social and political activities. History of women's struggle to enter the professions. Should be published.

231 EDMONDSON, LINDA HARRIET. *Feminism in Russia, 1900–1917.* Stanford, Calif.: Stanford University Press, 1984. 197 pp. Index. Bibliography.

The only book-length treatment of this subject in English. Excellent in placing Russian feminism in the comparative context; especially effective use of sources related to British suffragists and international women's organizations. Looking at the origins of the movement in Russia, Edmondson argues that feminism does not arise only in liberal democratic societies. Instead, in her view, women "have tended to become radicals on behalf of their own sex in times of social upheaval." Certainly, the history of the women's rights movement in Russia supports this; the 1905 Revolution sparked the creation of three major feminist groups. The bulk of this well-written book covers the period from 1905 through the 1908 Women's Congress. Along with Stites (entries 312–15), helps make this movement visible and gives it its rightful place in the history of the period.

232 EDMONDSON, LINDA [HARRIET], ed. *Women and Society in Russia and the Soviet Union.* Cambridge: Cambridge University Press, 1992. 233 pp. Index. Notes.

This volume contains ten articles, eight concerning the period immediately before and after the 1917 Revolution. Essays by Catriona Kelly on women in urban popular entertainment; by Charlotte Rosenthal on the significance of Silver Age women writers, especially poets; by Mary Schaeffer Conroy on women pharmacists before World War I; by Linda Edmondson on women's rights, civil rights and the question of citizenship in 1905; by Barbara Norton about E.D. Kuskova in the period between the February and October Revolutions; by Richard Abraham on Maria Bochkareva and the Women's Battalion in 1917; by Marina Ledkovsky (Astman) on Russian women writers after the Revolution; and by Elizabeth Waters on prostitution after 1917. The remaining two essays, by Sue Bridger ("Young women and perestroika") and Mary Buckley ("Glasnost and the woman question") bring in the perspectives of the last stages of Soviet rule. A significant contribution to scholarship about Russian and Soviet women.

233   EKLOF, BEN, and STEPHEN FRANK. *The World of the Russian Peasant: Post-Emancipation Culture and Society*. Boston: Unwin Hyman, 1990. 234 pp. Index. Bibliography.
Contains Rose Glickman's "Peasant Women and Their Work" and Barbara Engel's "The Woman's Side: Male Outmigration and the Family Economy in Kostroma Province" (entry 279).

234   ENGEL, BARBARA ALPERN. *Mothers and Daughters: Women of the Intelligentsia in Nineteenth-Century Russia*. Cambridge: Cambridge University Press, 1983. 230 pp. Index.
Primarily about female political activists, *nigilistki* (radical women of the 1860s), and revolutionary "heroines and martyrs" such as Sofia Perovskaia, Vera Figner, and Vera Zasulich. She identifies such "special qualities" of women activists as greater fervor, a greater penchant for self-sacrifice, and greater extremism than their male counterparts. She traces the roots of these differences to the family, to the Russian Orthodox tradition, and to the struggles for autonomy common to most educated women. A key work, and one of the few to apply current Western scholarship about gender to Russian history. Marred by a tendency to generalize from female revolutionary activists to all women of the intelligentsia.

235   ———. *Between the Fields and the City: Women, Work and Family in Russia, 1861–1914*. Cambridge: Cambridge University Press, 1993.
Engel here addresses the significance and consequences of peasant women's migration. Utilizing extensive archival data about peasant women, this work studies the impact of migration on the peasantry and the experience of peasants working in distant urban centers as well as nearby factories. The effects of industrialization and urbanization on family life, personal relations and the relationship of the migrant to the peasant household are explored. Engel discusses the mixed legacy of migration; for some it offered new and better opportunities; for many others it increased their hardship and risk. The focus on women and the family in this work provides a fresh perspective on the social history of late Imperial Russia.

236   ENGELSTEIN, LAURA. *The Keys to Happiness: Sex and the Search for Modernity in Fin-de-Siècle Russia*. Ithaca, N.Y.: Cornell University Press, 1992. 496 pp. Index. Bibliography.
Just published as this bibliography neared completion. Acclaimed by Richard Stites as a "blockbuster of a book. . . . Engelstein has expanded the whole

vocabulary of Russian social history by examining gender in the light of professionalism, modernization, elitism, disease control, jurisprudence, and cultural moods—particularly the sexual-cultural-class malaise that obsessed the Russian professional, liberal, and radical intelligentsia after the 1905 revolution." The first part of the title is taken from a popular pre-World War I novel.

237   EVANS, RICHARD J. *The Feminists: Women's Emancipation Movements in Europe, America, and Australasia, 1840–1920.* New York: Barnes and Noble Books, 1977. 266 pp. Index.

Comparative history. Information about Russian feminists primarily on pages 112–24 and 177–83. Marred by some omissions and errors, as in the statement that "the Kadets supported women's suffrage and equal rights," which makes no reference to the Kadet's heated internal battle to have a women's suffrage plank approved (this was finally done in January 1906). Also, there is no mention of Maria Pokrovskaia, editor and publisher of the feminist journal *Zhenskii vestnik* (Women's Herald) from 1904–17. Misspellings of key leaders' names (e.g., Chelkova for Chekhova). Russian language sources not used. Completely superseded by Stites' (entry 611) and Edmondson's (entry 224) accounts of Russian feminists but useful for comparative information.

238   FARNSWORTH, BEATRICE, AND LYNNE VIOLA. *Russian Peasant Women.* New York and Oxford: Oxford University Press, 1992. 304 pp. Notes.

A collection of fourteen essays, most originally published elsewhere, primarily spanning the period from the emancipation of the serfs (1861) to Gorbachev and glasnost. Most of the major current British and American scholars of peasant women represented. Articles by Mary Matossian ("The Peasant Way of Life," entry 53); Christine Worobec ("Temptress or Virgin?," entry 319); Rose Glickman ("Peasant Women and Their Work"); Cathy Frierson ("*Razdel*: The Peasant Family Divided," entry 290); Samuel Ramer ("Midwifery in the Nineteenth-Century Russian Countryside"); Brenda Meehan-Waters ("Russian Peasant Women and the Development of Women's Religious Communities in Prerevolutionary Russia"); three articles by Beatrice Farnsworth ("The Litigious Daughter-in-Law," entry 288; "Village Women Experience the Revolution," entry 656; and "Rural Women and the Law"); Lynne Viola ("*Bab'i Bunty* and Peasant Women's Protest During Collectivization," entry 721); Roberta Manning ("Women in the Soviet Countryside on the Eve of World War II, 1935–1940); Norton Dodge and Murray Feshbach ("The Role of Women in Soviet Agriculture," entry 644); and two essays by Susan Bridger ("Soviet Rural Women: Employment and Family Life" and "Rural Women and Glasnost"). Contains two sections, divided at the revolutionary year of 1917. Helpful introductory essays by the editors for the two sections. A significant resource for a too-long neglected topic.

239   GLENN, SUSAN A. *Daughters of the Shtetl: Life and Labor in the Immigrant Generation*. Ithaca, N.Y.: Cornell University Press, 1990. 312 pp. Index. Notes.
The first chapter surveys women's status in the Pale of Settlement, the emerging Zionist and socialist movements, and the impact of immigration.

240   GLICKMAN, ROSE. *Russian Factory Women: Workplace and Society, 1880–1914*. Berkeley: University of California Press, 1984. 325 pp. Index.
The only book in English on the subject. The product of extensive archival research, as well as a thorough survey of other primary and secondary sources. Covers the period 1880–1914. Although mostly devoted to factory workers, contains some discussion of peasants, prostitutes, and domestic servants. Discusses the roles of these women in the family and places them politically. Views female workers as "between feminism and socialism," with each movement claiming them but neither really representing them. Excellent source.

241   GOLDBERG (RUTHCHILD), ROCHELLE LOIS. "The Russian Women's Movement, 1859–1917." Ph.D. diss., University of Rochester, 1976. 394 pp.
Traces the history of feminist activity in Russia, from the first organized women's groups through the emergence of political feminism in 1905 and its demise as an independent movement after the Bolshevik Revolution. Chapters discuss major organizations such as the Women's Equal Rights Union, Women's Progressive Party, and the League for Women's Equality; the 1908 Women's Congress; and feminist "small deeds" activity from 1908 to 1917.

242   HUTTON, MARCELINE. "Russian and Soviet Women, 1897–1939: Dreams, Struggles, and Nightmares." 2 vols. Ph.D. diss., University of Iowa, 1986. 732 pp.
A wide-ranging study using a great variety of primary and secondary sources to argue for significant changes in the situation of women after the October Revolution. Good use of comparative data. Excellent interweaving of evidence from literature and history. Very well researched. An important source and clearly a labor of love, with a good overview of the situation of women in pre- and post-1917 Russia.

243   JOHANSON, CHRISTINE. *Women's Struggle for higher Education in Russia, 1855–1900*. Kingston, Ontario: McGill-Queen's University Press, 1987. 149 pp. Index. Bibliography.
Despite its reactionary reputation, the Russian government tolerated and sometimes even encouraged access to higher education for women on a scale unparalleled in the rest of Europe in the later half of the nineteenth century. The fight for this education, the radicalization of women studying abroad (especially in Zurich), courses for women doctors, and the conservative backlash after the

assassination of Alexander II and its limits are all surveyed in this book, based on a wide range of archival and other Russian sources.

244 LANGE, HELENE. *Higher Education of Women in Europe*. Translated by L. R. Klemm. New York: D. Appleton, 1897. 191 pp.
Brief survey of women's higher education in Russia. Useful comparative tables and statistics.

245 LINDENMEYR, ADELE. "Public Relief and Private Charity in Late Imperial Russia." Ph.D. diss., Princeton University, 1980. 345 pp.
Information on postreform charitable organizations and the "prominent but limited role" played by women in them. Also discusses the fight for women's suffrage planks in the Unions and the Union of Unions.

246 MOLOKHOVETS, ELENA. *Classic Russian Cooking. Elena Molokhovets' A Gift to Young Housewives*. Translated, introduced and annotated by Joyce Toomre. Bloomington: Indiana University Press, 1992. 680 pp. Index. Bibliography. Notes.
More than a cookbook, this work provides a revealing glimpse into many areas of Russian domestic life from 1861 to 1917. Joyce Toomre's extensive, well-researched introduction discusses such subjects as eastern, western, and Russian Orthodox influences on the development of cuisine, servants, ingredients, the history of Russian cookbooks, and the organization and layout of the Russian household. Almost 500 pages of recipes and explanations from Molokhovets follow the introduction.

247 MULLANEY, MARIE MARMO. *Revolutionary Women: Gender and the Socialist Revolutionary Role*. New York: Praeger, 1983. 401 pp. Index. Bibliography. Notes.
A study of five women revolutionaries, including two Russians (Angelica Balabanoff and Alexandra Kollontai, plus Eleanor Marx, Rosa Luxemburg and "La Pasionara" Dolores Ibarruri). Feminist analysis, with attention to both their public and private lives. No Russian-language sources used; nevertheless, provocative themes similar to Mullaney's 1984 article (see entry 302).

248 NORTON, BARBARA THERESE. "E. D. Kuskova: A Political Biography of a Russian Democrat, Part 1 (1869–1905)." Ph.D. diss., Pennsylvania State University, 1981. 299 pp.
Kuskova played an important role in the Liberation movement and in the 1905 Revolution. Norton, critical of the cursory treatment of Kuskova by historians and memoirists of all persuasions, thoroughly examines Kuskova's political and publicist activities. Her progression from populist to Marxist to Kadet to non-sectarian social democrat is surveyed. Argues convincingly for a reexamination of Kuskova's role in the Economist controversy and of the evolution of her political views through 1905 (a founder of the Kadet party, she left to form a

radical-democratic coalition). Emphasizes her commitment to democracy. Challenges view that women played a secondary role in the Russian opposition. Devotes little attention to Kuskova's connections to the nascent women's movement. Very useful survey of sources.

249   PORTER, CATHY. *Fathers and Daughters: Russian Women in Revolution*. London: Virago, in association with Quartet Books, 1976. 309 pp. Index.

Covers women's activism in Russia during the reign of Alexander II. An important contribution, inspired by the rebirth of the women's movement, but surpassed by the work of Engel and Stites.

250   ———. *Women in Revolutionary Russia*. Cambridge: Cambridge University Press, 1987. 48 pp.

Pamphlet geared to high-school students. Overall good information, despite some inaccuracy and oversimplification related to reading level. Suggestions for further reading do not include works by Engel or Stites or the four biographies (including Porter's own work) of Kollontai (entries 793, 794, 796, and 809).

251   RADKEY, OLIVER. *The Agrarian Foes of Bolshevism: Promise and Default of the Russian Socialist Revolutionaries, February to October 1917*. New York: Columbia University Press, 1958. 521 pp. Index.

Some mention of Breshko-Breshkovskaia and Spiridonova and their role in the events of this period.

252   RANSEL, DAVID, ed. *The Family in Imperial Russia: New Lines of Historical Research*. Urbana: University of Illinois Press, 1978. 342 pp. Index. Annotated bibliography.

Another excellent work from the late 1970s, with articles and information of use to women's studies scholars. Especially useful are essays by Jessica Tovrov on mother-child relationships in noble families, Barbara Alpern Engel on mother-daughter relations in the family intelligentsia, Richard Wortman on the evolution of the Russian empress's role as mother, Peter Czap on marriage and the peasant joint family under serfdom, Gregory Freeze on Alexander II's ecclesiastical reforms and their impact on clerical families, Stephen Dunn on the family in Russian folklore, Antonina Martynova on popular lullabies as a source of information about prerevolutionary village life, David Ransel on the women of the foundling system, Samuel Ramer on midwifery in rural nineteenth-century Russia, Nancy Frieden on medical reformers' attempts to change child-rearing practices, and Robert Johnson on the effects of the "rural-urban nexus" on family life. Includes an excellent selected and annotated bibliography of Russian and English sources on the family, demography, women, children, folklore, and working-class and clerical families, compiled by Harold Leich and June Pachuta. The introduction by Ransel sets the parameters for this collection and suggests future directions for research.

253 ———. *Mothers of Misery: Child Abandonment in Russia*. Princeton, N.J.:
      Princeton University Press, 1988. 330 pp. Index. Bibliography.
Provocative study. Traces the state's concern with, and attempts to ameliorate,
child abandonment—primarily by establishing foundling homes and a system
of fosterage. Argues that the comparatively high infant and childhood mortality rates among Russians were attributable to a flawed child-care culture characterized by very unsanitary conditions, maternal overwork, poor feeding
practices, and resignation toward children's illness and death. Finds that the
fosterage system became a lucrative source of extra income, primarily for peasant women. A case study in how "the government intended to achieve one pur-
pose but learned that the peasants could adapt the mechanism to other ends."

254 RAPPOPORT, A. S. *Home Life in Russia*. New York: Macmillan, 1913.
      287 pp. Index.
Observations about everyday life in prerevolutionary Russia. Peasant villages,
peasant women, family life, schools, women's education, literary women, workers, and home life are discussed. A good source for late-nineteenth- and early-
twentieth-century conditions in the countryside.

255 RIEMER, ELEANOR S., and JOHN C. FOUT, eds. *European Women:
      A Documentary History, 1789–1945*. New York: Schocken Books, 1980.
      258 pp. Index. Bibliography.
This anthology includes several documents about Russian and Soviet women.
One is an abridged version of an article by Dr. Maria Pokrovskaia (here called
Pokzovskaia) entitled "A Woman Doctor's Report on Working Conditions for
Women in Russian Factories." The article originally appeared in Pokrovskaia's
Zhenskii vestnik in 1913 and was translated and printed in the journal of the
international women's movement, *Jus suffragii*, in 1914. Its inclusion makes
this anthology the only contemporary English source that contains a translation
from Pokrovskaia's voluminous writings. Other documents include "Women
and Socialism in the Soviet Union: An "'Official' View" from Fanni Nurina's
1934 book, an excerpt from Kollontai's 1918 book *Communism and the Family*,
and two 1936 letters objecting to the prohibition of abortion, reprinted from
Pravda and Rudolf Schlesinger's *The Family in the USSR*. The bibliography is
dated but still helpful for those engaged in comparative research.

256 ROSS, DALE. "The Role of the Women of Petrograd in War,
      Revolution and Counter-Revolution, 1914–1921." Ph.D. diss., Rutgers
      University, 1973. 408 pp.
Covers the significant influence of women on events in Petrograd during this
period. Despite their general influence, Ross argues that women organized as
women "had *no* significant influence on the events of this period." Examines the
radical transformation of women's roles after the Revolution.

257   SANDERS, JONATHAN EDWARD. "The Union of Unions: Political, Economic, Civil and Human Rights Organizations in the 1905 Russian Revolution." Ph.D. diss., Columbia University, 1985. 1,308 pp.

Encyclopedic study. Chapter 6 devoted to the Women's Equal Rights Union and the Union for the Attainment of Full Equality for Jews. Makes provocative comparisons. First scholarly work in English to utilize material from the Women's Union archive. Discusses the fight for women's suffrage in the Union of Unions.

258   SATINA, SOPHIE. *Education of Women in Pre-Revolutionary Russia*. Translated by Alexandra F. Poustchine. Foreword by Myra Sampson. New York: Sophie Satin, 1966. 153 pp.

Useful survey of the topic. Most interesting are the author's memoirs of her days as a student in a private gymnasium in Moscow, from her entrance into the second class at the age of ten in 1889 to her graduation in 1896. Also includes memoirs of her student days at the Guerrier courses from 1900 to 1904 and her work at the courses thereafter. Information by two graduates about the Kiev and Kazan courses as well.

259   SCHIRMACHER, DR. KAETHE. *The Modern Women's Rights Movement: A Historical Survey*. Translated by Carl C. Eckhardt. New York: Macmillan, 1912. 280 pp. Index.

Section on the Slavic and Balkan countries, including fifteen pages on Russia.

260   STANTON, THEODORE. *The Woman Question in Europe*. New York: G. P. Putnam's Sons, 1884. 478 pp. Index.

Chapter on Russia written by Maria Tsebrikova (listed as Marie Zebrikoff in this book).

261   SUTTON, RICHARD CUMMER. "Crime and Social Change in Russia after the Great Reforms: Laws, Courts, and Criminals, 1874–1894." Ph.D. diss., Indiana University, 1984.

Evidence about women is primarily related to morality crimes and rape. Provides statistics indicating steep rise in convictions of women for "immoral behavior" in the late nineteenth century. Data provided on rural as well as urban crime, with information challenging traditional notions of the type and nature of crime in rural areas. No real discussion of prostitution.

262   TIAN-SHANSKAIA, OLGA SEMYONOVA. *Village Life in Late Tsarist Russia*. Edited by David L. Ransel. Translated by David L. Ransel with Michael Levine. Bloomington: Indiana University Press, 1993. 192 pp. Index. Notes.

The fruits of four years (1898–1902) of study of peasants in villages near the author's family estate in the Dankov district, Riazan province. Many observations about the role and treatment of women and children, including courting rituals, marriage and sexual relations, childbearing and childbirth, infanticide, work habits, the household economy, daily life and the prevalence of wife-beating. Tian-Shanskaia died in 1906; her friend Varvara Shneider edited and published this study in 1914. David Ransel has further edited and reorganized the manuscript. His introduction provides useful information about the development of ethnography, the intellectual climate of the times and about Tian-Shanskaia's life. Ransel psychologizes Tian-Shanskaia's negative portraits of peasant men and male violence, attributing her gloomy depictions to personal problems instead of the reality of the situation.

263   WOROBEC, CHRISTINE. "Family, Community, and Land in Peasant Russia, 1860–1905." Ph.D. diss., University of Toronto, 1984. 430 pp.
Disputes the "powerful social and political myth" that the traditional Russian peasant family was falling apart in this period. Instead, Worobec argues, continuity and stability characterized the traditional patriarchal multiple-family household, and "peasant traditionalism impeded the impact of modernization and cushioned its effects."

264   ———. *Peasant Russia: Family and Community in the Post-Emancipation Period*. Princeton, N.J.: Princeton University Press, 1991. 257 pp. Index. Bibliography.
A significant contribution to our understanding of the peasant world after emancipation. The first monograph to discuss in depth the role and status of women in the peasant community. Utilizes a wide range of sources, from court records to *zemstvo* (instruments of rural self-government established by Tsar Alexander II in 1864) reports to compilations of folk culture. Useful bibliographic essay discusses the author's methodological framework.

HISTORY AND SOCIAL SCIENCE ARTICLES

265   BERGMAN, JAY. "The Political Thought of Vera Zasulich." Slavic Review 38, no. 2 (June 1979): 243–58.
Zasulich's thought, reflecting the prevailing "ethos of social altruism and philanthropy" of the Russian intelligentsia of her time.

266   BERNSTEIN, LAURIE. "Yellow Tickets and State-Licensed Brothels: The Tsarist Government and the Regulation of Urban Prostitution." In *Health and Society in Revolutionary Russia*, edited by Susan Gross Solomon and John F. Hutchinson, pp. 45–65. Bloomington: Indiana University Press, 1990.
Derived from Chapters 1, 2, and 6 of Bernstein's dissertation, "Sonia's Daughters" (entry 221). History of licensing system, changing attitudes of the

Ministry of Internal Affairs to regulation at the turn of the twentieth century, and lack of workable alternatives to the existing system. Bernstein concludes that the tsarist government followed the lead of the Europeans in linking the prevention of venereal disease with the regulation of prostitutes and, like the Europeans, discovered that this approach controlled neither the diseases nor the prostitution.

267   BOBROFF, ANNE. "Russian Working Women: Sexuality in Bonding Patterns and the Politics of Daily Life." In *Powers of Desire: The Politics of Sexuality*, edited by Ann Snitow, Christine Stansell, and Sharon Thompson, pp. 206–27. New York: Monthly Review Press, 1983.

Anne Bobroff examines women workers' avoidance of "long-term, unified action in the public sphere." Using folklore, memoirs, newspaper accounts, and workers' oral histories, Bobroff explores gender-based differences in bonding patterns (women were expected to bond primarily with their husbands and children; for men, male unity remained primary). Bobroff analyzes adolescent rituals and group activity, courtship, and adult married life, making connections between the different cultural definitions of sexuality for women and men and their ability to engage in sustained political activity.

268   BOHACHEVSKY-CHOMIAK, MARTHA. "Women in Kiev and Kharkiv: Community Organizations in the Russian Empire." In *Imperial Russia, 1700–1917: State, Society, Opposition. Essays in Honor of Marc Raeff*, edited by Ezra Mendelsohn and Marshall Shatz, pp. 161–74. DeKalb: Northern Illinois University Press, 1988.

A study of Ukrainian women's organizations, focussing on the establishment of women's higher-education courses in Kiev and Kharkiv, Sunday adult literacy schools, and links between Ukrainian women activists and Russian feminists. Discusses cooperation between Ukrainian, Russian, and Jewish women in self-help and educational activities, resistance of nationalist groups to separate women's branches, and support of Russian feminists for national autonomy.

269   BROWN, JULIE VAIL. "Female Sexuality and Madness in Russian Culture: Traditional Values and Psychiatric Theory." *Social Research* 53, no. 2 (Summer 1986): 369–85.

Explores the understanding of the relationship between madness and female sexuality in Russian psychiatry. Argues for important cultural differences between the West and Russia. The Russians did not exalt the virgin and deny female sexuality; they affirmed the latter and linked it to the earth and fertility. Brief survey of attitudes toward premature sexual activity; *klikushestvo*, or peasant female hysteria; "deviant" sexual activity in religious sects; and the work of woman psychiatrist L. S. Pavlovskaia on radical female political activists and mental disorders. A rare and suggestive foray into an important but largely ignored topic.

270   ———. "Revolution and Psychosis: The Mixing of Science and Politics in Russian Psychiatric Medicine, 1905–1913." *Russian Review* 46, no. 3 (July 1987): 283–302.

An analysis of psychiatric practice in this turbulent period. Includes information on the work of Dr. L. S. Pavlovskaia, one of a small number of women psychiatrists. Pavlovskaia treated several women activists from a sympathetic point of view, emphasizing their "innate strength," in contrast to a male colleague who stressed their vulnerability. For more on this subject see Brown's article in *Social Research* (entry 269).

271   DEUTSCH, HELENE. "A Note on Rosa Luxemburg and Angelica Balabanoff." *American Imago* 40, no. 1 (Spring 1983): 29–33.

Laudatory remarks about these two revolutionary women and their fight for peace by one of the foremost female Freudians.

272   DONALD, MOIRA. "Bolshevik Activity Amongst the Working Women of Petrograd in 1917." *International Review of Social History* 27, pt. 2 (1982): 129–60.

Discusses the Bolshevik hostility to separate organizations for women, the short-lived attempt to set up a women's bureau, the concentration of advocates for organizing among women on the editorial board of *Rabotnitsa* (Working woman), and Kollontai's successful attempts to ally *soldatki* and laundresses' organizations with the Bolsheviks. Relies heavily on Kollontai's accounts of events. Although hostility between Bolsheviks and feminists is cited, only Kollontai and other Bolshevik sources are used; no feminist sources are cited.

273   DUDGEON, RUTH [ARLENE FLUCK]. "Women Students in Imperial Russia, 1872–1917." *Russian History* 9, pt. 1 (1982): 1–26.

Excellent survey of women's struggle for higher education, compressing information from Dudgeon's pathbreaking dissertation (entry 223).

274   DUNHAM, VERA SANDOMIRSKY. "The Strong Woman Motif." In *The Transformation of Russian Society*, edited by Cyril E. Black, pp. 459–83. Cambridge: Harvard University Press, 1960.

Examines the differences in the portrayal of the heroine in Russian and Soviet literature. Dunham argues that the norm is to show the "relaxed, non-neurotic quality of feminine strength." Stresses a recurring theme—the contrast between the strong woman and the weak or passive man—despite the reality that the women's strength is often tested by male acts of violence, such as rape. Speaks about the *tsel'nost* (fullness) of female characters. Postwar "new deference to the man" also noted.

275   EDMONDSON, LINDA. "Russian Feminists and the First All-Russian Congress of Women." *Russian History* 3, pt. 2 (1976): 123–49.

An excellent description and analysis of the largest prerevolutionary women's congress. Places the 1908 Congress in the context of the political forces unleashed by the 1905 Revolution and its aftermath. Disputes Stites's notion of a clear distinction between feminist and left political goals and activities. Argues for a more complex portrait of the feminist movement, noting the varied political perspectives within the movement.

276   ENGEL, BARBARA ALPERN. "Women as Revolutionaries: The Case of the Russian Populists." In *Becoming Visible: Women in European History*, edited by Renate Bridenthal and Claudia Koonz, pp. 346–69. Boston: Houghton Mifflin, 1977.
Presents thesis that radical women went from feminism to populism. Developed more fully in Engel's *Mothers and Daughters* (entry 234).

277   ———. "From Separatism to Socialism: Women in the Russian Revolutionary Movement of the 1870s." In *Socialist Women: European Socialist Feminism in the Nineteenth Century*, edited by Marilyn Boxer and Jean Quataert, pp. 51–74. New York: Elsevier North-Holland, 1978.
Engel argues that the women of the Chaikovskii circle were the first to play a significant, independent political role. She views their development as one that moved from feminist separatism to abandonment of their feminism in place of work with men and a commitment to revolution. This argument is more fully developed in later works, such as *Mothers and Daughters* (entry 234).

278   ———. "Women Medical Students in Russia, 1872–1882: Reformers or Rebels?" *Journal of Social History* 12, no. 3 (Spring 1979): 394–415.
In 1872 Russia became the first European nation to establish women's medical courses. Argues that female medical students cannot be characterized simply as radical or liberal. Information about the attitudes of government officials (largely negative) and society (generally positive) and the personal struggles of women to get an education. Did the medical students become revolutionaries? Engel finds a mixed record, but concludes that for the great majority, the fulfillment of their professional aspirations was more important than political activity.

279   ———. "The Women's Side: Male Out-Migration and the Family Economy in Kostroma Province." *Slavic Review* 45, no. 2 (Summer 1986): 257–71.
Engel shifts the focus from the male peasant migrant to the women and family remaining in the village in two districts (Soligalich and Chukhlonia) in Kostroma province. Based primarily on data from the Kostroma *zemstvo* and the observations of the *zemstvo* physician D. N. Zhbankov. Although some women, generally the most marginal, did migrate, 95 percent in these districts did not. Explores the significance of ties between the male out-migrants (a high percentage of whom were married) and their families. Examines the effects of

the out-migrant marriage relationship on the women involved (chief among them were greater independence for the women, a more significant contribution by the women to the family economy, much less physical violence against women, higher literacy, lower birth rates and infant mortality, and a generally higher standard of living). This pioneering contribution raises provocative questions about relations between the sexes in the countryside in the face of changing economic conditions and suggests avenues for future research.

280   ———. "Women in Russia and the Soviet Union." *Signs* 12, no. 4 (Summer 1986): 781–96.
Bibliographical essay reviewing Rose Glickman's *Russian Factory Women* (entry 240; incorrectly cited by Engel as *The Russian Factory Woman*), Linda Harriet Edmondson's *Feminism in Russia* (entry 231; incorrectly cited by Engel as *The Feminist Movement in Russia*), the collection of essays in *Soviet Sisterhood* (entry 550), the Soviet feminist articles in Tatyana Mamonova's *Woman and Russia* (entry 574), and the Soviet writings on women in Gail Lapidus's *Women, Work and Family in the Soviet Union* (entry 566). A very useful survey, highlighting the key issues and debates in Western scholarship about women in Russia and the Soviet Union.

281   ———. "Women, Gender and Political Choice in the Revolutionary Movement of the 1870s." Research Paper no. 66. The Marjorie Mayrock Center for Soviet and East European Research. Jerusalem: Hebrew University of Jerusalem, 1988. 23 pp.
Engel argues that gender was critical in shaping the consciousness of women in the revolutionary movement of the 1870s. These women, largely from the gentry class, were, like women of all classes, bound by law and custom to the family. Their choice to enter the public sphere involved far more personal disruption and sacrifice of family ties than did that of men. The struggle to be part of the movement for social change shaped populist women's attitudes about sexual relations, pregnancy, and children. Ironically, as Engel shows, the very struggle on the part of the women activists for autonomy made it difficult for them to organize working and peasant women, for whom traditional family ties remained more compelling.

282   ———. "St. Petersburg Prostitutes in the Late Nineteenth Century: A Personal and Social Profile." *Russian Review* 48 (January 1989): 21–44.
Engel is the most prolific of the scholars in Russian women's history and a pioneer in applying insights of new feminist historical scholarship to Russia. In this article she turns her attention to a segment of the female working class. On the basis of limited data (the 1899 census of prostitutes in the Russian Empire) and two studies by St. Petersburg physicians Petr Oboznenko and Aleksandr Fedorov, Engel "explore[s] the socio-economic and personal profiles of registered prostitutes in St. Petersburg at the end of the nineteenth century" and compares them with French and English prostitutes. She finds significant dif-

ferences in the length of time Russian prostitutes plied their trade (longer than the English, shorter than the French) and concludes that "the more marginal" peasant women were most likely to become prostitutes when they migrated to the city. Contemporary Russian-feminist writing about prostitution, including the work of Dr. Maria Pokrovskaia, is not included.

283   ———. "Women, Work and Family in the Factories of Rural Russia." *Russian History* 16, nos. 2–4 (1989): 223–37.
Examines "the impact of customary gender roles on the deployment of women's labor between household and factory, and the effect of women's factory labor on relations within the peasant household." Focuses on the Vladimir-Kostroma textile region and uses data provided by *zemstvo* studies. Emphasizes continued ties between women workers and their home villages, but also notes that greater economic freedom is possible for single women earning factory wages. Also discusses changes in women worker's sexual mores and argues for greater sexual independence among female factory workers. Concludes that while factory labor has certainly changed the peasant family, the rural patriarchal system has essentially stayed intact.

284   ———. "Peasant Morality and Pre-Marital Relations in Late 19th Century Russia." *Journal of Social History* 23, no. 4 (Summer 1990): 695–714.
Discusses changes in peasant sexual morality within the traditional patriarchal system at a time of increasing economic change. Challenges those historians who argue for continuity in peasant sexual behavior. Based primarily on materials from the Tenishev Archive. Argues that there was greater sexual independence on the part of younger peasants but notes that this was much more the case for males than for females.

285   ENGELSTEIN, LAURA. "Morality and the Wooden Spoon: Russian Doctors View Syphilis, Social Class, and Sexual Behavior, 1890–1905." *Representations* 14 (Spring 1986): 169–209. (Also in Gallagher, Catherine, and Thomas Lacquer, eds. *The Making of the Modern Body: Sexuality and Society in the Nineteenth Century*, pp. 169–208. Berkeley: University of California Press, 1987.
Examines theories of transmission of syphilis and their social and political resonance in late-nineteenth- to early-twentieth-century Russia. Describes cultural differences, political perspectives, and their influence on the conception of this disease. Covers debate between public health physicians, who viewed the disease as a social problem and supported theories of nonvenereal transmission, and proponents of venereal transmission. Proposes that the erosion of belief in the morality of village life was a key factor in weakening the case for nonvenereal transmission. Exposes the system of regulation of prostitutes as "a system of controlling women, not disease." Argues for the "distinctive symbolic function of syphilis in Russia."

286 ———. "Gender and the Juridical Subject: Prostitution and Rape in Nineteenth-Century Russian Criminal Codes." *Journal of Modern History* 60 (September 1988): 458–95.
An analysis of the 1895 draft criminal code. Argues that changes in the 1903 text reflect "a strong liberalizing tendency among Russian bureaucrats and influential public figures" as well as their attitudes towards society and the state. Engelstein discusses changes in the perception of rape, various forms of sexual conduct, including male homosexuality and prostitution, and compares these with European legal concepts. Concludes that "the legal reconstitution of women's dependent status on a modern basis, within the general context of greater individual autonomy, was consistent with Russia's hesitant acceptance of contemporary legal ideas."

287 ———. "Lesbian Vignettes: A Russian Triptych from the 1890s." *Signs* 15, no. 4 (1990): 813–31.
Translates and puts into context St. Petersburg obstetrician-gynecologist I. M. Tarnovskii's three vignettes of contemporary lesbianism, involving women of different social class and standing—two peasant women, two women of the intelligentsia, and two prostitutes. A valuable source about a topic rarely discussed in Russia from that time to the present.

288 FARNSWORTH, BEATRICE. "The Litigious Daughter-in-Law: Family Relations in Rural Russia in the Second Half of the Nineteenth Century." *Slavic Review* 45, no. 1 (Spring 1986): 49–64.
Examines the position of the daughter-in-law in the peasant family by reviewing records of court disputes in the peasant courts. Farnsworth finds that complaints brought by daughters-in-law against in-laws and by wives against husbands were much more frequent than the reverse. She challenges the notion that peasant women accepted violence directed against them as the norm, citing numerous court cases in which women protested such treatment. In suggesting areas for further study, Farnsworth highlights the crying need for more research about peasant women.

289 FIESELER, BEATE. "The Making of Russian Female Social Democrats, 1890–1917." *International Review of Social History* 34, no. 2 (1989): 193–226.
Revised version of a paper given at the 1988 Akron Conference on Women in the History of the Russian Empire. Analysis of the social composition of women in the Russian Social-Democratic Labor (Rabochaia in Russian) Party (RSDRP). Finds that women activists came from "higher social backgrounds," were relatively well educated (more so than their male counterparts), and were primarily professionals and students.

290 FRIERSON, CATHY A. "Razdel: The Peasant Family Divided." *Russian Review* 46, no. 1 (January 1987): 35–52.
Discusses family and household division and argues that they are not new,

postemancipation phenomena, nor can they be explained solely by economic factors. No specific concern with gender. Focuses on the peasant man; nevertheless, provides some useful information about the role and status of women in the *razdel* (division or partition of land within the peasant commune). Household disputes described as "conflict among the men" and "haggling among the women."

291   GROBERG, KRIS. "The Education of Jewish Girls in Nineteenth Century Russia." *Women: East-West Forum*, no. 5 (May 1988): 11–13.
Addresses questions and issues raised by materials found in the course of the author's research. Survey of options for education of Jewish girls, from religious schools (*khadorim*) to tutors to secular Russian crown schools. Barriers of religious custom and class.

292   HARUKI, WADA. "Vera Figner in the Early Post-Revolutionary Period, 1917–23." *Annals of the Institute of Social Science* (University of Tokyo), no. 25 (1983–84): 43–73.
Uses a wide range of sources, including archival (Figner's personal *Fond*) and personal interviews to describe and analyze this long-lived (1852–1942) populist radical's experience in the first years of Bolshevik rule. Does not mention Figner's participation at the head of the largest women's suffrage demonstration, organized by feminists in March 1917.

293   HELDT MONTER, BARBARA. "*Rassvet* (1859–1862) and the Woman Question." *Slavic Review* 36, no. 1 (March 1977): 76–85.
Discusses the first comprehensive Russian women's journal, its contents, and its impact. For Heldt Monter, *Rassvet* served to awaken its female readers to the issues of the day, particularly to the woman question.

294   JOHANSON, CHRISTINE. "Autocratic Politics, Public Opinion, and Women's Medical Education during the Reign of Alexander II, 1855–1881." *Slavic Review* 38, no. 3 (September 1979): 426–43.
The initiation and growth of women's medical education as an illustration of the policies and practices of the reign of Alexander II. Illuminates a neglected aspect of the tsar's reforms.

295   KARLINSKY, SIMON. "Russia's Gay Literature and Culture: The Impact of the October Revolution." In *Hidden From History*, edited by Martin Bauml Duberman, Martha Vicinus, and George Chauncy, Jr., pp. 347–64. New York: New American Library, 1989.
Karlinsky challenges the "simplistic and schematic" notion that sexual liberation in Russia began with the Bolshevik October Revolution of 1917. He argues that homosexuality became more visible after Alexander II's reforms of the 1860s, and especially between 1905 and 1917 in literary circles. Disputing the notion that the Bolsheviks legalized homosexuality, Karlinsky argues instead that the Russian Left was especially homophobic and that the Bolsheviks sup-

pressed widespread male homosexuality in the Caucasus and Central Asia, propounding the view that homosexuality was a sickness to be cured. In this view, the recriminalization of male homosexuality in 1933–34 was a logical outcome of rampant radical homophobia. (For an alternate view, see Lauritsen and Thorstad [entry 567]). Though focused primarily on men, this article is one of the few sources of information about Russian lesbians.

296 KNIGHT, AMY. "The *Fritschi*: A Study of Female Radicals in the Russian Populist Movement." *Canadian-American Slavic Studies* 9, no. 1 (Spring 1975): 1–17.
Disputes those who minimize or ignore women's contribution to the nineteenth-century Russian revolutionary movement, citing the example of the women's revolutionary group the *Fritschi*. The members of this group were Varvara Aleksandrova, Dora Aptekman, Sofiia Bardina, Vera and Lidiia Figner, Betia Kaminskaia, Aleksandra Khorzhevskaia, Ol'ga and Vera Liubatovich, Evgeniia, Mariia, and Nadezhda Subbotina, Anna Toporkova, and Evgeniia Tumanova. Argues that the *Fritschi* and other like-minded women helped "strengthen" many populist "values and ideals." Views motivation for many women's radical activity as "largely a personal need to prove their own worth and independence."

297 KUCHEROV, SAMUEL. "The Case of Vera Zasulich." *Russian Review* 11, no. 2 (1952): 86–96.
Account of the trial of Vera Zasulich. A number of translated excerpts from the trial, from the memoirs of Presiding Judge A. F. Koni.

298 McNEAL, ROBERT. "Women in the Russian Radical Movement." *Journal of Social History* 5, no. 2 (Winter 1971–72): 143–63.
One of the first contemporary historians to note the relatively large number of Russian women radical activists. Some useful biographical information contrasts the comparatively prominent position of women among the Populists and Socialist Revolutionaries with the more male-dominated Social Democrats.

299 MEEHAN-WATERS, BRENDA. "From Contemplative Practice to Charitable Activity: Russian Women's Religious Communities and the Development of Charitable Work, 1861–1917." In *Lady Bountiful Revisited: Women, Philanthropy, and Power*, pp. 142–56. New Brunswick, N.J.: Rutgers University Press, 1990.
Surveys the history of these communities against the larger socio-economic and cultural context of Russian society in the period from 1861 to 1917. The author documents a shift from "contemplative practice to charitable activity" in this period, analyzes the role of women in building and sustaining these communities, and compares and contrasts Russian and Western practice with respect to religious orders and philanthropy.

300   MIROVICH, ZENEIDE. "Russia." *The International Woman Suffrage Alliance: Report of Second and Third Conferences*, pp. 97–103. Copenhagen, 1906.
Report by one of the leading Women's Equal Rights Union activists to the largest international feminist organization. Rare contemporary account in English of Russian feminist activity.

301   ———. "Russia." *The International Woman Suffrage Alliance: Report of Fourth Conference*, pp. 116–18. Amsterdam, June 15–20, 1908.
Women's Equal Rights Union activity during the early years of repression after the 1905 Revolution. Another rare primary account in English.

302   MULLANEY, MARIE MARMO. "Gender and the Socialist Revolutionary Role, 1871–1921: A General Theory of the Female Revolutionary Personality." *Historical Reflections* 11, no. 2 (Summer 1984): 99–152.
Critiques the literature on revolutionary behavior for "its unstated assumptions about gender." Focuses on the specificity of the female revolutionary experience as distinct from the male, based on five European female revolutionaries active between 1871–1921 (two Russians—Angelica Balabanoff and Alexandra Kollontai—plus Rosa Luxemburg, Eleanor Marx, and Louise Michel). Mullaney identifies such factors as strong female role models, a "sense of specialness" as children, supportive fathers, a rejection of power hunger and revolutionary asceticism, a strong female support network, and an acceptance of self-sacrifice as significant. A strong, thought-provoking feminist analysis.

303   NORTON, BARBARA [THERESE]. "*Esche raz Ekonomizm*: E. D. Kuskova, S. N. Prokopovich, and the Challenge to Russian Social Democracy." *Russian Review* 45, no. 2 (April 1986): 183–207.
Disputes the notion that Kuskova and Prokopovich played a major role in formulating Russian economism.

304   ———. "The Making of a Female Marxist: E. D. Kuskova's Conversion to Russian Social Democracy." *International Review of Social History* 34, no. 2 (1989): 227–47.
Documents the political development of this leading social democrat. Argues that Kuskova saw Marxism as the only viable analysis of and program of action to cure Russia's ills. Kuskova deserves more attention than she has received.

305   RAMER, SAMUEL C. "The Transformation of the Russian Feldsher, 1864–1914." In *Imperial Russia, 1700–1917: State, Society, Opposition. Essays in Honor of Marc Raeff*, edited by Ezra Mendelsohn and Marshall S. Shatz, pp. 136–60. Dekalb: Northern Illinois University Press, 1988.
Documents the changes in the role and training of *feldshers* (often the only medical practitioners available to peasents), especially after restrictions against

women were lifted in 1871. In time women predominated, by 1910 making up 70 percent of *feldsher* students, most training to be midwives. Jewish women were 20 percent of this total, in part because their diplomas freed them to live outside the Pale of Settlement.

306   ———. "Traditional Healers and Peasant Culture in Russia, 1861–1917." In *Peasant Economy, Culture, and Politics of European Russia, 1861–1917*, edited by Esther Kingston-Mann and Timothy Mixter, with the assistance of Jeffrey Burds, pp. 207–32. Princeton, N.J.: Princeton University Press, 1991.
Information about the *znakhari* (the most prevalent name for traditional healers) and the predominance of women in their ranks.

307   RANSEL, DAVID. "Problems in Measuring Illegitimacy in Pre-revolutionary Russia." *Journal of Social History* 16, no. 2 (Winter 1982): 111–23.
Makes the case that illegitimacy rates were not dropping in late-nineteenth- and early-twentieth-century Russia, particularly in Russian cities in the 1890s.

308   RUANE, CHRISTINE. "The Vestal Virgins of St. Petersburg: Schoolteachers and the 1897 Marriage Ban." *Russian Review* 50 (April 1991): 163–82.
Surveys the situation of women schoolteachers in Russia, emphasizing the intersection of gender and work. Employers preferred young female teachers because they were a cheap, compliant work force. Discusses the struggle to overturn the 1897 ban on marriage for St. Petersburg's female teachers. Examines how feminist support finally overturned the ban in 1913 and changed conditions for women teachers. Views the repeal as indicative of a change in attitude about sex discrimination. Some comparative data. Discusses ambivalent attitudes of male leaders of teachers' organizations.

309   SHATZ, MARSHALL S. "Michael Bakunin and his Biographers: The Question of Bakunin's Sexual Impotence." In *Imperial Russia, 1700–1917: State, Society, Opposition. Essays in Honor of Marc Raeff*, edited by Ezra Mendelsohn and Marshall S. Shatz, pp. 219–40. Dekalb: Northern Illinois University Press, 1988.
Examines the question of Bakunin's relations with women and argues strongly against assertions of this revolutionary's impotence.

310   SLAUGHTER, JANE. "Humanism versus Feminism in the Socialist Movement: The Life of Angelica Balabanoff." In *European Women on the Left*, edited by Jane Slaughter and Robert Kern, pp. 179–94. Westport, Conn.: Greenwood, 1981.
Useful survey of the life of this Russian revolutionary, antiwar activist, and secretary of the Third International.

311   SPRINGER, BEVERLY TANNER. "Anna Kulisioff: Russian
       Revolutionist, Italian Feminist." In *European Women on the Left*, edited
       by Jane Slaughter and Robert Kern, pp. 13–27. Westport, Conn.:
       Greenwood, 1981.
Surveys the key elements of the political work and writing of Kulisioff.

312   STITES, RICHARD. "M. L. Mikhailov and the Emergence of the
       Woman Question in Russia." *Canadian Slavic Studies* 3, no. 2 (Summer
       1969): 178–99.
Mikhailov was an articulate proponent of ideas about women's equality that
were prevalent in the late 1850s and early 1860s. His thought was influenced
by the French feminist Jenny D'Hericourt.

313   ———. "Women's Liberation Movements in Russia, 1900–1930."
       Canadian-American Slavic Studies 7, no. 4 (Winter 1973): 460–74.
Survey of this subject, covered much more fully in Stites's book (entry 611).

314   ———. "Wives, Sisters, Daughters, and Workers: A Review Article."
       Russian History 3, pt. 2 (1976): 237–44.
Review of Mazour's *Women in Exile* (entry 205), Engel and Rosenthal's *Five
Sisters* (entry 344), Porter's *Fathers and Daughters* (entry 249), and Nadezhda
Karpetskaia's *Rabotnitsy i velikii Oktiabr'*. Finds Mazour disappointing in its lack
of historical and social analysis, praises *Five Sisters*, finds Porter superficial and
misleading, and calls Karpetskaia "one-dimensional and one-sided."

315   ———. "Prostitutes and Society in Pre-Revolutionary Russia."
       Jahrbücher für Geschichte Osteuropas 31, no. 3 (1983): 348–64.
Excellent survey, placing Russian prostitution in the wider European context.
Discusses social background, nationality, motivation, conditions of work, male
clients, and white slavery. Covers official, feminist, and intelligentsia responses
to the problem.

316   WAGNER, WILLIAM G. "The Trojan Mare: Women's Rights and
       Civil Rights in Late Imperial Russia." In *Civil Rights in Imperial Russia*,
       edited by Olga Crisp and Linda Edmondson, pp. 65–84. Oxford:
       Clarendon/Oxford University Press, 1989.
Examines jurists' support for women's rights as part of a larger effort to replace
the authoritarian, patriarchal family with the concept of the "mutual rights and
obligations of the conjugal family" as the basis of Russian civil law. Discusses
limited success of these efforts.

317   WHITAKER, CYNTHIA. "The Women's Movement during the Reign
       of Alexander II: A Case Study in Russian Liberalism." *Journal of Modern
       History* 48, no. 2 (June 1976): 35–69. On-demand supplement.
Explores the reasons for the extraordinary comparative success of the women's

movement in Russia during Alexander II's reign (1855–81) and its significance as "an unexplored example of Russian liberalism." Good comparative information. Some exaggeration in the beginning about the extent of women's legal equality in Russia, but overall the best short treatment of this subject to date.

318   WOROBEC, CHRISTINE. "Customary Law and Property Devolution among Russian Peasants in the 1870s." *Canadian Slavonic Papers* 26, nos. 2–3 (June–September 1984): 220–34.

Argues that the peasant partible system of inheritance has been overlooked by scholars, although it was "a key to the understanding of peasant traditionalism." Inheritance strategies seen as creating "a significant degree of stability in the nineteenth-century countryside in spite of the abolition of serfdom and the growth of capitalism." Discusses property rights of women and their inalienable right to keep their dowries.

319   ———. "Temptress or Virgin? The Precarious Sexual Position of Women in Postemancipation Ukrainian Peasant Society." *Slavic Review* 49, no. 2 (Summer 1990): 227–38.

A rare study in English of Ukrainian peasant attitudes toward female sexuality. A key aspect of these attitudes is the notion of woman as temptress and insatiable sexual aggressor. Double sexual standard, premarital sex, and illegitimacy discussed. Wide range of sources, including bawdy peasant songs. Needs greater gender-consciousness in use of language (e.g., the term *young girls* is used, but *young women* would be more accurate, especially considering that the term *young men* is used for males of the same age).

320   WORTMAN, RICHARD. "Images of Rule and Problems of Gender in the Upbringing of Paul I and Alexander I." In *Imperial Russia, 1700–1917: State, Society, Opposition. Essays in Honor of Marc Raeff*, edited by Ezra Mendelsohn and Marshall S. Shatz, pp. 58–75. Dekalb: Northern Illinois University Press, 1988.

Argues that Paul and Alexander were torn between the influences of the tutors who sought to instill in them Enlightenment values and of the male role models at court and on Western European thrones. To Wortman, the ideal of the good prince "is in many respects a tamed, feminized image." Views Alexander III and Nicholas II as deprived of an alternative, "feminine" image of benevolence to temper autocratic power. Paul rebelled against this ideal with his extreme authoritarianism; Alexander sought to combine authoritarianism and benevolence.

AUTOBIOGRAPHIES AND BIOGRAPHIES

321   ALEXANDRA, EMPRESS OF RUSSIA. *Letters of the Tsaritsa to the Tsar, 1914–1916*. Introduction by Sir Bernard Pares. New York: Robert M. McBride, 1924. Reprint. Westport, Conn.: Hyperion, 1979. 478 pp. Index.
Alexandra's letters to Nicholas II, written in English. Pares's introduction provides biographical details.

322   ALKANA, LINDA ANNE KELLY. "Suzanne Voilquin: Feminist and Saint-Simonian." Ph.D. diss., University of California, Irvine, 1985. 259 pp.
Devotes some attention to this French feminist's ill-fated attempt to introduce Western notions of midwifery in Russia in the 1840s.

323   BALABANOFF, ANGELICA. *My Life as a Rebel*. New York: Harper, 1938. 324 pp. Reprint. Bloomington: Indiana University Press, 1973. 324 pp. Index.
Life in émigré circles and in the Zimmerwald movement. Balabanoff did not become a Bolshevik until 1917. For a time she served as secretary of the Comintern, under the watchful eyes of then-director Zinoviev ("next to Mussolini, the most despicable individual I have ever met"). Disillusioned by Bolshevik tactics and terror, she left Russia in 1921. Portraits of Georgii Plekhanov, Lenin, Klara Zetkin, Rosa Luxemburg, Trotsky, Louise Bryant, John Reed, and Emma Goldman, among others.

324   BARIATINSKAIA, PRINCESS ANATOLE MARIE. *My Russian Life*. London: Hutchinson, 1923. 351 pp. Index.
Memoirs of woman from a prominent aristocratic family about life at the imperial court and the traumas and dislocations of war and revolution.

325   BASHKIRTSEFF, MARIE. *The Journal of Marie Bashkirtseff*. Translated by Mathilde Blind. New Introduction by Roszika Parker and Griselda Pollock. London: Virago, 1985. 716 pp.
Russian by nationality, born in Ukraine in 1859, at age eleven Bashkirtseff and her brother were taken to France by their mother after their parents separated. From age twelve to her death at twenty-five she kept a diary. A prolific writer, Bashkirtseff left eighty-four handwritten notebooks chronicling her development, her career as an artist, her romances, and her political activity (she became a militant suffragist with links to the socialist feminist journal *La Citoyenne*). Her frank entries (even after her mother's excisions) caused a sensation when the journal was published in the late 1880s and early 1890s.

326   BERGMAN, JAY. *Vera Zasulich: A Biography*. Stanford, Calif.: Stanford University Press, 1983. 261 pp. Index.

The only biography in English of the woman whose attempt to assassinate General Trepov, the governor of St. Petersburg, sparked a series of terrorist acts, culminating in the assassination of Alexander II in 1881. Utilizes Western archival sources from the Hoover Institution, the International Institute of Social History, and the Bakhmetoff Collection at Columbia, but no Soviet archival sources, which the author claims were not worth investigating. Originally the author's doctoral dissertation, this book contains a good deal of useful information.

327 BOTCHKAREVA, MARIA. *Yashka: My Life as Peasant, Officer and Exile, as Set Down by Isaac Don Levine*. New York: Frederick A. Stokes, 1919. 340 pp.

Memoirs of the commander of the Women's Battalion of Death, hailed by suffragist leader Emmeline Pankhurst as the "Russian Joan of Arc." Enlisted by special permission of the tsar in a reserve army regiment in 1914, Botchkareva formed the Women's Battalion after the February Revolution. A bitter opponent of the Bolsheviks, she escaped to the United States in 1918.

328 BRESHKO-BRESHKOVSKAYA, CATHERINE. *The Little Grandmother of the Russian Revolution: Reminiscences and Letters of Catherine Breshkovsky*. Edited by Alice Stone Blackwell. Boston: Little, Brown, 1917. 348 pp.

Born in 1844 in Vitebsk of gentry parents, Breshkovsky found the inequitable treatment of the peasants intolerable and gave up her marriage, child, and privileged position to join a revolutionary group. Her memoirs chronicle horrendous prison conditions, her part in the formation and activities of the Socialist Revolutionary party, and her 1904 visit to the United States. Includes correspondence with supporters in the United States (many of them, like Alice Stone Blackwell, feminists).

329 ———. *Hidden Springs of the Russian Revolution: Personal Memoirs*. Edited by Lincoln Hutchinson. Foreword by A. F. Kerensky. Stanford, Calif.: Stanford University Press, 1931. 369 pp. Index.

Memoirs of this extraordinary woman—a populist, revolutionary activist, and Socialist Revolutionary party organizer—dating from her participation in the Going to the People movement in 1873 to the 1917 Revolutions.

330 BROIDO, EVA. *Memoirs of a Revolutionary*. Translated and edited by Vera Broido. London: Oxford University Press, 1967. 150 pp.

Eva Broido's autobiography. Born in 1876, Broido grew up in the Jewish Pale and escaped it by becoming a pharmacist. She married the chemical engineer Mark Broido. Both Mensheviks, they experienced prison and exile for much of the prerevolutionary period. Eva Broido was secretary-general of the Menshevik Central Committee. This memoir stops at the time of the February Revolution, when Broido was in exile in Minusinsk. Subsequently, Broido left the country and returned to Russia in 1927. She is thought to have died in June 1941.

331   BURGIN, DIANA L. "After the Ball Is Over: Sophia Parnok's Creative Relationship with Marina Tsvetaeva." *Russian Review* 47, no. 4 (October 1988): 425–44.
Examines symbolic images of the lesbian relationship between Parnok and Tsvetaeva in their poetry. Considers Tsvetaeva to have "planted the seed" of creativity in Parnok, as Parnok produced her best poetry after their love affair ended. Discusses Parnok's reaction to the friendship between Mandelstam and Tsvetaeva.

332   ———. "Signs of a Response: Two Possible Parnok Replies to Her 'Podruga,'" *Slavic and East European Journal* 35, no. 2 (1991): 214–27.
Comparison of the love affair between Tsvetaeva and Parnok with two other contemporary lesbian relationships—those of Renee Vivien and Natalie Clifford Barney in France and of Virginia Woolf and Vita Sackville-West in England. Develops notion of the "lyrical dialogue" between the two Russians as expressed in their verse.

333   ———. "Sophia Parnok and the Writing of a Lesbian Poet's Life." *Slavic Review* 51, no. 2 (Summer 1992): 485–96.
Burgin argues that Parnok consciously lived and wrote as a lesbian and that this awareness informed all aspects of her life. Parnok's "successful struggle to inscribe her lesbian "I" into Russian poetry, to make a voice like hers heard, constitutes one of the most radical and original aspects of her lyrics. . . ." In her study of Parnok, Burgin has done much to break down the very strong taboos against discussing lesbianism or lesbian themes in the work of Russian women writers.

334   CAROTENUTO, ALDO. *A Secret Symmetry: Sabina Spielrein between Jung and Freud*. Translated by Arno Pomerans, John Shepley, and Krishna Winston. New York: Pantheon, 1982. 250 pp. Index. Notes.
Biography of this Russian-Jewish woman, at eighteen or nineteen first a patient of Jung's, then his lover (he was about twelve years older) from 1904 to 1909 while in medical school, and finally an established psychoanalyst and scholar in her own right. She influenced both Jung and Freud; the latter borrowed heavily from her in his *Beyond the Pleasure Principle* and possibly in other works. Returning to Russia for good in 1923, Spielrein gained membership in the Russian Psychoanalytic Society, taught at the local university in Rostov-on-Don, founded a children's home, published a few articles in Western psychoanalytic journals, and completely disappeared in 1937, no doubt a purge victim.

335   CARR, EDWARD HALLETT. *The Romantic Exiles: A Nineteenth-Century Portrait Gallery*. London: Gollancz, 1933. Reprint. New York: Octagon Books, 1975. 391 pp.

The lives, loves, and politics of revolutionary exiles Natalie and Alexander Herzen. Natalie and Nicholas Ogarev, Sergei Nechaev, and Mikhail Bakunin also appear, but this book is especially notable for its exploration of the personal lives of the Herzens.

336 CHAGALL, BELLA. *First Encounter*. Translated by Barbara Bray. Illustrated by Marc Chagall. New York: Schocken, 1982. 348 pp. Glossary.
The author recounts her life in Vitebsk in prerevolutionary Russia. Many details about Jewish family life and her relationship with Marc Chagall. Translation of *Burning Lights*, which first appeared in Yiddish.

337 CHARTERS, ANN, and SAMUEL CHARTERS. *I Love: The Story of Vladimir Mayakovsky and Lili Brik*. New York: Farrar, Straus & Giroux, 1979. 398 pp. Index.
Very informative. Based on interviews with Brik, Nora Polonskaia (Mayakovsky's last mistress), the translator Rita Rait, and Tatiana Yakovleva (the émigré Mayakovsky almost married). Offers more than Jangfeldt (entry 740) on Brik's life after Mayakovsky's suicide. Details about the Lili Brik-Mayakovsky-Osip Brik triangle. The authors generally refer to women by their first names and men by their last names.

338 CHUKOVSKAYA, LYDIA. *To the Memory of Childhoood*. Translated by Eliza Kellogg Klose. Evanston, Illinois: Northwestern University Press, 1988. 168 pp. Notes. Biographical Glossary.
Memoirs of the author's pre-Revolutionary childhood living in Kuokkala, a dacha area close to St. Petersburg, but then part of Finland. Mostly impressions of Chukovskaya's father, the beloved author of Russian children's books Kornei Chukovsky. Chukovskaya was deeply attached to her father; her mother hardly figures at all in these reminiscences.

339 DAVIES, JESSIE. *Anna of all the Russias: The Life of Anna Akhmatova (1889–1966)*. Liverpool: Lincoln Davies, 1988. 148 pp. Index. Bibliography. Notes.
Narrative popular biography of the poet, based largely on interviews with and memoirs of close friends and admirers. Many anecdotes reveal the poet's sharp sense of humor in the face of adversity.

340 DESIND, PHILIP. *Jewish and Russian Revolutionaries Exiled to Siberia (1901–1917)*. Lewiston, N.Y.: Edwin Mellen Press, 1991. 734 pp. Index. Bibliography.
Autobiography of Jewish Byelorussian revolutionary Israel Pressman, including the story of the Izmailovich sisters, Russian revolutionary daughters of a tsarist general.

341   DOSTOEVSKY, ANNA. *Dostoevsky: Reminiscences*. Edited and
      Translated by Beatrice Stillman. Introduction by Helen Muchnic. New
      York: Liveright, 1975. 448 pp. Index. Biographical glossary.
Translation of the second Russian edition (1971) of the memoirs of
Dostoevsky's wife. In both Russian editions only the part of the 798-page manuscript describing the fourteen years with Dostoevsky have been included, plus
a response to Nikolai Strakhov's charge that Dostoevsky had proudly confessed
to raping a ten-year-old girl. Pages 3 to 13 provide brief details about Anna
Snitkina's childhood and youth.

342   DURLAND, KELLOGG. *The Red Reign, the True Story of an Adven-
      turous Year in Russia*. New York: Century Company, 1908. 533 pp.
Report of a visit to Maria Spiridonova.

343   ELWOOD, R. C. *Inessa Armand: Revolutionary and Feminist*.
      Cambridge: Cambridge University Press, 1992. 304 pp. Index.
      Bibliography.
The author seeks to rescue Armand from exclusive association with Lenin as his
disciple and/or alleged mistress. An exploration of Armand's political development, her early attraction to Tolstoyan and feminist ideas as well as her
Bolshevik party work. Emphasis on Armand's independence, her relationships
with Bolsheviks other than Lenin and Krupskaia. Elwood stresses the complex
nature of the Armand-Lenin connection, considers but rejects the widely held
speculation that Armand and Lenin were lovers.

344   ENGEL, BARBARA ALPERN, and CLIFFORD ROSENTHAL, eds.
      and trans. *Five Sisters: Women against the Tsar*. New York: Alfred A.
      Knopf, 1975. 254 pp. Reprint. Boston: Allen & Unwin, 1987. Index.
Excerpts from the memoirs of five revolutionary activists of the 1870s: Vera
Figner, Vera Zasulich, Praskovia Ivanovskaia, Olga Liubatovich, and Elizaveta
Kovalskaia. Essay discusses the particularly important role played by women in
the Russian revolutionary century.

345   ESHELMAN, NANCY GORMAN. "Angelica Balabanoff and the
      Italian Socialist Movement: From the Second International to
      Zimmerwald." Ph.D. diss., University of Rochester, 1977. 579 pp.
This critical biography about this important socialist provides some informa-
tion about Balabanoff's early years in Russia, her role in the international
Socialist movement, her continued ties to Russian Marxists such as Plekhanov
and Lenin, and her hostility to feminism. Does not cover Balabanoff's return to
Russia in 1917 or her subsequent activities until her death in 1965.

346   FEINSTEIN, ELAINE. *A Captive Lion: The Life of Marina Tsvetayeva*.
      New York: E. P. Dutton, 1987. 289 pp. Index. Bibliography.

Popular biography by a translator of Tsvetaeva's verse. Relies on Karlinsky's earlier biography (entry 357) and works by other Tsvetaeva scholars.

347 FEN, ELISAVETA. *A Girl Grew Up in Russia*. London: Readers Union, 1972. 317 pp.

Fen, daughter of a provincial governor in Belorussia, describes her life from the age of eleven, when she is sent off to boarding school, to her departure from home for her university education in Petrograd in 1917. The momentous events of this period (World War I, social unrest) form the backdrop for Fen's description of the daily life of a young woman of the gentry.

348 FITZLYON, KYRIL, and TATYANA BROWNING. *Before the Revolution: A View of Russia under the Last Tsar*. London: Allen Lane, 1977. 203 pp.

Photographs of Russian society during the reign of Nicholas II, including some of non-Russian nationalities.

349 FOOTMAN, DAVID. *Red Prelude: The Life of the Russian Terrorist Zhelyabov*. New Haven, Conn.: Yale University Press, 1945. 267 pp. Index.

Mention of the relationship between Zhelyabov and Perovskaia and their work together.

350 GOOD, JANE E., and DAVID R. JONES. *Babushka: The Life of the Russian Revolutionary Ekaterina K. Breshko Breshkovskaia (1844–1934)*. Newtonville, Mass.: Oriental Research Partners, 1991. 253 pp. Index of names.

The first English biography of this remarkable revolutionary activist, utilizing Western archival sources and a rare 1964 interview with Kerensky. Breshkovskaia, age seventy-three at the time of the 1917 Revolutions, had a long history of radical activity, dating from the 1860s. Leaving her husband and son to devote herself to the cause of the people, she endured persecution and prison, helped found the Socialist Revolutionary party, became a revolutionary hero in the West, and lived in the Winter Palace during Kerensky's brief tenure. Her vehement opposition to Lenin and the Bolshevik Revolution cost her dearly in terms of the repression of the Socialist Revolutionaries within the Soviet Union and the loss of many of her left-leaning Western supporters. She spent the last years of her life in relative obscurity in Czechoslovakia.

351 GRABBE, ALEXANDER. *The Private World of the Last Tsar, 1912–1917, in the Photographs and Notes of General Count Alexander Grabbe*. Edited by Paul and Beatrice Grabbe. London: Collins, 1985. 191 pp. Bibliography.

Photographs of the imperial family by an aide-de-camp to the tsar.

352   GRAY, PAULINE. *The Grand Duke's Woman*. London: MacDonald & Jane's, 1976. 201 pp. Index.
The tale of the romance and marriage of Nicholas II's brother Michael and the commoner Natalya Cheremetevskaya, written by the latter's granddaughter. Also recounts Cheremetevskaya's life in exile after Michael's arrest and subsequent murder.

353   HAIGHT, AMANDA. *Anna Akhmatova: A Poetic Pilgrimage*. New York: Oxford University Press, 1976. Reprint. Oxford: Oxford University Press, 1990. 213 pp. Index.
Biography by the British scholar who met Akhmatova in 1964 and was close to her until the poet's death in 1965.

354   HAIMSON, LEOPOLD, ed. *The Making of Three Russian Revolutionaries*. In collaboration with Ziva Galili y Garcia and Richard Wortman. Introduction by Leopold Haimson. Notes by Ziva Galili y Garcia. Cambridge: Cambridge University Press, 1987. 515 pp. Index.
Contains an interview with the Menshevik Lidia Dan. Information about her childhood in a Russian-Jewish assimilated middle-class family in the late nineteenth century, and about the Social Democratic party, Mensheviks, and Bolsheviks through 1905.

355   HINGLEY, RONALD. *Nightingale Fever: Russian Poets in Revolution*. New York: Alfred A. Knopf, 1981. 269 pp. Index.
Akhmatova, Mandelstam, Pasternak, Tsvetaeva, and the interweaving of their lives and work against the backdrop of the enormous changes of the period from 1889 to 1966.

356   IZWOLSKY, HELENE. *No Time to Grieve: An Autobiographical Journey*. Philadelphia: Winchell, 1985. 297 pp. Index.
Iswolsky, born into the aristocracy, recounts her life as the daughter of the last tsarist ambassador to France, her friendships within the émigré community (with Berdiaev, Kerensky, Tsvetaeva), and the spiritual journey that led to her conversion to Catholicism, her close friendship with Dorothy Day, and her membership in the Catholic worker community.

357   KARLINSKY, SIMON. *Marina Tsvetaeva: The Woman, Her World and Her Poetry*. Cambridge: Cambridge University Press, 1986. 289 pp. Index. Appendix on sources.
Well-researched account, including contemporary Soviet as well as Western scholarship. Full account of all aspects of Tsvetaeva's life, including her sexual relationships with women.

358   KELLY, RITA MAE CAWLEY. "The Role of Vera Ivanovna Zasulich in the Development of the Russian Revolutionary Movement." Ph.D. diss., Indiana University, 1967. 324 pp.

Assesses Zasulich's political thought, her evolution as a revolutionary, and her relationship to the male leaders of the revolutionary movement. Serious attention to Zasulich's ideas, including those about the role of women in the revolutionary movement and her hostility to feminism. This account ends in 1904.

359   KENNEDY, DON H. *Little Sparrow: A Portrait of Sophia Kovalevsky*. Athens: Ohio University Press, 1983. 341 pp. Index.
A narrative account of Kovalevskaia's life. Contains much useful information. Author displays limited understanding of gender issues in relation to Kovalevskaia's career and personal life. Kennedy does not read Russian; his wife translated the Russian sources. Ann Hibner Koblitz, the best biographer in English of Kovalevskaia, notes that "Kennedy made no use of the archives of the Swedish Academy of Sciences, archival information in the USSR, and many published primary and secondary sources in Russian. The omissions and inaccuracies caused by these gaps in his research become more serious as the book goes on" (entry 361).

360   KOBLITZ, ANN HIBNER. "Science, Women, and Revolution in Russia." *Science for the People* 14, no. 4 (July/August 1982): 14–18, 34–37.
Covers the general ethos of the sixties and seventies among the educated elite, the Nihilists, the intelligentsia's identification with science and progress, and women's struggles to obtain higher education. The high proportion of women drawn to science and medicine challenges the notion that these disciplines were considered "unfeminine" and conservative.

361   ———. *A Convergence of Lives: Sofia Kovalevskaia, Scientist, Writer, Revolutionary*. Boston: Birkhauser, 1983. 305 pp. Index. Bibliography. Bibliographical notes.
By far the best, most thorough treatment of all aspects of Kovalevskaia's life, including her contributions to the field of mathematics. Helpful bibliographic notes and bibliography indicate the thoroughness of Koblitz's scholarship.

362   KOVALEVSKAYA, SOFYA. *A Russian Childhood*. Translated, edited, and introduced by Beatrice Stillman. With an analysis of Kovalevskaya's mathematics by P. Y. Kochina, USSR Academy of Sciences. New York: Springer-Verlag, 1978. 250 pp. Index.
An accurate translation of Kovalevskaya's reminiscences from her childhood to 1865. The last chapter describes the relationship of Kovalevskaya and her sister Anyuta Korvin-Krukovskaya with Dostoevsky. Also includes Kovalevskaya's "An Autobiographical Sketch" and Polubarinova-Kochina's discussion of Kovalevskaya's mathematical work. Useful introduction by Stillman.

363   KOVALEVSKY, SONIA. *Biography and Autobiography*. Vol. 1, *Memoir*, by A. C. Leffler. Vol. 2, *Reminiscences of Childhood*, by Sonia Kovalevsky, translated by Louise Von Cossel. London: Walter Scott, 1895. 317 pp.
British edition of the Leffler biography and the autobiography of

Kovalevsky/Kovalevskaia (1840–91). These memoirs stop before the beginning of her brilliant scholarly career. Leffler picks up the narrative at that point and weaves her version of events.

364   ———. *Sonya Kovalevsky: Her Recollections of Childhood*, with a biography by Anna Carlotta Leffler, Duchess of Cajanello. Translated by Isabel F. Hapgood and A. M. Clive Bayley. New York: Century, 1895. 318 pp.
A fictionalized account of Kovalevskaia's life. Many errors made in the translation. As Ann Hibner Koblitz notes: "Virtually all biographical sketches of Kovalevskaia in Western Europe and America treat Anna Carlotta Leffler's idiosyncratic and unreliable account as the unbiased truth. Although Anna Carlotta herself did not intend for her 'poem' to be the last word on her friend, until the present time many of Kovalevskaia's actions, thoughts, and motivations may have been seen through the distorting haze of Leffler's sketch" (entry 337).

365   KRUPSKAIA, NADEZHDA KONSTANTINOVNA. *Reminiscences of Lenin*. Translated by Bernard Isaacs. New York: International Publishers, 1970. 553 pp. Index.
Memoirs by Lenin's coworker and wife from 1893–1919. Obviously tailored to the Stalinist times during which they were written. Uncritical of Lenin, they inflate Stalin's role and omit Trotsky almost entirely. Not unexpectedly, offers little about Krupskaia's personal life, although some can be inferred between the lines.

366   ———. *Memories of Lenin*. Translated by E. Verney. Introduction by Andrew Rothstein. London: Lawrence & Wishart, 1970. 318 pp. 318 pp.
British edition of Krupskaia's memoirs.

367   LAVIGNA, CLAIRE. "Anna Kuliscioff: From Russian Populism to Italian Reformism, 1873–1913." Ph.D. diss., University of Rochester, 1971. 402 pp.
The life of a Russian radical, born Anna Rosenstein, one of the principal founders of the Italian Socialist party in 1892. Part of the Going to the People movement in 1873, she left Russia in 1877. From 1885 to her death in 1925 she shared an intense political and personal partnership with the Italian Socialist leader Filippo Turati.

368   LAZEBNIK, EDITH. *Such a Life*. New York: William Morrow, 1978. 287 pp.
Memoir of life in the *shtetl* (Jewish village in Eastern Europe) by a woman who immigrated to the United States before the 1917 Revolution.

369   LUXEMBURG, ROSA. *"The Russian Revolution" and "Leninism or Marxism?"* Introduction by Bertram D. Wolfe. Ann Arbor: University of Michigan Press, 1961. Reprint, with new introduction by Bertram D. Wolfe. Westport, Conn.: Greenwood, 1981. 109 pp.

Translation of two essays by the leading revolutionary theorist, both sharply critical of Lenin's authoritarianism. Luxemburg originally entitled her essays "Organizational Questions of Russian Social Democracy." Scottish Communists renamed them in a 1935 English version.

370 McNEAL, ROBERT. *Bride of the Revolution: Krupskaya and Lenin*. Ann Arbor: University of Michigan Press, 1972. 326 pp. Index.
The definitive biography of Krupskaya has yet to be written, but this provides more information than any other English source about her. Marred by a sarcastic tone and uncritical acceptance of the Armand-Lenin love-affair story. McNeal also fails to view the Krupskaya-Lenin relationship in the context of the egalitarian ideal of marriage so cherished by the radical intelligentsia.

371 MALIA, MARTIN. *Alexander Herzen and the Birth of Russian Socialism*. Cambridge: Harvard University Press, 1961. 486 pp. Paperback ed. New York: Grosset & Dunlap, Universal Library, 1965. 486 pp. Index.
Acclaimed biography of this leading democrat and critic of tsarism. Refers to Herzen's advocacy of feminism thusly: "Although against a backdrop of serfdom the passion this issue generated in Russia appears a pure luxury, the radicals of Herzen's generation made feminism a paramount concern."

372 MARIE, GRAND DUCHESS OF RUSSIA. *Education of a Princess: A Memoir*. Translated under the editorial supervision of Russell Lord. New York: Viking, 1930. 388 pp. Index.
Autobiography of the niece of Alexander III, cousin of Nicholas II. Information about the upbringing of women of her class, the participation of her brother Dmitri in the plot to kill Rasputin, life at the tsarist court, the effects of the Bolshevik Revolution, and her escape to Romania.

373 MASSIE, ROBERT K. *Nicholas and Alexandra*. New York: Atheneum, 1968. 584 pp. Index.
Sympathetic portrait of the last tsar. Concludes that Nicholas was too much influenced by his wife.

374 MATICH, OLGA. *Paradox in the Religious Poetry of Zinaida Gippius*. Munich: Wilhelm Fink Verlag, 1972. 127 pp. Index.
Gippius, in the introduction to her first book of poetry, equated poetry and prayer. In this study of Gippius, Matich seeks to "reveal the very intense religiosity of her poetry and disprove the poet's already legendary decadent reputation." She succeeds in the former more than in the latter.

375 MAXWELL, MARGARET. *Narodniki Women: Russian Women Who Sacrificed Themselves for the Dream of Freedom*. New York: Pergamon Press, 1990. 341 pp. Index. Bibliography.
Positive portraits of Vera Zasulich, Vera Figner, Sofia Perovskaya, Katerina Dolgorukaya, Maria Spiridonova, Katya and Sanya Izmailovich, Catherine

Breshko-Breshkovskaya, Mariya Shkolnik, Lydiya Ezerskaya, Rebecca Fialka, and Irina Kakhovskaya. Based on research in both Russian and English sources. Particularly interesting on the fate of left Socialist Revolutionary women Zasulich and Figner after the Revolution. Tendency to name women by first names, men by last; refers to the twenty-eight-year-old Zasulich as a "young girl" (surprising in a book published as part of the feminist Athene series).

376   MEINCKE, EVELYN. "Vera Ivanovna Zasulich: A Political Life." Ph.D. diss., State University of New York at Binghamton, 1984. 730 pp. Argues for greater attention to Zasulich, who "played a pivotal role in every major ideological crisis in Russian revolutionary history for almost forty years." Discusses her mediating role in several revolutionary disputes, including those between Plekhanov and Lenin during the Iskra period. Later, Meincke argues that by her actions and writing, Zasulich encouraged splits between the terror and anti terror factions of the radical camp, between Marxists and populists, between Bolsheviks and Mensheviks, and between supporters and defenders of World War I.

377   MULLANEY, MARIE MARMO. "The Female Revolutionary, the Woman Question and European Socialism, 1871–1921." Ph.D. diss., Rutgers University, 1980. 645 pp.
Discusses the intersection of gender and revolutionary activity in the cases of five women—Louise Michel, Eleanor Marx, Alexandra Kollontai, Rosa Luxemburg, and Angelica Balabanoff. Each is examined in an analytical biography as an example of a general type within the socialist movement. Significant similarities are elucidated. Traditional male-defined theories of the revolutionary personality are critiqued (see also entries 247 and 302).

378   NARISHKIN-KURAKIN, ELIZABETH. *Under Three Tsars: The Memoirs of the Lady-in-Waiting Elizabeth Narishkin-Kurakin*. Edited by Rene Fulop-Miller. Translated by Julia E. Loesser. New York: E. P. Dutton, 1931. 231 pp.
Autobiography of this confidante of Russian royalty until the departure of the deposed Nicholas and Alexandra from Petrograd in 1917.

379   NICHOLAS II, EMPEROR OF RUSSIA. *Letters of the Tsar to the Tsaritsa, 1914–1917*. London: John Lane, Bodley Head, 1929. Reprint. Westport, Conn.: Hyperion, 1979. 325 pp. Index.
Translation from the Russian text (edited by M. N. Pokrovsky) of the tsar's letters, originally written in English.

380   NOVIKOFF, MADAME OLGA. *Russian Memories*. Introduction by Stephen Graham. London: Herbert Jenkins, 1917. 310 pp. Index.
Autobiography of Novikoff, called by Disraeli "the M.P. for Russia in England." She came to England with the goal of improving Anglo-Russian

relations and became acquainted with Gladstone and Carlyle, among others. The exact nature of her missions to England may never be clear, but her influence on Anglo-Russian relations deserves further study.

381 ORR, MIRIAM ELAINE NEIL. "Tillie Olsen's Vision: A Different Way of Keeping Faith." Ph.D. diss., Emory University, 1985. 295 pp.

First chapter discusses the Russian-Jewish context of Olsen's upbringing. Her parents immigrated to the United States after the 1905 Revolution.

382 PACHMUSS, TEMIRA. *Zinaida Hippius [Gippius]: An Intellectual Profile*. Carbondale: Southern Illinois University Press, 1971. 491 pp. Index. Bibliography. Notes.

Part of Pachmuss's attempt to make known Gippius's works to those who read English. Criticized by Simon Karlinsky for seeking to make Gippius "as conventional and innocuous as possible" by editing and censoring the writer's diaries and letters. Nevertheless, an important contribution and one of the few English sources on this significant writer.

383 PERLINA, NINA. "Olga Friedenberg on Myth, Folklore and Literature." *Slavic Review* 50 (Summer 1991): 371–83. Response by Kevin Moss, pp. 383–84.

An effort to make Friedenberg's wide-ranging scholarship and work in semantic paleontology more well known to American scholars. Discusses the complementarity of Friedenberg's and Bakhtin's ideas.

384 PETHYBRIDGE, ROGER, ed. *Witnesses to the Russian Revolution*. London: George Allen & Unwin, 1964. 308 pp. Index.

Excerpts from eye witness accounts from the period 1905–17, including those of Krupskaia, Princess Paley, A. Allilueva. Small excerpt from the letters of Alexandra to Nicholas II.

385 PITCHER, HARVEY. *Chekhov's Leading Lady: A Portrait of the Actress Olga Knipper*. London: John Murray, 1979. 288 pp. Index.

Biography of the leading Moscow Art Theater actress, married to Chekhov for three years (1901–04). Pitcher is sure that Knipper considered her marriage the most important event in her ninety-one years. Consistently refers to Knipper by her first name and Chekhov and other men by their last names. Describes the triangle of Chekhov, Knipper, and his sister, Masha, as well as the sixty-year friendship between the two women.

386 POOLE, ERNEST. *Katherine Breshkovsky: For Russia's Freedom*. Chicago, Charles Kerr, 1905. 29 pp.

An interview with Breshkovsky about the roots of the 1905 Revolution and the goals of the Socialist Revolutionary party.

387   RAPPAPORT, KAREN. "S. Kovalevsky: A Mathematics Lesson."
      American Mathematical Monthly 88, no. 8 (October 1981): 564–74.
Disputes those who dismiss Kovalevsky's mathematical work as insignificant or
completely influenced by the work of her mentor, Weier-Strass. Shows that
Kovalevsky's research on the motion of a rigid body about a fixed point won
her recognition and prizes at the time and deserves more serious attention
today.

388   SCEPANSKY, ANNE JOHNSON. "Vera Ivanovna Zasulich: From
      Revolutionary Terror to Scientific Marxism." Ph.D. diss., George
      Washington University, 1974. 460 pp.
Seeks to view the revolutionary movement "through the eyes" of Zasulich.
Good information on Zasulich's early years, the reaction to her shooting of
Trepov, her acquittal, and the extent of the collaboration between Zasulich and
Plekhanov. Some attention to gender as a motivator for Zasulich's revolution-
ary activities.

389   SCOTT, MARK CHAPIN. "Her Brother's Keeper: The Evolution of
      Women Bolsheviks." Ph.D. diss., University of Kansas, 1980. 396 pp.
A study of eighty-three Bolshevik women. Analysis of their early backgrounds,
family relations, the formation of their views, "the radical political influence of
formal education," their work or professions, the influence of Tolstoyan ideas,
the Going to the People movement and terrorism, the women's revolutionary
activity, government action against them, the women's participation in the
October Revolution and Civil War, and their postrevolutionary activity.

390   STEINBERG, I. N. *In the Workshop of the Revolution*. New York and
      Toronto: Rinehart, 1953. 306 pp. Index.
Steinberg, a leader of the Socialist Revolutionaries, describes the actions of several women terrorists such as Yevstolia Ragozinikova, Dora (Fanya) Kaplan,
and Maria Spiridonova. Contains Spiridonova's "Open Letter to the
Bolsheviks," written while she was imprisoned in the Kremlin in 1918.

391   STILLMAN, BEATRICE. "Sofya Kovalevskaya: Growing Up in the
      Sixties." *Russian Literature Triquarterly*, 9 (Spring 1974): 276–302.
Early version of the introductory essay in Stillman's translation of
Kovalevskaya's autobiography, *A Russian Childhood* (entry 364).

392   SUKLOFF, MARIE. *The Life Story of a Russian Exile*. Translated by
      Gregory Yarros. New York: Century, 1914. 251 pp. Photographs.
A memoir that provides some detail about the lives of Jewish farmers in the
Pale of Settlement. The author, born in a *shtetl*, learned to read and write when
she was thirteen in a Bund study group, joined a Socialist Revolutionary circle,
and was imprisoned at age seventeen.

393 TUVE, JEANETTE E. *The First Russian Women Physicians.* Newtonville, Mass.: Oriental Research Partners, 1984. 147 pp. Index. Bibliography.
The only work in English about this important topic. A narrative history using many Russian sources. Follows the changes in women's access to medical careers through the lives of several pioneering female doctors, such as Nadezhda Suslova, Maria Bokova, Anna Shabanova, Maria Pokrovskaia, and Vera Lebedeva. Marred by misspellings, typographical errors, and some factual inaccuracies. For example, although she was its president for almost its entire existence, Shabanova did not found the Russian Women's Mutual Benevolence Society (this was the work of the first generation of feminists, primarily Stasova and Filosofova). Nevertheless, provides much useful information.

394 TYRKOVA-WILLIAMS, ARIADNA. *From Liberty to Brest-Litovsk: The First Year of the Russian Revolution.* London: Macmillan, 1919. 526 pp. Reprint. Hyperion Press, 1977. 526 pp. Index.
Unsympathetic chronicle of the ascent of the Bolsheviks in 1917. Tyrkova, a Kadet and an active feminist, is mum about her or others' women's rights activity in this period. The only real discussion of women is devoted to the Women's Battalion, led by Botchkareva.

395 VALENTINOV, N. (N. V. VOLSKY). *Encounters with Lenin.* Translated by Paul Rosta and Brian Pearce. Foreword by Leonard Schapiro. London: Oxford University Press, 1968. 273 pp. Bibliographical footnotes.
Personal relations among the Bolsheviks before the Revolution. Relationships between women and men revolutionaries.

396 VIROUBOVA, ANNA. *Memories of the Russian Court.* New York: Macmillan, 1923. 400 pp.
Memoirs of life at court by this close friend and confidante of Empress Alexandra. Viroubova, widely believed to have introduced Rasputin into the Russian Court, claims that he was already well known to Nicholas and Alexandra before she met him.

397 VODOVOZOVA, E. N. *A Russian Childhood.* Translated by Anthony Brode and Olga Lane. London: Faber & Faber, 1960. 216 pp.
Memoir of life in a gentry family before the Revolution, with a widowed mother and a sister with an abusive husband. Last half describes Vodovozova's student days at the Smol'nyi Institute.

398 VYRUBOVA, ANNA. *The Romanov Family Album.* Introduction by Robert Massie. Picture research and descriptions by Marilyn Pfeifer Swezey. New York: Vendome, 1982. 127 pp. Bibliography.
Glimpses of Romanov family life through informal pictures of Nicholas II, Alexandra, and their children.

399   WOLFE, BERTRAM D. "Lenin and Inessa Armand." *Slavic Review* 22,
        no. 1 (March 1963): 96–114.
The source of the recurring assertions that Lenin and Armand were lovers. For
a rebuttal, see Stites's "Kollontai, Inessa, and Krupskaia" (entry 711).

400   YABLONSKAYA, M. N. *Women Artists of Russia's New Age*. Translated
        by Anthony Parton and Felicity O'Dell Vnukova. New York: Rizzoli,
        1990. 248 pp. Index.
Biographical sketches of leading pre- and postrevolutionary artists such as Olga
Rozanova, Liubov Popova, and Alexandra Exter. Laudatory about women and
the avant-garde movement. In the *Women's Review of Books* Karen Rosenberg
criticized Yablonskaya's failure to confront the movement's "pro-masculine ideology," noting that "Russian futurists often gendered the avant-garde as masculine and rejected the Symbolism of Balmont and other Russian poets as
feminine." Weak on Stalinism's impact on women artists.

401   ZETKIN, KLARA. "Lenin at the Third Congress of the Comintern."
        In *We Have Met Lenin*, pp. 9–10. Moscow: Foreign Languages
        Publishing House, 1939.
Adulatory reminiscence of Lenin in this collection of same by various foreign
Communists.

402   ZLOBIN, VLADIMIR. *A Difficult Soul: Zinaida Gippius*. Edited, anno-
        tated, and with an introductory essay by Simon Karlinsky. Berkeley:
        University of California Press, 1980. 197 pp. Index. Bibliography.
Biography of Gippius, an early symbolist poet, a leader in the turn-of-the-cen-
tury religious revival in the liberal educated class, and an early rebel against traditional sex roles. Introduction by Simon Karlinsky discusses Gippius's platonic
marriage to Dmitri Merezhkovsky, her infatuation with the homosexual Dmitri
Filosofov (son of the leading Russian feminist Anna Filosofova), and the
unorthodox relationship of this trio and its effect on the literature and art of the
period. Vladimir Zlobin, heir and executor of Gippius's and Merezhkovsky's
estate, was close to the couple for over twenty-five years and part of the homosexual subculture that was a feature of Russian artistic circles in the Silver Age.

The Tolstoy Family

So much has been written about Sofia Andreevna Tolstaia and her husband
Leo Tolstoy that these sources provide our most well-documented glimpse into
family relations among nineteenth-century Russian gentry. Both the Tolstoys
left diaries and letters, and all their grown children left memoirs, as did several
close relatives and friends. Sofia Tolstaia's diaries are the most extensive source
in English for a Russian gentrywoman's view of married life.

403   ASQUITH, CYNTHIA. *Married to Tolstoy*. London: Hutchinson, 1960; Boston: Houghton Mifflin, 1961. 288 pp.
Chronicles "the drama of the long heaven and hell shared by the Tolstoys." A more balanced account than most.

404   BENSON, RUTH CREGO. *Women in Tolstoy: The Ideal and the Erotic*. Urbana: University of Illinois Press, 1973. 141 pp. Bibliography.
Argues that Tolstoy's attitude toward women was complex in that he was both drawn to and repelled by them. Recognizing this ambivalence is key to understanding Tolstoy.

405   COLLINS, JOHN S. *Marriage and Genius: Strindberg and Tolstoy*. London: Cassell, 1973. 310 pp. Index.
A useful summary and analysis of Tolstoy's relations with his wife and children and of his general attitude toward marriage. Divided into two sections, the first on Strindberg, the second on Tolstoy. Comparisons must be inferred; nevertheless, a unique juxtaposition of these two authors.

406   DE COURCEL, MARTINE. *Tolstoy: The Ultimate Reconciliation*. Translated by Peter Levi. New York: Charles Scribner's Sons; London: Collier Macmillan, 1988. 458 pp. Index.
More balanced than most accounts of the Tolstoy marriage.

407   EDWARDS, ANNE. *Sonya: The Life of Countess Tolstoy*. New York: Simon & Schuster, 1981. 512 pp. Index.
This narrative, sympathetic to Sonya, draws on the voluminous reminiscences of the Tolstoy family.

408   FEILER, LILY. "The Tolstoi Marriage: Conflict and Illusions." *Canadian Slavonic Papers* 23, no. 3 (September 1981): 245–60.
Challenges the view of Tolstoy biographers about the idyllic first fifteen years of their marriage. Shows that from the beginning Sonia and Lev had very different concepts of marriage: for him marriage was a means of satisfying his lust; for her it meant completely sharing her life with another person. Portrays Sonia as an insightful, sensitive human being married to a man supremely insensitive to her personal and sexual needs.

409   KUZMINSKAYA, TATIANA ANDREEVNA. *Tolstoy as I Knew Him. My Life at Home and at Yasnaya Polyana*. Translated by Nora Sigerist, Joan Levinson, Elizabeth Kresky, Boris Egor, Glenora W. Brown, and Azizeh Azodi. Introduction by Ernest Simmons. New York: Macmillan, 1948. 439 pp.
Autobiography of the younger sister of Sofia Andreevna Tolstaia, a regular summer guest at the Tolstoy estate at Yasnaya Polyana and model for Natasha Rostova in *War and Peace*.

410   MAUDE, AYLMER, ed. *Family Views of Tolstoy*. Translated by Louise
          and Aylmer Maude. Boston: Houghton Mifflin, 1926. 220 pp. Index.
Entries by Tolstoy's niece about her mother, Tatiana Kuzminskaia, the model
for Natasha in *War and Peace*; by daughter Tatiana on Tolstoy and the land
question; by eldest son, Sergei, on his father's humor and love of music; and by
youngest daughter, Alexandra, on Tolstoy's flight from home and subsequent
death.

411   POLNER, TIKHON. *Tolstoy and His Wife*. Translated by Nicholas
          Wreden. New York: W. W. Norton, 1945. 222 pp.
Chronicles the history of the Tolstoy marriage, mostly from Tolstoy's point
of view.

412   SADLER, CATHERINE EDWARDS. *Sasha: The Life of Alexandra
          Tolstoy*. New York: G. P. Putnam's Sons, 1982. 138 pp. Index. bibliog-
          raphy.
Biography of "Sasha" Tolstoy, the author's youngest daughter and his spiritual
heir, from her childhood to 1929, when she left the Soviet Union.

413   SMOLUCHOWSKI, LOUISE. *Lev and Sonya: The Story of the Tolstoy
          Marriage*. New York: G. P. Putnam's Sons, 1987. 288 pp. Biblio-
          graphy.
Sympathetic portrait of Sonya and the Tolstoy marriage. Argues that her
strength and personality have been underestimated, maligned, or ignored in the
focus on the great writer. Emphasizes the Tolstoys' love and partnership, and
Lev's failure to apply his worldview to his personal life.

414   SUKHOTINA-TOLSTAIA, TATIANA. *The Tolstoy Home: Diaries of
          Tatiana Sukhotin-Tolstoy*. Translated by Alec Brown. London: Harvill,
          1950. 352 pp.
Diaries of the Tolstoys' eldest daughter. More favorable to her father than to
her mother.

415   ———. *Tolstoy Remembered*. Translated by Derek Coltman.
          Introduction by John Bayley. London: Michael Joseph, 1977. 255 pp.
Memoirs by Tolstoy's oldest daughter, with an afterword by Tatyana Albertini,
her only child.

416   TOLSTAIA, SOFIA ANDREEVNA. *The Diary of Tolstoy's Wife,
          1860–1891*. Translated by Alexander Werth. New York: Payson &
          Clarke; London: Gollancz, 1928. 272 pp. Notes.

417   ———. *Countess Tolstoy's Later Diary, 1891–1897*. Translated by
          Alexander Werth. London: Gollancz; New York: Payson & Clarke,
          1929. 267 pp.

These two volumes represent a less-complete version of Tolstaia's diaries than the Porter edition (entry 419).

418 ――――. *The Final Struggle, Being Countess Tolstoy's Diary for 1910, with Extracts from Leo Tolstoy's Diary of the Same Period*. Translated and introduced by Aylmer Maude. Preface by S. L. Tolstoy. New York: Octagon, 1980. 407 pp. Index.

Covers Tolstoy family relations in the year of Tolstoy's death. Maude, Tolstoy's biographer and English translator (he knew Tolstoy from 1888–1910), portrays Tolstaia as "mentally unbalanced." Referring to the Tolstoy's well-known marital conflict in his preface, eldest son Sergei, while more sympathetic, ascribes his mother's behavior to "hysteria." This book is organized chronologically, with entries from Tolstaia's daybook and diary, Tolstoy's diary, and his private diary, "For Myself Alone." Tolstaia's entries reveal much about the beliefs and expectations of a woman of her class background.

419 ――――. *The Diaries of Sophie Tolstoy*. Edited by O. A. Golinenko, S. A. Rozanova, B. M. Shomova, I. A. Pokrovskaya, and N. I. Azarova. Translated by Cathy Porter. Introduction by R. F. Christian and C. Porter. New York: Random House, 1985. 1,043 pp. Index.

Sofia Andreevna Tolstaia married Leo Tolstoy when she was eighteen and he thirty-four. Although she was Tolstoy's invaluable helpmate in transcribing and deciphering his writing, Sofia confined her own writing mostly to her diary. The definitive treatment of her life and her role in the Tolstoy family remains to be written, but much can be gleaned from this book—the first complete English translation of Tolstaia's diaries, with excerpts from her "daily diaries." Introductions by Tolstoy expert Christian and feminist historian and translator Porter recast Sofia in a more sympathetic light.

420 TOLSTOY, ALEXANDRA. *The Tragedy of Tolstoy*. Translated by Elena Varneck. New Haven, Conn.: Yale University Press, 1933. 294 pp. Index.

Memoirs of Alexandra's early years, up to the time of her father's death at the age of eighty-two, when she was twenty-six.

421 ――――. *I Worked for the Soviet*. New Haven, Conn.: Yale University Press, 1934. 254 pp. Index. Reprint, with some additions.

422 ――――. *Tolstoy: A Life of My Father*. Translated by Elizabeth Reynolds Hapgood. New York: Harper, 1953. Reprint. New York: Octagon, 1973. 543 pp. Index.

Biography of Tolstoy by his youngest daughter. Championing her father in the bitter Tolstoy marriage, Alexandra (Sasha) helped him leave home for the fateful journey that ended with his death in the Astapovo railroad station. As might be expected, Sasha is quite critical of her mother.

423   ———. *Out of the Past*. Edited by Katherine Strelsky and Catherine
        Wolkonsky. New York: Columbia University Press, 1981. 430 pp.
        Index. Bibliography.
Mostly about life after the Bolshevik Revolution, political persecution, harassment by various commissars, flight to Japan and refuge there, eventual emigration to the United States, and "First Steps in America" (1931–39).

424   TOLSTOY, COUNTESS ALEXANDRA ANDREYEVNA, and LEV
        TOLSTOY. *The Letters of Tolstoy and His Cousin Alexandra, 1857–1903*.
        Translated by Leo Islavin. New York: E. P. Dutton, 1928; London:
        Methuen, 1929. 232 pp. Index.
Intimate, trusting correspondence between Countess Alexandra (tutor of
Alexander II's only daughter) and Tolstoy.

425   TOLSTOI, COUNT LEON L. *The Truth about My Father*. New York:
        D. Appleton, 1924. 229 pp. Index.
Contains a chapter on Tolstoy's ideas about marriage and women.

426   TOLSTOY, ILYA. *Reminiscences of Tolstoy*. Translated by George
        Calderon. London: Chapman & Hall, 1914. 405 pp.; New York:
        Century, 1914. 310 pp.
Early edition of Ilya Tolstoy's memoirs, without explanatory notes or index.

427   ———. *Tolstoy, My Father: Reminiscences*. Translated and annotated by
        Ann Dunnigan. Chicago: Cowles, 1971. 322 pp. Index.
Memoirs by the Tolstoys' third child. Sympathetic to his mother, little inclined
to idealize his father: "The world bowed down before the great Tolstoy, read
him, and revered him. But someone had to feed Tolstoy, make his shirts and
trousers, take care of him when he was ill."

428   TOLSTOY, LEO. *Childhood. Boyhood. Youth. The Incursion*. Translated
        and edited by Leo Weiner. London: J. M. Dent & Sons, 1904. Reprint.
        New York: AMS Press, 1968. 497 pp.
Stories about gentry family life with autobiographical elements (especially in
Childhood).

429   ———. *Tolstoy's Love-Letters, with a Study of the Autobiographical Elements
        in Tolstoy's Work by Paul Biryukov*. Translated by S. S. Koteliansky and
        Virginia Woolf. London: Hogarth, 1923. 134 pp.
Letters from Tolstoy to his fiancée Valeria Arsenieva, written in 1846 and
1847, until the breaking off of their engagement.

430   ———. "What Is Art?" and "Essays on Art." Translated By Aylmer
        Maude. Oxford: Oxford University Press, 1930. 339 pp.
In "An Afterword to Chekhov's Story 'Darling'" (1905) Tolstoy expresses his
view of the woman question.

431 ———. *Tolstoy's Letters*. Vol. 1, *1828–1879*. Vol. 2, *1880–1910*.
      Selected, edited, and translated by R. F. Christian. New York: Charles
      Scribner's Sons, 1978. Vol. 1, 336 pp.; vol. 2, 400 pp. Index.
Selected letters from the author's voluminous correspondence with family,
friends, and literary and political luminaries.

432 ———. *Collected Works*.
Countless editions of Tolstoy's novels, short stories, essays, letters, and diaries,
with their remarkable portraits of women. Although Tolstoy is often viewed as
a misogynist, feminist literary scholar Barbara Heldt praises his creation of
complex female characters.

433 TOLSTOY, SERGEI. *Tolstoy Remembered by His Son*. Translated by
      Moura Budberg. London: Weidenfeld & Nicholson, 1961. 234 pp.
      Index.
Good detail about early life in the Tolstoy household (from 1862 to 1881).

FICTION, POETRY, AND LITERARY CRITICISM

434 AKHMATOVA, ANNA. *Poems of Akhmatova*. Selected, translated, and
      introduced by Stanley Kunitz with Max Hayward. Boston: Atlantic
      Monthly Press, 1973. 173 pp.
Forty poems, with the Russian and English texts of each printed side by side.
Includes "Requiem," excerpts from "Poem without a Hero," and "Lot's Wife."
Translator's Note by Stanley Kunitz.

435 ———. *"Tale without a Hero" and "Twenty-Two Poems"*. Translated by
      Jeanne van der Eng-Liedmeier and Kees Verheul. The Hague: Mouton,
      1973. 141 pp.
Includes several essays by the translators about Akhmatova's poetry.

436 ———. *"Requiem" and "Poem Without a Hero"*. Translated, introduced,
      and annotated by D. M. Thomas. Athens: Ohio University Press, 1976.
      78 pp.
Translations of two of Akhmatova's best-known poems.

437 ———. *Selected Poems*. Edited and translated by Walter Arndt. Includes
      "Requiem" (translated by Robin Kemball) and *"A Poem without a Hero"*
      (translated and annotated by Carl Proffer). Ann Arbor, Mich.: Ardis,
      1976. 202 pp.
Contains "Bulrushes," "Verses," "Samizdat," "Requiem," "Poem without a
Hero," and other uncollected verse. Helpful explanatory notes and chronology.

438 ———. *Way of All the Earth*. Translated by D. M. Thomas. London: Martin, Secker & Warburg, 1979. 96 pp. Notes.
Translations of poems from the cycles *Evening, Rosary, By the Seashore, White Flock, Plantain, Anno Domini, Reed*, and *The Seventh Book*, as well as other poems dating from 1909 to 1963. Helpful endnotes.

439 ———. *Poems*. Selected and Translated by Lyn Coffin. Introduction by Joseph Brodsky. New York: W. W. Norton, 1983. 100 pp.
Over one hundred of Akhmatova's poems, including "Requiem." The poems, illustrating Akhmatova's prodigious output, date from 1909 to 1965.

440 ———. *Poems*. Moscow: Raduga, 1988. 272 pp. Chronology. Notes.
English-Russian edition of Akhmatova's poems, including selections from the books *Evening* (1912), *Rosary* (1914), *A White Birds' Flight* (1917), *The Plantain* (1921), *Anno Domini* (1921–22), *Reeds* (1924–40), *The Seventh Book* (1936–64). Also excerpts from the long poems "Requiem" and "Northern Elegies" and some individual poems, including a number published posthumously.

441 ———. *Selected Early Love Lyrics by Anna Akhmatova*. Translated by Jesse Davies. Liverpool: Lincoln Davies, 1988. 48 pp.
Translations of twenty poems dating from 1911 to 1921, with parallel Russian text.

442 ———. *Selected Poems*. Translated and introduced by Richard McKane. Newcastle upon Tyne: Bloodaxe Books, 1989. 336 pp. Translator's notes.
Translations of poems from *Evening, Rosary, White Flock, Wayside Grass, Anno Domini, Reed*, and *The Seventh Book*, as well as "A Half Century of Quatrains," "Requiem," "Poem without a Hero," and several other epic and long poems, and parts of "Prologue: A Play." Also includes the poet's "Briefly about Myself" and "Fragments from Memoirs." Helpful endnotes.

443 ———. *The Complete Poems of Anna Akhmatova*. 2 vols. Edited and introduced by Roberta Reeder. Translated by Judith Hemschemeyer. Somerville, Mass.: Zephyr, 1990. Vol. 1, 650 pp.; vol. 2, 871 pp. Index. Bibliography.
An exhaustive collection of the poems of Russia's premier female poet. A true labor of love, this work is a very successful joint effort between Hemschemeyer, who knows little Russian, and Russian scholar Roberta Reeder. Both volumes are well-designed and readable, with English and Russian versions of each poem on facing pages. Reeder's introduction provides useful biographical information.

444 ANDREW, JOE. "The Lady Vanishes: A Feminist Reading of Turgenev's *Asya*." *Irish Slavonic Studies* 8 (1987): 87–96.
Earlier version of a chapter in *Women in Russian Literature* (entry 190).

445 BARKER, ADELE. "Pushkin's 'Queen of Spades': A Displaced Mother Figure." *American Imago* 41, no. 2 (Summer 1984): 201–9.
Analyzes the oedipal theme in Pushkin's story (Hermann's fixation on the Countess even after her death).

446 CHERNYSHEVSKY, NIKOLAI. *What Is to Be Done? A Romance*. Translated by Benjamin R. Tucker. Revised and abridged by Ludmilla B. Turkevich. Vintage Russian Library. New York: Random House, 1961.
One scholar calls this a "censored and truncated" version of the seriously flawed Tucker translation.

447 ———. *What Is to Be Done? Tales about New People*. Original translation by Benjamin Tucker, expanded by Cathy Porter. London: Virago, 1982. 378 pp.
Based on the Tucker translation, with all its inaccuracies, this expanded version still omits much previously censored material.

448 ——— *What Is to Be Done? Tales of New People*. Translated by Laura Beraha. Moscow: Raduga, 1983.
A new and complete translation. Criticized by Kathryn Feuer for employing outdated and jarring British and American slang.

449 ———. *A Vital Question; or, What Is to Be Done?* Translated by Nathan Haskell Dole and S. S. Skidelsky. Facsimile ed. Introduction by Kathryn Feuer. Ann Arbor, Mich.: Ardis, 1986.
Reprint of the Dole-Skidelsky translation, with all its flaws and with the sexually explicit passages excised.

450 ———. *What Is to Be Done?* Translated by Michael Katz. Annotated by William G. Wagner. Ithaca, N.Y.: Cornell University Press, 1989. 449 pp.
The best English translation of this landmark utopian novel. Completely new, it restores all material omitted in the Tucker (entry 447) and Dole-Skidelsky (entry 449) versions. Introduction by Katz and Wagner provides key elements of the historical and literary background; annotations are helpful. Women's liberation themes, as reflected in the various female and male characters, are discussed. Readers of this translation will get a sense of the full range, including the erotic content, of this highly influential book.

451   CLAYTON, J. DOUGLAS. "Towards a Feminist Reading of *Evgenii Onegin.*" *Canadian Slavonic Papers* 29, no. 2/3 (June/September 1987): 255–65.

Attempts to begin the long-overdue analysis of the role of women and the erotic in Pushkin. Argues that erotic elements were ignored or censored by Victorian and Soviet puritans.

452   COSTLOW, JANE. "Speaking the Sorrow of Women: Turgenev's 'Neschastnaia' and Evgeniia Tur's 'Antonina.'" *Slavic Review* 50, no. 2 (Summer 1991): 328–35.

Views the story "Neschastnaia" as "part of the complex operation by which Russia's melancholic bachelor gained legitimacy as the revealer of Russian femininity." Discusses the influence of Tur and other women writers on Turgenev's work. Costlow contends that Turgenev's condemnation of Tur's writing helped empty the field of competitors; she concludes that his "embrace of 'feminine' writing depend[ed] on Tur's silence." Costlow issues a call to rescue nineteenth-century Russian women writers from a "premature literary grave."

453   De MAEGD-SOEP, CAROLINA. *The Emancipation of Women in Russian Literature and Society: A Contribution to the Knowledge of the Russian Society during the 1860s.* Adapted and translated by the author and Jos Coessens. Slavica Gandensia Analecta. Ghent, Belgium: Ghent State University, 1970. 402 pp. Index.

Discusses the movement for women's emancipation as it affected the family, work, and education, as well as the more independent women who emerged. Surveys works of Goncharov, Turgenev, and Chernyshevsky.

454   EVANS, MARY. *Reflecting on Anna Karenina.* London: Routledge, 1980. 99 pp.

Rare feminist critique of Tolstoy's novel.

455   FORRESTER, SIBELAN. "Bells and Cupolas: The Formative Role of the Female Body in Marina Tsvetaeva's Poetry." *Slavic Review* 51, no. 2 (Summer 1992): 232–46.

Forrester argues that for Tsvetaeva, "women's language and physical experience were central to her concern with poetry and poetic creation."

456   GIPPIUS, ZINAIDA N. *The Green Ring: A Play in Four Acts.* Translated by S. S. Koteliansky. London: Daniel, 1920. 104 pp.

English version of Gippius's *Zelenoe kol'tso* (1916).

457   GUNTER, SUSAN ELIZABETH. "The Influence of Turgenev's Heroines on the Women of Henry James's 1880's Novels." Ph.D. diss., University of South Carolina, 1986. 206 pp.

Argues that Turgenev's most important influence on Henry James was in the treatment of women, particularly in the 1880s. In Gunter's view, during that period "James borrowed wholesale both feminine types and individuals from Turgenev to create his gallery of formidable heroines."

458   HELDT, BARBARA. *Terrible Perfection: Women and Russian Literature.* Bloomington: Indiana University Press, 1987. 174 pp. Index.
A provocative and pioneering work. The first study of its kind that challenges traditional interpretations on all fronts and applies a feminist perspective to a range of topics, primarily in nineteenth- and twentieth-century Russian literature. The first section discusses portrayals of women by such male authors as Pushkin, Dostoevsky, Turgenev, Chekhov, Gogol, and Tolstoy. Heldt dwells on the similarities in their portrayals of women and argues that only Tolstoy developed toward feminism, which she defines as "a world view which releases women from the burden of male-definition and even shows the latter to be a grave error." The second part, "In Search of Self-Definition," is devoted to women's autobiographies, specifically those of Dashkova, Durova, Sokhanskaia, Labzina, Vodovozova, Liubov Blok, and Tsvetaeva, with brief mention also of Kovalevskaia. Heldt contends that these works represent "a full expression of self that is rarely seen in fiction" and decries critics' lack of attention to them. The final section focuses on four modern women poets—Sofiia Parnok (1885–1933), Mariia Shkapskaia (1891–1952), Anna Akhmatova (1889–1966) and Marina Tsvetaeva (1892–1941). The latter two are well known; Parnok is included for her love poems to other women, and Shkapskaia for her portrayal of the mother and mother-child love. The conclusion includes a withering critique of *Doctor Zhivago.* Overall, Heldt has taken a giant step forward in rediscovering, rehabilitating, and reframing the place of women and women's writing in Russian and Soviet literature. A truly germinal work.

459   ———. "Men Who Give Birth: A Feminist Perspective on Russian Literature." In *Discontinuous Discourses in Modern Russian Literature,* edited by Catriona Kelly, Michael Makin, and David Sheperd, pp. 157–67. Houndmills, Basinstoke, Hampshire, England: Macmillan, 1989.
Argues for the necessity of feminist criticism of Russian literature, noting that the "construction of sexual identity and the exercise of sexual authority within a text may be factors difficult to determine. But without a feminist criticism, the discussion of their recurring patterns and voices will continue to be haphazard, imprecise and self-indulgent." Surveys the treatment of childbirth by major Russian and Soviet authors from Turgenev and Tolstoy to Sholokhov and Pasternak. Analyzes the "transference of the female experience to the male domain," culminating in *Doctor Zhivago.*

460   JOHANSON, CHRISTINE. "Turgenev's Heroines: A Historical Assessment." *Canadian Slavonic Papers* 26, no. 1 (March 1984): 24–34.
Analyzes "the historical authenticity of Turgenev's portrayal of the social posi-

tion, family life, and marital relations of gentry women in mid-nineteenth-century Russia." Johanson concludes that Turgenev, in the character of Kukshina, "made the progressive woman a subject of comic disdain." But overall, in her view, Turgenev shows much more about class stratification than about divisions by sex.

461   KANZER, MARK. "Dostoevsky's Matricidal Impulses." *Psychoanalytic Review* 35, no. 2 (April 1948): 115–25.
The matricidal theme as developed in *Crime and Punishment*.

462   KELLY, CATRIONA, MICHAEL MAKIN, and DAVID SHEPERD. *Discontinuous Discourses in Modern Russian Literature*. Houndmills, Basingstoke, Hampshire, England: Macmillan, 1989. 178 pp. Index.
Contains essays by Catriona Kelly on "Petrushka and the Pioneers: The Russian Carnival Puppet Theatre after the Revolution," Michael Makin on "Text and Violence in Tsvetaeva's Molodets," Joe Andrew on "Radical Sentimentalism or Sentimental Radicalism? A Feminist Approach to Eighteenth-Century Russian Literature," and Barbara Heldt on "Men Who Give Birth: A Feminist Perspective on Russian Literature" (entry 459). One of the still too rare literary collections that takes gender issues seriously. Heldt's germinal essay is particularly significant in this regard.

463   KETCHIAN, SONIA. *The Poetry of Anna Akhmatova: A Conquest of Time and Space*. Verse translation by F. D. Reeve. Munich: Verlag Otto Sagner, 1986. 225 pp. Index.
Ketchian surveys the entire work of Akhmatova, discussing how it fits together and how it relates to world literature and culture. Compares Akhmatova with Pushkin; argues that the two were similar in that they "conquered both time and space."

464   KIREMIDJIAN, DAVID. "Crime and Punishment: Matricide and the Woman Question." *American Imago* 33, no. 4 (Winter 1976): 403–33.
Psychoanalytic interpretation, discussing also Dostoevsky's attitude toward feminism and his general portrayal of women. Critique of the Wasiolek and Snodgrass analysis of the matricidal theme in the novel (entry 484).

465   KOKHANOVSKAYA, NADEZHDA STEPANOVNA. *"The Rusty Linchpin" and "Luboff Archipovna."* After the Russian of Mme. Kokhanovsky. Boston: D. Lothrop, 1887. 296 pp.
Translation of two sentimental stories by this writer.

466   KUPRIN, ALEXANDRE. *Yama [The Pit]: A Novel in Three Parts*. Translated by Bernard Guilbert Guerney. New York: A. Koren, 1922. Reprint. Westport, Conn.: Hyperion, 1977. 406 pp.

Classic realistic novel of prostitution in Russia, first published between 1909 and 1915.

467 LEITER, SHARON. *Akhmatova's Petersburg*. Philadelphia: University of Pennsylvania Press, 1983. 215 pp. Subject, name, and poem indexes. Bibliography.

The changing image of Petersburg-Leningrad in Akhmatova's work. Argues that Akhmatova "was the last great poet of the Petersburg tradition" and that she transformed the myth of the city, bringing it into the twentieth century. Her life and the history of the city are intricately intertwined.

468 LUKER, NICHOLAS, ed. and trans. *An Anthology of Russian Neo-Realism: The "Znanie" School of Maxim Gorky*. Ann Arbor: Ardis, 1982. 283 pp.

Includes Leonid Andreev's classic, "The Seven Who Were Hanged," the portrait of two female and three male terrorists and two others who join them on the gallows. Also includes a translation of chapters 38 and 39 of Mikhail Artsybashev's novel *Sanine*, controversial for its bold examination of contemporary sexual mores.

469 McCORMACK, KATHRYN LOUISE. "Images of Women in the Poetry of Zinaida Gippius." Ph.D. diss., Vanderbilt University, 1982. 206 pp.

Applies feminist criticism to study of Gippius's poetry and prose. Specifically discusses her theories of the polarity between women and men. Defines four predominant images of women in her poetry: females in traditional male roles, woman as abstraction, the religious woman, and the androgyne.

470 MATHEWSON, RUFUS W. *The Positive Hero in Russian Literature*. Stanford, Calif.: Stanford University Press, 1975. 369 pp. Index.

Problems in the portrayal of male heroes in Russian and Soviet literature.

471 MATICH, OLGA. "A Typology of Fallen Women." In *American Contributions to the Ninth International Congress of Slavists*, edited by Paul Debreczeny, pp. 325–43. Columbus, Ohio: Slavica, 1983.

Typology of fallen women in relation to men, with four categories: female victim/male victimizer, female victim/male redeemer, female redeemer/male victim, and female victimizer/male victim.

472 MOSER, CHARLES. *Antinihilism in the Russian Novel of the 1860s*. The Hague, London and Paris: Mouton, 1964. 215 pp. Index.

Information about the place of the woman question in the radical movment. Discussion of emancipated young women (*Nigilistki*) and their portrayal in literature.

473   NEATROUR, ELIZABETH BAYLOR. "Miniatures of Russian Life and
      Works of N. A. Teffi." Ph.D. diss., Indiana University, 1972. 387 pp.
An effort at remedying the long neglect of the work of this talented writer. A
systematic study and analysis of her works plus a short biography.

474   NIKOLSKAYA, TANYA. "'The Contemporary Woman' in Early
      Twentieth Century Russian Literature." *Irish Slavonic Papers* 8 (1987):
      107–13.
Attitudes of such writers as Sologub, Mark Krinitsky, Nemirovich-Danchenko,
and Bryusov to women. Brief discussion of works by Verbitskaya,
Vinnichenko, Shchepkina-Kupernik, Nagrodskaya, Anna Mar, Vera Rudich,
Nadezhda Sanzhar, and Kollontai.

475   PACHMUSS, TEMIRA. *Selected Works of Zinaida Hippius [Gippius]*.
      Urbana: Illinois University Press, 1972. 315 pp. Index.
Although her interpretation of Gippius' ideas and life has been challenged,
Temira Pachmuss is singlehandedly responsible for making Gippius' work
accessible in English. Works included are: "Heavenly Words," "Fate," "It's All
for the Worse," "The Pilgrim," "He Is White," "There Is No Return," "The
Eternal Woman," "The Strange Law," "Memoirs of Martynov," "Julien or Not
Julien," "Rest, Heart," "With the Star," and "Metamorphosis."

476   ———, ed. and trans. *Women Writers in Russian Modernism: An
      Anthology*. Urbana: The University of Illinois Press, 1978. 340 pp.
      Index. Bibliography.
An important effort to rediscover and rehabilitate eight Russian women writers important to understanding the history of Modernism. The eight are:
Zinaida Gippius, Mirra Lokhvitskaya, Anastasiya Verbitskaya, Poliksena
Solovyova, Lidiya Zinovyeva-Annibal, Cherubina de Gabriak, Nadezhda Teffi,
and Adelaida Gertsyk. The section for each writer is prefaced by helpful biographical notes, and the introduction aids in placing these writers in context.

477   PARNOK, SOPHIA. "Eight Poems." Translated by Rima Shore.
      Conditions 6 (1980): 171–75.
Poems included here are "Fortune Telling" (based on Russian bridal laments),
"Dreams of Sappho," "For Ludmila Erarskaya" (Parnok's lover after
Tsvetaeva), and several untitled works. Poems date from 1915 to a month
before Parnok's death on 26 August 1933.

478   PETERSON, DALE. "From Russia with Love: Turgenev's Maidens
      and Howells's Heroines." *Canadian Slavonic Papers* 36, no. 1 (March
      1984): 24–34.
Argues that William Dean Howells and Henry James derived the independent

heroines in their novels from Turgenev's strong women.

479   PETERSON, RONALD E. *The Russian Symbolists: An Anthology of Critical and Theoretical Writings.* Ann Arbor, Mich.: Ardis, 1986. 223 pp. Notes.
Contains two essays by Zinaida Gippius, "Decadence and Society" and "Peredonov's Little Tear." The first was written in 1905 under Gippius' male pseudonym, Anton Krayny. Also included is Andrei Bely's "A Review of Gippius' Literary Diary."

480   ROSENTHAL, CHARLOTTE. "Zinaida Vengerova: Modernism and Women's Liberation." *Irish Slavonic Studies* 8 (1987): 97–105.
Vengerova as an examplar of the modernist ethic, justifying challenges to traditional norms and resulting in a flowering of female poetic writing. For Rosenthal, Vengerova's rejection of political feminism and emphasis on the personal and spiritual represents a rebellion against the traditional self-sacrificing female family role.

481   ROSSLYN, WENDY. *The Prince, the Fool and the Nunnery: The Religious Theme in the Early Poetry of Anna Akhmatova.* Amersham, England: Avebury Publishing, 1984. 256pp. Index. Bibliography.Notes.
An examination of the "inner world" of the poet through examination of her early poems, namely those in the books *Evening, Rosary, White Flock, Plantain,* and *Anno Domini.* Celebrates the poet's passive resistance against Soviet tyranny. Concludes that Akhmatova ultimately triumphed over her circumstances not through religion but through "an acute moral sensitivity, unfailing conscience, and above all, to poetry."

482   SHORE, RIMA. "Remembering Sophia Parnok (1885–1933)." *Conditions* 6 (1980): 177–93.
Sophia Parnok, a gifted poet, avowed lesbian, and lover of Marina Tsvetaeva, long sunk in obscurity, is rediscovered in this first English examination of her life and work. Between 1913 and 1916 Parnok wrote under the male pseudonym Andrei Polyanin; otherwise she wrote under her own name. Shore discusses the sexism and homophobia behind the liberal facade of the Russian intelligentsia and its effect on Parnok's work and her recognition as a poet.

483   SIEGEL, GEORGE. "The Fallen Woman in Nineteenth Century Russian Literature." *Harvard Slavic Studies* 5 (1970): 81–107.
"Chronicles the theme of the fallen woman in the works of Gogol ("Nevsky Avenue"), Chernyshevsky (*What Is to Be Done?*), Nekrasov's poetry, Garshin and Krestovsky's stories, and the works of Chekhov, Dostoevsky, and Tolstoy. Discusses themes of degradation, the sexual double standard, rehabilitation, and the widespread nature of prostitution.

484 SNODGRASS, W. D. "Crime for Punishment: The Tenor of Part One." *Hudson Review* 13, no. 2 (Summer 1960): 202–53.
Touches on the theme of matricide in Dostoevsky's novel.

485 TSVETAEVA, MARINA. *Marina Tsvetaeva. A Captive Spirit: Selected Prose*. Edited and translated by J. Marin King. Ann Arbor, Mich.: Ardis, 1980. 491 pp. Index.
Translation of about one-third of Tsvetaeva's prose. Includes "A Living Word about a Living Man," "Koktebel,'" "Max and the Folk Tale," "A Captive Spirit," "An Otherworldly Evening," "My Father and His Museum," "Charlottenberg," "The Uniform," "The Laurel Wreath," "The Opening of the Museum," "The Intended," "The Tower of Ivy," "The House at Old Pimen," "Mother and Music," "The Devil," "My Pushkin," "Two Forest Kings," and "Pushkin and Pugachev."

486 ———. *The Demesne of the Swans*. Translated, with introduction, notes, and commentaries, by Robin Kemball. Ann Arbor, Mich.: Ardis, 1980. 211 pp.
Definitive version of the Russian text. Bilingual edition. Helpful introduction; extensive notes and commentaries.

487 ———. *Selected Poems*. Translated by Elaine Feinstein. London: Hutchinson, 1986. 108 pp. Bibliography.
Poems from 1915 to 1938, beginning with "I Know the Truth" and ending with "Poems to Czechoslovakia."

488 ———. *Selected Poetry*. Translated and introduced by David McDuff. Newcastle upon Tyne: Bloodaxe Books, 1987. 160 pp. Bibliography.
Sixty-one poems dating from 1913 to 1939, from the collections *Poems of Youth*, *Bon Voyages*, *Swans' Encampment*, *The Craft*, and *After Russia*, as well as twenty-three uncollected poems.

489 WEEKS, LAURA D. "'I Named Her Ariadna . . .': The Demeter-Persephone Myth in Tsvetaeva's Poems for Her Daughter." *Slavic Review* 49, no. 4 (Winter 1990): 568–84.
Analyzes the "indissoluble union of mother and daughter," as well as Tsvetaeva's mythmaking. Explores the archetype underlying the poet's verses for her first daughter, and the death-and-rebirth theme as reflected in the lives of Tsvetaeva and Ariadna.

490 "Women in Russian Literature." Edited by Carl B. Proffer and Ellendea Proffer. *Russian Literature Triquarterly* no. 9 (Spring 1974): 1–601.
A pathbreaking collection of articles, translated poetry, prose, drama, criticism, texts, documents, and review articles. Not surprisingly, Anna Akhmatova has the most (27) poems included, followed by Marina Tsvetaeva. Also included are nine poems by early nineteenth century writer Nadezhda Teplova as well as

poems by Anna Bunina, Mirra Lokhvitskaia, Elena Guro, Yunna Moritz, Bella Akhmadulina, and Nataliia Gorbanevskaia. Odoevsky's *Princess Mimi*, excerpts from Karolina Pavlova's *A Double Life*, Lydia Zinovieva-Annibal's *Thirty-Three Abominations*, Teffi's *The Dog*, Natalya Baranskaia's *The Retirement Party*, and Anna Mass's *Lyuba's Wedding* round out the prose sections. Pisemsky's "Baal" is the drama selection. N. V. Nedobrovo's essay on Akhmatova, an interview with Victor Gorenko, the poet's brother, and some unpublished letters from Akhmatova to him, Akhmatova's remembrances of Mandelstam and Modigliani, and Pasternak's unpublished letters to and reviews of Akhmatova add to our knowledge of the esteemed poet. This issue also includes an unpublished letter by Alexander Fadeev to Marina Tsvetaeva, nine unpublished poems by Nataliia Gorbanevskaia, and twelve unpublished letters from Karolina Pavlova to Alexei Tolstoi. Review articles include Sidney Schultze, "A Further Feminist Look at Russian Grammars." Articles included are: Owen Ulph, "I-330: Reconsiderations on the Sex of Satan"; Beatrice Stillman, "Sofya Kovalevskaya: Growing Up in the Sixties" (see entry 391); Milica Banjanin, "The Prose and Poetry of Elena Guro"; Sam Cioran, "The Russian Sappho: Mirra Lokhvitskaya"; Barbara Heldt, "From an Introduction to Pavlova's *A Double Life*"; Jane Andelman Taubman, "Tsvetaeva and Akhmatova: Two Female Voices in a Poetic Quartet"; Josephine Pasternak, "*Patior*"; Jane Gary Harris, "Pasternak's Vision of Life: The History of a Feminine Image"; Marina Ledkovsky, "Avdotya Panaeva: Her Salon and Her Life"; Antonia Glasse, "The Formidable Woman: Portrait and Original"; Edythe Haber, "Nadezhda Teffi"; Xenia Gasiorowska, "Happiness in Recent Soviet Fiction"; and Andrew Donskov, "Pisemsky's Talent as a Playwright."

The Soviet Period, 1918–1991

HISTORIES AND GENERAL WORKS

491 ALEXIYEVICH, SVETLANA. *War's Unwomanly Face*. Translated by Keith Hammond and Lyudmila Lezhnera. Moscow: Progress Publishers, 1988. 248 pp.

The author spent four years searching out and recording the stories of some of the over 800,000 Soviet women who fought in World War II. Their stories document the heroism and suffering of those who survived and remember the contributions of those who did not. The material is organized impressionistically; this makes it difficult to pinpoint in time and sometimes place. This book is the most comprehensive of the war memoirs about women but keeps to the official line. It portrays heroism in its many forms but fails to mention the negative aspects of the war—corruption, incompetence, desertion, political intimidation—which are now well known. Nor is there any analysis of the evolution of Soviet policy about women in combat. Still, this book helps illuminate an area that deserves more study.

492 ALT, HERSCHEL, and EDITH ALT. *Russia's Children: A First Report on Child Welfare in the Soviet Union*. New York: Bookman Associates, 1959. 240 pp. Index.

Two social workers of Russian-Jewish immigrant backgrounds travel to Leningrad, Moscow, and Kiev in the summers of 1956 and 1957. They visit schools, childcare centers, clinics, hospitals, and mental hospitals. Some useful anecdotal information about women and children for a period in which there were few such books.

493 AMINOVA, R. *The October Revolution and Women's Liberation in Uzbekistan*. Translated by B. M. Meerovich. Moscow: Nauka, 1977. 239 pp. Bibliography.

Valuable study of this topic, the subject of far too little scholarly attention. Uses archival sources. Particularly good on early efforts to emancipate Uzbek women. Critical of efforts of trade unions and bureaucrats for often ignoring or resisting these efforts. Mostly discusses the 1920s; little about the Stalin and post-Stalin eras.

494 ATTWOOD, LYNNE. *The New Soviet Man and Woman: Sex Role Socialization in the USSR*. Bloomington: Indiana University Press, 1990. 263 pp. Index. Bibliography.

The British scholars of the Women in Eastern Europe group almost single-handedly kept the field of Soviet women's studies alive in the 1980s; U.S. scholars published virtually no monographs in that area. Lynne Attwood tackles the important subject of sex-role socialization thoroughly and with insight. Mary Zirin writes, "Lynne Attwood's book shows where Francine Gray is getting her views of women's life in the Soviet Union. In a quiet, clear, devastating exposition, Attwood meticulously traces the historical pattern: the development of Russian-Soviet psychological theories of the largely biological basis of sexual identity and their use, abuse, or neglect at various periods in pedagogy and daily life. . . . Glasnost was just getting underway when Attwood wrote the book, but the ironically titled *New Soviet Man and Woman* gives us a solid theoretical underpinning for following developments both in the official line and in the 'egalitarian' and burgeoning feminist movements of the turbulent '90s."

495 BELOFF, NORA. *Inside the Soviet Empire: The Myth and the Reality*. New York: Times Books, 1979. 188 pp. Index.

A British writer and a female friend spend five weeks touring the Soviet Union by car and get detained at the border as they attempt to leave.

496 BENNIGSEN, ALEXANDRE, and S. ENDERS WIMBUSH. *Mystics and Commissars: Sufism in the Soviet Union*. Berkeley: University of California Press, 1985. 195 pp. Index. Glossary. Annotated bibliography.

The few pages (67–69) devoted to women in the Sufi brotherhoods suggest interesting leads for further research about this little-explored topic. Glossary and annotated bibliography helpful.

497 BEREDAY, GEORGE, WILLIAM BRICKMAN, and GERALD READ, with the assistance of Ina Schlesinger. *The Changing Soviet School*. Boston: Houghton Mifflin, 1960. 514 pp. Index.

Impressions of the post-Stalin educational system by three educators after a one-month visit in 1958. Covers predominance of female teachers, special schools, sample lessons, and sex-role socialization.

498 BERMAN, HAROLD J. *Justice in Russia: An Interpretation of Soviet Law*. Cambridge: Harvard University Press, 1950. 322 pp. Index.
Chapter 12 discusses law and the family. Contains excerpts from court cases.

499 ———. *Justice in the USSR*. Rev. ed. Cambridge: Harvard University Press, 1963. 450 pp. Index.
A revision of the 1950 book *Justice in Russia* (entry 498). Chapter 14, "Law and the Family," contains some examples from court cases and a general overview of Soviet family law. This book does not specifically address gender issues.

500 ———. *Soviet Criminal Law and Procedure: The RSFSR Codes*. Translated by Harold J. Berman and James W. Spindler. Cambridge: Harvard University Press, 1972. 399 pp. Index. Glossary of legal terms.
Translation of the 1960 Russian Soviet Federated Socialist Republic (RSFSR) criminal codes, as amended through 1 March 1972. The 1960 codes for the first time made it a crime to obstruct women's exercise of their equal rights. This second edition differs from the first in including amendments from July 1965 to March 1972.

501 BILSHAI, VERA. *The Status of Women in the Soviet Union*. Translated by Robert Macilhone. Edited by D. Skvirsky. Moscow: Foreign Languages Publishing House, 1957. 105 pp.
Translation of *Reshenie zhenskogo voprosa v SSSR (The resolution of the woman question in the USSR)*. As is evident from the Russian title, this is a positive account of Soviet efforts at achieving women's equality. A popular work with no footnotes or list of references.

502 BINYON, MICHAEL. *Life in Russia*. New York: Pantheon, 1983. 286 pp. Index.
Chapter 2, "Women and Families," contains nothing new, with the exception of some anecdotal information. This chapter also has a page and a half (pages 47–49) on homosexuality, referring only to males.

503 BLEKHER, FEIGA. *The Soviet Woman in the Family and Society (A Sociological Study)*. Translated by Hilary and Ron Hardin. New York: John Wiley & Sons, 1980. 234 pp. Index.
A very useful survey covering work, marriage, and family, as well as some historical background. Particularly helpful discussion of the specifics of everyday Soviet life.

504 BODROVA, VALENTINA, and RICHARD ANKER, eds. *Working Women in Socialist Countries: The Fertility Connection*. Geneva: International Labour Office, 1985. 234 pp. Bibliography.
See Anker's comparative survey (compares data from Bulgaria, Cuba,

Czechoslovakia, Hungary, Poland, and the Uzbek SSR) and chapter 6, by a group of Soviet (Russian and Uzbek) scholars on Uzbekistan. Useful statistical data and bibliography.

505 BRIDGER, SUSAN ALLOTT. *Women in the Soviet Countryside: Women's Roles in Rural Development in the Soviet Union*. Cambridge: Cambridge University Press, 1987. 259 pp. Index. Bibliography.
Excellent survey of the subject. Includes a historical survey of change in the countryside. Chapters discuss the status of women in the rural work force, the changing nature of the family, sex roles, policies affecting rural population growth, education, gender differences in leisure time, the gender gap in religious belief, and observance and women's participation in local politics, including the role of the *Zhensovety* (Women's Councils).

506 BRINE, JENNY, MAUREEN PERRIE, and ANDREW SUTTON, eds. *Home, School and Leisure in the Soviet Union*. London: George Allen & Unwin, 1980. 279 pp. Index.
Contains a section on housing, the family, and the role of women. Essays by G. D. Andrusz on housing ideals, structural constraints, and the emancipation of women; by Alix Holt on housework; and by Barbara Holland on the realities of abortion and the conflict between Soviet pronatalism and women's reproductive rights. Useful bibliographies at the end of each article.

507 BROIDO, VERA. *Lenin and the Mensheviks: The Persecution of Socialists under Bolshevism*. Aldershot, England: Gower/Maurice Temple Smith, 1987. 216 pp. Index.
Information about the fate of women Mensheviks after the Revolution.

508 BRONFENBRENNER, URIE, with the assistance of John C. Condry, Jr. *Two Worlds of Childhood: U.S. and U.S.S.R.* New York: Basic Books, 1970. Paperback ed. New York: Pocket Books, 1973. 196 pp. Index.
The famous comparison of U.S. and Soviet childrearing, with many still-timely observations. Finds Soviet children more conformist but also "less anti-adult, rebellious, aggressive and delinquent." Emphasis on the traditional nuclear family as healthy; blames "father absence and the mother-centered family" for juvenile delinquency.

509 BROWN, DONALD R. *The Role and Status of Women in the Soviet Union*. New York: Teachers College Press, 1968. 139 pp.
The proceedings of the first Mary Winston Symposium at Bryn Mawr College. Contents include three essays ("Workers [and Mothers]: Soviet Women Today" by Mark Field, "The Changing Image of Women in Soviet Literature" by Vera Dunham, and "The Changing Soviet Family" by Urie Bronfenbrenner), as well as shorter essays by Patricia Carden on women students, David Heer on childbearing in the Soviet family, and Rachel Dunaway

Cox on marriage and the family. Introductory remarks by Henry Roberts; concluding comments by Robert Feldmesser. Comments by other discussants included, as well as bibliographies and useful statistical tables.

510   BROWNING, GENIA. *Women and Politics in the USSR: Consciousness Raising and Soviet Women's Groups*. Sussex, England: Wheatsheaf; New York: St. Martin's Press, 1987. 178 pp. Index.
Far too little has been written in the eighties about women in the USSR. This book, focusing primarily on the *Zhensovety*, makes an important contribution, although the narrative does not discuss in any detail the changes wrought by *glasnost*. Useful bibliography.

511   BRYANT, LOUISE. *Mirrors of Moscow*. New York: Thomas Seltzer, 1923. 209 pp.
Portraits, generally sympathetic, of major Bolshevik leaders, including Kollontai (pages 111–28), noting their conventional private lives. Bryant comments that Kollontai herself is far from perfect and that "her inconsistencies are her most feminist trait as well as her most alluring characteristic."

512   BUCKLEY, MARY. *Women and Ideology in the Soviet Union*. Ann Arbor: University of Michigan Press, 1989. 266 pp. Index. Bibliography. Notes.
Historical overview and contemporary analysis of the subject. Although the Bolsheviks never wavered from their stated commitments to women's equality, as Buckley shows, the practical approach to this issue varied in different historical periods, from the *Zhenotdel* (Women's Sections) and social experiments of the 1920s to the Stalinist declaration that the woman question had been resolved. Khrushchev addressed the failure to bring women into leadership positions in his secret 1956 speech; this aspect of the speech has been virtually ignored. Discusses the Brezhnev years, the "lively debate about women's roles," and the impact of Gorbachev's policies until 1988. A significant contribution about a subject that deserves more attention.

513   BUCKLEY, MARY, ed. *Perestroika and Soviet Women*. Cambridge: Cambridge University Press, 1992. 183 pp. Index. Notes.
A useful collection surveying the last decade of the Soviet Union. Eleven essays, including an introductory overview by Mary Buckley. Other essays by Judith Shapiro on the industrial labor force, Sue Bridger on women and agricultural reform, Mary Buckley on political reform, feminist writer Ol'ga Lipovskaia on new women's organizations, Solomea Pavlychko on new Ukrainian women's groups, Genia Browning updating her work on the *zhensovety* (Women's Councils), Natalia Rimashevskaia on the "new women's studies," Elizabeth Waters on glasnost and children's homes, Hilary Pilkington on girls in Soviet youth culture. Barbara Heldt, in the last essay of the volume, introduces the concept of "gynoglasnost," in reference to the too-frequent appropriation of

woman as symbol by male writers across the political spectrum. She contrasts this to the still small sound of women's authentic voices.

514   CELMINA, HELENE. *Women in Soviet Prisons*. New York: Paragon
      House, 1985. 238 pp.
The author, a Latvian, was imprisoned in 1947 for a year, and in 1962 for four years, on trumped-up charges. She eventually was able to emigrate to the West. This book is primarily her memoir about her years in prison and the camps.

515   CENTRAL STATISTICAL BOARD OF THE COUNCIL OF MIN-
      ISTERS OF THE USSR. *Women in the USSR: Brief Statistics*. Moscow:
      Foreign Languages Publishing House, 1960. 100 pp.
A range of useful statistics about Soviet women. Aside from basic population information, includes data on the percentage of women in different jobs, the comparative pre- and postrevolutionary distribution of women in the labor force, women executives and specialists, women deputies to local and regional Soviets and to the Supreme Soviet, and educational levels among women. Concludes with information about mothers and children. The last table lists the number of hero-mothers (women who have had a large number of children) of the Soviet Union. (The usual caveats about Soviet statistics should be heeded. Job categories, particularly that of engineer, do not mean the same things in the East and West.)

516   ———. *Women and Children in the USSR: Brief Statistical Returns*.
      Moscow: Foreign Languages Publishing House, 1963. 195 pp.
Official Soviet statistics on demographics, education, women at work and in the family, sports, health, and entertainment.

517   CHAMBERLIN, WILLIAM HENRY. *Soviet Russia: A Living Record
      and a History*. Boston: Little, Brown, 1929. Rev. ed., 1931. 486 pp.
      Index.
Chapter on women and interviews with peasants and workers whose lives have been changed by the Revolution. The work of the *Zhenotdel* is described.

518   CHAO, PAUL. *Women under Communism: Family in Russia and China*.
      Bayside, New York: General Hall, 1977. 231 pp. Index.
Contains section entitled "The Development of the Soviet Family and Women's Status." Useful comparative information.

519   CLEMENTS, BARBARA EVANS, BARBARA ALPERN ENGEL,
      and CHRISTINE D. WOROBEC, eds. *Russia's Women: Accommo-
      dation, Resistance, Transformation*. Berkeley: University of California
      Press, 1991. 353 pp. Index. Bibliography.
Selected papers from the Conference on the History of Women in the Russian Empire, held in Akron in 1988. Divided into two sections entitled "Traditional

Society" and "Transforming Tradition." Includes the following papers: N. L. Pushkareva, "Women in the Medieval Russian Family of the Tenth through Fifteenth Centuries"; Eve Levin, "Childbirth in Pre-Petrine Russia: Canon Law and Popular Tradition"; Nancy Shields Kollmann, "Women's Honor in Early Modern Russia"; Valerie A. Kivelson, "Through the Prism of Witchcraft: Gender and Social Change in Seventeenth-Century Muscovy"; Rodney A. Bohac, "Widows and the Russian Serf Community"; David Ransel, "Infant-Care Cultures in the Russian Empire"; Rose Glickman, "The Peasant Woman as Healer"; Judith Pallot, "Women's Domestic Industries in Moscow Province, 1800–1900"; Laura Engelstein, "Abortion and the Civic Order: The Legal and Medical Debates"; Alfred Meyer, "The Impact of World War I on Russian Women's Lives"; Elizabeth Waters, "The Female Form in Soviet Political Iconography, 1917–32"; and Wendy Goldman, "Women, Abortion, and the State." General overviews by the editors place the essays in their larger historical context.

520   COHEN, STEPHEN, ed. *An End to Silence: Uncensored Opinion in the Soviet Union from Roy Medvedev's Underground Magazine, "Political Diary."* Translated by George Saunders. New York: W. W. Norton, 1982. 375 pp. Index.
Contributions by Irina Kakhovskaya on the fate of her circle of Socialist Revolutionaries and the last days of Spiridonova, Stalin's attitudes toward women, prison memoirs of Yelena Vladimirova, Olga Bergolts' poem "Days of Shame and Sorrow" (about the Terror), a letter from a wife of a prison-camp official attacking Solzhenitsyn's and Dyakov's prison-camp memoirs, and Raissa Lert's critique of neo-Stalinist Russophobia.

521   CONQUEST, ROBERT. *Kolyma: The Arctic Death Camps*. London: Macmillan, 1978. 256 pp. Index.
Contains some information on women in the camps.

522   Constitution (Fundamental Law) of the Union of Soviet Socialist Republics, Moscow, 1977.
The 1977 Constitution, adopted at the Ninth Convocation of the Supreme Soviet on 7 October 1977.

523   CROLL, ELISABETH J. *Socialist Development Experience: Women in Rural Production and Reproduction in the Soviet Union, China, Cuba, and Tanzania*. Brighton, England: Institute of Development Studies at the University of Sussex, 1979. 48 pp.
Examines the ways in which changes introduced by socialism have affected "the productive and reproductive activities of peasant women." Useful comparative information for the time period surveyed.

524   DANIELS, ROBERT V. *The Conscience of the Revolution: Communist Opposition in Soviet Russia*. Cambridge: Harvard University Press, 1960. 526 pp. Bibliography. Index.
Contains several brief mentions of Kollontai as a Menshevik and, later, leader of the Workers Opposition.

525   De WITT, NICHOLAS. *Education and Professional Employment in the USSR*. Washington, D.C.: National Science Foundation, 1961. 856 pp. Index.
A comprehensive survey of the Soviet educational system, including a discussion of the role of women. Also includes information about female employment and the status of women in the professions (pages 490–96). Many useful tables.

526   DESFOSSES, HELEN, ed. *Soviet Population Policy: Conflicts and Constraints*. New York: Pergamon, 1981. 210 pp. Index.
Eight essays by noted specialists in the field of population policy. Particularly important for information about women are David Heer's "Fertility and Female Work Status in the USSR" and "Soviet Population Policy: Four Model Futures," Helen DesFosses' "Pro-Natalism in Soviet Law and Propaganda," and Alfred J. Di Maio Jr.'s "Evolution of Soviet Population Thought: From Marxism-Leninism to the *Literaturnaya Gazeta* Debate." Thirty-five tables provide useful information, including comparative percentages of women in the labor force in the United States and the USSR in different age groups in 1970. Very helpful source.

527   DEWAR, MARGARET. *Labour Policy in USSR, 1917–1928*. London: Royal Institute of International Affairs, 1956. 286 pp. Index. Bibliography. Appendixes.
Some information on the effect of New Economic Policy on women, especially in terms of the high rate of unemployment. Appendixes include a reprint of the 1903 Russian Social Democrats' labor platform and all decrees, ordinances, and instructions on labor from October 1917 to October 1928.

528   DODGE, NORTON T. *Women in the Soviet Economy: Their Role in Economic, Scientific and Technical Development*. Baltimore: Johns Hopkins Press, 1966. 331 pp. Index.
Classic book on this subject. Thorough examination of the topic, including sections on demographic factors and work; labor force participation; social, economic, and legal factors affecting employment; work and family; education; occupational indexes for all levels, from unskilled to highly skilled; and a separate chapter on scientific and technological achievements. Wide variety of data provided in 178 statistical tables and 29 lists of Figures. Needs a sequel, that updates this data to the nineties. A very worthwhile scholarly project.

529   DUNAYEVSKAYA, RAYA. *Women's Liberation and the Dialectics of Revolution: Reaching for the Future. A 35-Year Collection of Essays— Historic, Philosophic, Global.* Atlantic Highlands, N.J.: Humanities Press International, 1985. 294 pp. Index.

Included in this anthology is an essay on Natalia Sedova Trotsky. The author is a Russian-born Marxist-humanist philosopher who worked in 1937–38 in Mexico as Trotsky's secretary and then broke with him. Introduction discusses briefly the role of women in the February Revolution of 1917.

530   *Equality of Women in the USSR: Materials of International Seminar (Moscow, September 15–October 1, 1956).* Moscow: Foreign Languages Publishing House, 1957. 362 pp.

Account of this conference, including reports by various Soviets (all women but one) on such topics as political, civil, and economic rights, social welfare, public health, education, science, culture, and art. Covers visits to court, schools, and factories. If the Soviets or their foreign visitors had anything critical to say, it is not printed here.

531   FEIFER, GEORGE. *Justice in Moscow.* New York: Simon & Schuster, 1964. 353 pp.

Chapter 7 describes a Soviet divorce trial.

532   FILTZER, DONALD. *Soviet Workers and Stalinist Industrialization.* Armonk, N.Y.: M. E. Sharpe, 1986. 338 pp. Index.

Contains short appendix on the growth of the female work force, arguing that Stalinist policies were never aimed to liberate women but simply to manipulate them in order to gain needed labor power and to promote a conservative influence in the family.

533   FISHER, WESLEY ANDREW. *The Soviet Marriage Market: Mate-Selection in Russia and the U.S.S.R.* New York: Praeger, 1980. 299 pp. Index. Bibliography.

A wide-ranging survey discussing courtship, marriage rates, marital status, age at marriage, and intermarriage between different ethnic and occupational groups and persons of different educational levels.

534   *Fundamentals of Legislation of the USSR and the Union Republics on Marriage and the Family.* Moscow: Novosti, 1975. 31 pp.

The text of the law enacted on 27 June 1968.

535   GEIGER, H. KENT. *The Family in Soviet Russia.* Cambridge: Harvard University Press, 1968. 381 pp. Index. Bibliography.

A thorough, dispassionate account of Soviet family life, including chapters on Marxist theory and Soviet practice, changes brought about by the Revolution and its effect on everyday life, and relationships between husbands and wives and parents and children. Statistics dated, but basic themes still very timely.

536 GITELMAN, ZVI. *Jewish Nationality and Soviet Politics: The Jewish Sections of the CPSU, 1917–1930*. Princeton, N.J.: Princeton University Press, 1972. 573 pp. Index. Bibliography.
Information about Esther Frumkin, a leader of the *Evsektsiia* (Jewish section) of the Communist party. Little else specifically about women.

537 GOLDMAN, WENDY ZEVA. "The 'Withering Away' and the Resurrection of the Soviet Family, 1917–1936." Ph.D. diss., University of Pennsylvania, 1987. 431 pp.
Analysis of the development of Soviet family policy and the application of legal changes and their effect on the urban working class and rural peasants. Accepts the argument that the 1918 and 1926 Family Codes represent sweeping and innovative changes reversed in large part by the Family Law of 1936.

538 GOLOMSHTOK, IGOR, and ALEXANDER GLEZER. *Soviet Art in Exile*. Edited by Michael Scammell. Introduction by Sir Roland Penrose. New York: Random House, 1977. 172 pp. Bibliography.
A few women represented here (Galina Bitt, Valentina Kropovnitskaya, Lydia Masterkova, and Valentina Shapiro). Biographical information and list of exhibitions also included.

539 GRAY, FRANCINE DUPLESSIX. *Soviet Women: Walking the Tightrope*. New York: Doubleday, 1990. 213 pp.
A largely anecdotal survey of the subject. Gray made several trips of unspecified duration to the USSR, visiting Moscow, Leningrad, Riga, Tbilisi, Tashkent, Samarkand, and Irkutsk. The Soviet women described are largely from the professional, privileged class. Though some hold very important jobs, Gray finds them hostile to feminism. A key theme is that Soviet women are powerful superwomen who have overwhelmed their passive men. Offers no explanation of the absence of women at the highest levels of the political structure or the prevalence of patriarchal customs and attitudes. No index.

540 HALLE, FANNINA W. *Woman in Soviet Russia*. New York: Viking, 1933. 409 pp. Index. Annotated bibliography.
First published in Germany in 1932, this is the best combination of eyewitness account and background research of any of the books of its type. Halle, born and brought up in Russia, was, like most female observers of the time, quite enthusiastic about the Soviet experiment in women's equality, and quick to contrast it with conditions for women under tsarist rule.

541 ———. *Women in the Soviet East*. Translated by Margaret M. Green. London: Secker & Warburg. New York: E. P. Dutton, 1938. 363 pp. Index.
Almost all the books written about Soviet women have ignored or mentioned briefly women of nationalities other than Russian. A rare account of the massive changes for women taking place among the Islamic peoples of the USSR in the 1920s and 1930s and the resistance to them.

542   HALYCHYN, STEPHAINE, ed. *500 Ukrainian Martyred Women*. New York: United Ukrainian Women's Organizations of America, 1956. 159 pp. Bibliography.
Proceedings of a meeting held in New York on 26 February 1956 to commemorate the deaths of five hundred Ukrainian women on 26 June 1954 during an uprising in the Kingir labor camp in Siberia (the uprising was put down by tanks). Also contains some information about the Ukrainian famine, the treatment of Ukrainian peasants, the fate of the Ukrainian nationalist and feminist Lyudmyla Starytska Chernyakivska, women insurgents, and life in the labor camps.

543   HANSSON, CAROLA, and KARIN LIDEN. *Moscow Women: Thirteen Interviews*. Translated by Gerry Bothmer, George Blecher, and Lone Blecher. Introduction by Gail Warshofsky Lapidus. New York: Pantheon, 1983. 194 pp.
The authors, two Swedes, conducted these interviews in the spring of 1978 and smuggled their tapes out some time later. The women interviewed are the kind most likely to talk to foreigners—generally well-educated, urban, largely Russian, and from the intelligentsia, with the requisite material resources and survival skills. Common problems center around the double burden of paid work and domestic obligation; traditional sex roles are rarely challenged. The book is organized thematically into sections entitled "Women in the Work Force," "Salaries and the Cost of Living," "Daily Life in Moscow," "Day Care," "Women in Politics and Women's Politics," "Birth Control and Abortions," "One Child or Several?" "Pensions," and "Divorces." Helpful introduction and brief fact sheet for each section by Lapidus.

544   HAYDEN, CAROL EUBANKS. "Feminism and Bolshevism: The Zhenotdel and the Politics of Women's Emancipation in Russia, 1917–1930." Ph.D. diss., University of California, Berkeley, 1979. 454 pp.
Important study, some of which was reworked and published in a *Russian History* article (entry 667).

545   HEITLINGER, ALENA. *Women and State Socialism: Sex Inequality in the Soviet Union and Czechoslovakia*. Montreal: McGill-Queen's University Press, 1979. 241 pp. Index. Bibliography.
Helpful comparative study written from a feminist perspective. Investigates Marxist theory, historical background, and the *Zhenotdel*. Part of the book devoted to issues of family versus commune, housework, employment and politics, childbirth, childcare, and birth control for Soviet women. Concludes with a section on Czech women that covers similar topics. Ascribes failure to achieve real sexual equality in the USSR to the low level of economic development, Stalinist industrialization policies, failure to address forcefully inequalities in the family, the persistence of traditional attitudes and sex-role stereotyping, and the nature of the state socialist power structure. Useful bibliography.

546 HINDUS, MAURICE. *Humanity Uprooted*. New York: Jonathan Cape & Harrison Smith. 1929. 369 pp.
Hindus, born in a Russian village, emigrated at age fourteen. His observations on the Soviet Union in its first decade cover the New Morality, changes in the family, Red love, the status of women and the village in the first throes of collectivization.

547 ———. *House without a Roof: Russia After Forty-Three Years of Revolution*. Garden City, N.Y.: Doubleday, 1961. 562 pp. Index.
Veteran Soviet observer returns to a changed country during the post-Stalin thaw. Includes chapter entitled "Women—The Heroic Sex"; impressions of village life.

548 ———. *The Kremlin's Human Dilemma: Russia after Half a Century of Revolution*. Garden City, N.Y.: Doubleday, 1967. 395 pp. Index.
Sober reassessment. Useful chapters on village life and the "rediscovery" of sex.

549 ———. *Red Bread: Collectivization in a Russian Village*. Foreword by Ronald Grigor Suny. Bloomington: Indiana University Press, 1988. 372 pp.
Originally published in 1931, a generally favorable report on collectivization, including its impact on women, both peasants and organizers.

550 HOLLAND, BARBARA, ed. *Soviet Sisterhood*. Bloomington: Indiana University Press, 1985. 272 pp. Index. Bibliographies.
Eight essays by nine British scholars, many the beginnings of later books. Mary Buckley writes about "Soviet Interpretations of the Woman Question," Lynne Atwood covers "The New Soviet Man and Woman—Soviet Views on Psychological Sex Differences," Susan Allott writes about "Soviet Rural Women: Employment and Family Life" (see entry 505, under Susan Bridger), and Genia Browning discusses "Soviet Politics—Where are the Women?" Maggie McAndrew critiques Soviet women's magazines, and Jo Peer contributes a perceptive analysis of the demographic crisis, highlighting the paradox between women's economic and social power in the work force and their powerlessness in their personal lives. Barbara Holland and Teresa McKevitt discuss Soviet maternity care, and, finally, Alix Holt's "The First Soviet Feminists" insightfully surveys this initial burst of feminist activity, covering the period 1979–82. Holt includes information about the reaction to the feminists by the Soviet government, dissidents, the Western women's movement, and the Western Left.

551 HUMPHREY, CAROLINE. *Karl Marx Collective: Economy, Society and Religion in a Siberian Collective Farm*. Cambridge: Cambridge University Press, 1983. 522 pp. Index. Bibliography.
The first book by a Western anthropologist based on fieldwork in a Soviet com-

munity—specifically, at two Buryat collective farms. Instructive history of the area and its customs. Describes the theory and practice of collective farm life, including the division of labor and changes in wedding rituals in the Soviet period.

552   HUTTON, MARCELLINE. "Russian and Soviet Women, 1897–1939: Dreams, Struggles, and Nightmares." Ph.D. diss., University of Iowa, 1986. 732 pp.
See entry 242.

553   HYER, JANET, ed. "Soviet Women." *Canadian Woman Studies* 10, no. 4 (Winter 1989): 1–103.
A collaborative effort, this issue includes articles by Soviet, U.S., and Canadian scholars and activists. Includes poems, photos, a brief and very general historical overview, an article about women workers, and interviews with a Soviet fashion designer, an Estonian woman pastor, and a Finnish Communist émigré to Karelia, among other women. Acknowledging Soviet women's ambivalent, if not hostile, reaction to feminism, contributor Nina Belyaeva asks: "Can I give my son the whole world if I only look out the kitchen window?"

554   INKELES, ALEX, and KENT GEIGER, eds. *Soviet Society: A Book of Readings*. Boston: Houghton Mifflin, 1961.
Essays by leading Soviet specialists of the day. Little attention given to gender issues, except in the section on family. See Vera Dunham's essay "Sex: From Free Love to Puritanism" for a highly critical look at Soviet sexual relationships through the prism of literature.

555   JANCAR, BARBARA WOLFE. *Women under Communism*. Baltimore: Johns Hopkins University Press, 1978. 291 pp. Index. Bibliography.
Compares public policy about women with the realities in the USSR, Eastern Europe (excepting Albania), China, and Cuba (short appendix). Measures these countries' performances against a general standard of equality involving two criteria: "ability to make demands upon the government and actual participation in policy making." By these criteria women have not won equality. But in interviews with female émigrés, many observed that "they had to go to the West to find real discrimination and bias against women." Overall, Jancar is pessimistic, claiming that the monolithic nature of Communist states prevents women from achieving the consciousness necessary to demand equality. The Western and Communist approaches to women's liberation are considered complementary on a continuum measured by industrial development, with the United States and Sweden at the top. Marred by some glaring errors (e.g., Bulat Okudzhava is listed as a leading female dissident). One of several U.S. scholars to publish books about women in the late 1970s, Jancar has, like Stites and Lapidus, since turned her attention to other topics.

556 JUVILER, PETER. *Revolutionary Law and Order: Politics and Social Change in the USSR*. New York: Free Press, 1976. 274 pp. Index.
Brief discussions of crimes against women and female criminals.

557 KIM, SAM GON. *Black Americans' Commitment to Communism: A Case Study Based on Fiction and Autobiographies by Black Americans*. Lawrence: University of Kansas, 1986. 313 pp.
Chapter 3 discusses impressions of the Soviet Union and includes some information about Emma Harris, an African-American woman living in Moscow since the 1900s. According to one account, she and her Russian husband prospered financially by running a house of prostitution in prerevolutionary Russia. After escaping arrest by the Bolsheviks, she befriended several African-American Communists (Westerners) and introduced them to some of the realities not acknowledged in Soviet propaganda.

558 KINGSBURY, SUSAN MYRA, and MILDRED FAIRCHILD. *Factory, Family, and Woman in the Soviet Union*. New York: G. P. Putnam's Sons, 1935. 334 pp. Index.
Two Bryn Mawr professors went to the Soviet Union for nine months in 1929 and 1930 and again in 1932, visiting factories, construction sites, new socialist cities, peasant villages, and collective farms. This general survey, mostly favorable, contains some good eyewitness accounts.

559 KOROLYOV, YURI. *Soviet Family and the Law*. Moscow: Novosti, 1977. 64 pp.
Pamphlet summarizing Soviet laws on marriage and the family.

560 KRUPSKAIA, NADEZHDA K. *On Education*. Moscow: Foreign Languages Publishing House, 1957. 254 pp.
Krupskaia was a highly respected Soviet educational theorist in the 1920s and early 1930s. This is a sample of her writings, heavily censored.

561 KURGANOFF, IVAN A. *Women in the USSR*. Translated by R. V. Piontkovsky. London, Ontario: S.B.O.N.R. Publishing, 1971. 154 pp. Bibliography.
Survey of the status of Soviet women by this émigré researcher. Highly critical. Some useful statistics and quotes.

562 LANE, DAVID. *The Socialist Industrial State*. Boulder, Colo.: Westview, 1976. 230 pp. Index. Bibliography.
Pages 193–97 discuss male and female differentiation. Lane argues that considerable progress has been made by Soviet women but acknowledges continued "structural inequality."

563   ———, ed. *Politics and Society in the USSR*. New York: New York
       University Press, 1978. 622 pp. Index. Appendixes.
Some information on women in sections on the economy, the Party, and the
family. Appendix H contains the text of the 1968 Marriage and Family Law.

564   ———. *Soviet Society under Perestroika*. Boston, Mass.: Unwin Hyman,
       1990. 401 pp. Index. Bibliography.
Textbook with survey chapters and readings. Chapter 7, entitled "Reproducing
Society, Gender, Family, and Generations," provides a very basic survey of the
gender role debate, briefly discussing capitalist, feminist, and Marxist perspectives. Useful comparative data on female participation in the labor force, birth
rate, and divorce. Short discussion of position of women under *perestroika*.

565   LAPIDUS, GAIL WARSHOFSKY. *Women in Soviet Society: Equality,
       Development, and Social Change*. Berkeley: University of California Press,
       1978. 381 pp. Index. Bibliography.
The most comprehensive study of Soviet women ever done in English or,
probably, any language. Places woman question in historical and comparative
perspective, outlining the trends of female participation in the work force, the
patterns of women's employment, the development of support institutions such
as child care facilities, women's political participation, and changes within the
family. Helpful discussion of public policy concerns about female employment,
low birthrate, structural inequality. Useful tables and statistics, but only to
1976. Downplays ideology and leans toward economic determinism in explain-
ing Soviet policies toward women, especially their large-scale entry into the
labor force. Concludes that Western feminists will lead the way in challenging
male authority and traditional sex roles. Lapidus's current research focuses on
nationalities issues. An updated version of this book, covering Gorbachev's
reforms and the post-Soviet period, is much needed.

566   ———. *Women, Work, and Family in the Soviet Union*. Armonk, N.Y.:
       M. E. Sharpe, 1982. 311 pp. Bibliography.
The Soviets, after years of proclaiming the woman question resolved, in the
end faced the reality of the complex issues surrounding women's attainment of
real equality in society. In her introduction Lapidus sketches the major themes:
balancing work and family, the distribution of women workers in the labor
force, working conditions, protective labor, and the low birthrate. The bulk of
the book consists of translations of articles by Soviet scholars, organized around
the following themes: levels and patterns of female employment, the impact of
female employment on the family, and a policy for the 1980s. Although the
book was completed before Gorbachev's accession to power, many of the
themes continue to be significant and timely even after the collapse of the
Soviet Union.

567　LAURITSEN, JOHN, and DAVID THORSTAD. *The Early Homosexual Rights Movement (1864–1935)*. New York: Times Change Press, 1974. 93 pp. Index. Bibliography.

A survey of early gay-rights activity, focusing primarily on Germany, but with a short overview (pages 62–70) of shifting Bolshevik attitudes toward homosexuality, from decriminalization immediately after the Revolution to recriminalization under Stalin in 1934. No specific mention of lesbianism. Agrees with and depends on Reich's analysis in *The Sexual Revolution* (entry 589).

568　MCAULEY, ALISTAIR. *Economic Welfare in the Soviet Union*. London: Allen & Unwin; Madison: University of Wisconsin Press, 1979. 389 pp. Index. Bibliography.

Contains some limited information on women.

569　――――. *Women's Work and Wages in the Soviet Union*. London: Allen & Unwin, 1981. 228 pp. Index. Bibliography.

Excellent discussion of this topic. Covers the period to the late 1970s, a little later than Sacks (entry 595). Forty-eight statistical tables and twelve graphs and charts supplement the text, which covers such topics as socialist theory on equality, male and female earnings, female employment and participation, horizontal and vertical segregation in the work force, agriculture, education, protective legislation, combining the roles of worker and mother, and Soviet views on inequality in the workplace. Disputes Lapidus (entries 565 and 566) on Soviet adherence to the ideals of emancipation.

570　MACE, DAVID, and VERA MACE. *The Soviet Family*. New York: Doubleday, 1963. Paperback ed. Dolphin, 1964. 387 pp. Index. Annotated bibliography.

The Maces, prominent marriage counselors, travelled 3,500 miles around the Soviet Union. They combine personal experience and research and provide a useful annotated bibliography of a wide range of English sources. Chapter entitled "The New Soviet Women" covers familiar ground. Useful primarily for anecdotal material.

571　MADISON, BERNICE Q. *Social Welfare in the Soviet Union*. Stanford, Calif.: Stanford University Press, 1968. 298 pp. Index. Bibliography.

The only book about this important topic. Provides a historical background to Soviet social welfare policies of the 1960s. Includes chapters on Soviet psychosocial theories, family and child welfare policies and services, income maintenance, treatment of individual problems, old-age services, vocational rehabilitation, and unwed mothers and their children. Includes case studies that show a move to a more balanced integration of collective and individual treatment. No gender-consciousness in narrative, but much good information about the reality of the Soviet safety net in relation to women.

572   MALLY, LYNN. *Culture of the Future: The Proletkult Movement in Revolutionary Russia*. Berkeley: University of California Press, 1990. 306 pp. Index.
Discussion of this popular movement, symbol of the widespread impact of cultural revolution in the immediate post revolutionary period. Provocative material about the gaps between theory and practice in attempts to implement the ideology of women's liberation.

573   MAMONOVA, TATYANA, with the assistance of Margaret Maxwell. *Russian Women's Studies: Essays on Sexism in Soviet Culture*. New York: Pergamon, 1989. 178 pp. Index.
Tatyana Mamonova remains the foremost spokeswoman of Russian feminism in the West. She is closest to the mainstream of Western feminism, and her religious feminist opposites in the Maria group have either turned to other issues or lapsed into obscurity. This work is a collection of short essays on a wide variety of topics. Sections on history; the attitudes of classical male Russian writers toward women; women in art and science; sex; and "Women, the cold war, and peace."

574   MAMONOVA, TATYANA, ed., with the assistance of Sarah Matilsky. *Women and Russia: Feminist Writings from the Soviet Union*. Translated by Rebecca Park and Catherine A. Fitzpatrick. Foreword by Robin Morgan. Boston: Beacon, 1984. 273 pp.
Collection of writings by Soviet women from several issues of *Almanac: Woman and Russia*. Some were published earlier in the Sheba edition of the first *Almanac* (entry 522). Mamonova, the driving force behind the publication of the *Almanac* and the first feminist *samizdat*, was expelled from the USSR in 1980, along with several other members of her group. Sections on women workers; everyday life; foremothers; women, birth, and the family; socialization; relationships between women; dropouts and dissidents; women and the state; and women and peace. Short introductory notes to each section by Matilsky.

575   MANDEL, WILLIAM. *Russia Re-Examined: The Land, the People and How They Live*. New York: Hill & Wang, 1964. 255 pp. Index.
Chapter on the status of Soviet women, by a sympathetic observer.

576   ———. *Soviet Women*. Garden City, N.Y.: Anchor Press/Doubleday, 1975. 350 pp. Index. Bibliography.
One of the few books on the subject, and one with a distinctly pro-Soviet slant. Mandel mixed interesting personal vignettes from his many trips to the USSR with useful statistical information to paint a very favorable picture of the situation of Soviet women. Citing progressive laws on women's equality and abortion, Mandel offers example after example of women artists, engineers, ship captains, legislators, and physicians who succeeded in the Soviet system.

Unfortunately, this study is marred by an almost total blindness to anything negative in Soviet society (e.g., prostitution, rape, ethnic rivalry, anti-Semitism). Reacting to the simplistic anticommunism of the cold war era, Mandel presented a flawed picture of his own.

577 MASSELL, GREGORY J. *The Surrogate Proletariat: Moslem Women and Revolutionary Strategies in Soviet Central Asia, 1919–1929*. Princeton, N.J.: Princeton University Press, 1974. 448 pp. Index. Bibliography.
There is no book-length study of women in Soviet central Asia. Massell's study, although concerned primarily with the Bolshevik use of women's liberation as a political strategy, makes an important contribution to our understanding of the massive changes in the lives of many central Asian women after the Bolshevik Revolution. Massell argues that in the absence of a central Asian proletariat, the Bolsheviks supported women's equality, hoping thereby to gain mass support and create a substitute or surrogate proletariat.

578 MAYNE, JUDITH. *Kino and the Woman Question: Feminism and Soviet Silent Film*. Columbus: Ohio State University Press, 1989. 211 pp.
A study of the period between the appearance of Sergei Eisenstein's *Strike* (1925) and Freidrich Ermler's *Fragment of an Empire* and Dziga Vertov's *Man with a Movie Camera* (1929). In Mayne's view these films, along with V. I. Pudovkin's *Mother* (1926) and Abram Room's *Bed and Sofa* (1927), "embody the most distinctive features of Soviet film practice." In particular, they explore the position of women within the new socialist society. This study seeks to expand feminist film criticism beyond its preoccupation with Hollywood as the norm. Other films, such as Eisenstein's *Potemkin* (1925) and *October* (1927), as well as Alexander Dovzhenko's *Earth* (1930), are also analyzed. Interesting application of feminist criticism. No sources in Russian used.

579 MEGO, DEBORAH KAREN. "The Acculturation, Psycho-Social Development and Jewish Identity of Soviet Jewish Émigrés." Ph.D. diss., California School of Professional Psychology, Berkeley, 1988. 167 pp.
Gender differences among the variables examined. Scores of older and younger women on Erikson subscale indicate differences in socialization for those who grew up in the Soviet Union.

580 MEYER, DONALD. *Sex and Power: The Rise of Women in America, Russia, Sweden and Italy*. 2d ed. Middletown, Conn.: Wesleyan University Press, 1989. 721 pp. Index. Bibliography.
Comparative survey relying heavily on secondary sources in English. Touches on early history of the Bolshevik Revolution, Kollontai's theories, Stalin's reliance on female labor during collectivization and industrialization, and the tension between the individual and the political as portrayed in Soviet literature.

581   MOSES, JOEL C. *The Politics of Female Labor in the Soviet Union*.
      Western Societies Program Occasional Paper No. 10. Ithaca, N.Y.:
      Center for International Studies, Cornell University, 1978. 76 pp.
Traces the "almost unprecedented" open political debate about women in the
Soviet work force in national and regional publications. Wide range of Soviet
sources consulted.

582   ———. *The Politics of Women and Work in the Soviet Union and the
      United States: Alternative Work Schedules and Sex Discrimination*.
      Berkeley, Calif.: Institute of International Studies, 1983. 181 pp. Index.
An important discussion and analysis, especially timely now as the former
USSR moves toward a market economy with a reduced need for labor power
in many of the old sectors of the economy, and women are often the first fired
and last hired. Comparison with the U.S. experience helpful. Moses argues that
the issue of alternative work schedules transcends traditional political divisions.

583   MOSKOFF, WILLIAM. *Labor and Leisure in the Soviet Union: The
      Conflict Between Public and Private Decision-Making in a Planned
      Economy*. London: Macmillan, 1984. 225 pp. Index. Bibliography.
Discussion of household time budgets, the double burden, part-time work for
women, women and the service sector, and the role of women in rural areas.
Marred by the omission of any discussion about sexism as a major factor in
maintaining women's heavy work and domestic burdens.

584   MYLES, BRUCE. *Night Witches: The Untold Story of Soviet Women in
      Combat*. London: Panther Books, 1983. 272 pp.
The story of Soviet women's air regiments in World War II. Information about
(among others) Lily Litvak, the "Rose of Stalingrad," the fighter pilot who
downed a German flying ace.

585   PANKHURST, JERRY G., and MICHAEL PAUL SACKS, eds.
      Contemporary Soviet Society: Sociological Perspectives. New York: Praeger,
      1980. 272 pp. Index.
Sacks surveys the contribution of women in his essay, mostly condensing material from his book (entry 595). Louise Shelley discusses female offenders in her
piece on crime and delinquency, and David Heer discusses population policy.
An article on rural life barely mentions women.

586   PETROVA, LIDIA, and EKATERINA SHEVELIOVA. *Together with
      Women Everywhere*. Moscow: Novosti, 111 pp.
Written during the Vietnam War. Mostly pictures, including a few of the
Moscow World Congress of Women and of Nina Popova, then chair of the
Soviet Women's Committee. Contains a short essay on Soviet women and the
international peace movement.

587 RADKEY, OLIVER H. *The Sickle under the Hammer*. New York: Columbia University Press, 1963. 525 pp. Index. Bibliography.
Contains limited information about the charismatic women leaders Spiridonova and Breshko-Breshkovskaia.

588 RADKEY, OLIVER H. *Russia Goes to the Polls: The Election to the All-Russian Constituent Assembly, 1917*. With a foreword by Sheila Fitzpatrick. Ithaca, N.Y.: Cornell University Press, 1989. 171 pp. Index. Bibliography.
Table 3 shows the feminist vote in Petersburg province. The feminists are lumped under special interest groups ("sundry elements with axes to grind, such as feminists").

589 REICH, WILHELM. *The Sexual Revolution: Toward A Self-Governing Character Structure*. Translated from the German by Theodore Wolfe. New York: Farrar, Straus & Giroux, 1969. 273 pp. Bibliography.
Reich began as a Freudian but moved to create a synthesis between Freudianism and Marxism, arguing for the role of the state in the shaping of individual personality. Part 2, "The Struggle for the 'New Life' in the Soviet Union," extends Reich's thesis that there is a direct connection between political and sexual revolution. Surveys Soviet social and sexual experimentation of the 1920s and decries the sexual reaction under Stalin.

590 ROLLINS, NANCY. *Child Psychiatry in the Soviet Union: Preliminary Observations*. Cambridge, Mass.: Harvard University Press, 1972. 293 pp. Index. Bibliography.
Rollins spent four months studying her topic in Moscow, Leningrad, and Kiev during the winter of 1968–69. A balanced account including case studies, this book provides rare information in English about several prominent women in the field, including the mother of Soviet child psychiatry, Grunya Efimovna Sukhareva.

591 ROSENHAN, MOLLIE SCHWARTZ. "Women's Place and Cultural Values in Soviet Children's Readers: An Historical Analysis of the Maintenance of Role Division by Gender, 1920s and 1970s." Ph.D. diss., University of Pennsylvania, 1981, 669 pp.
Analysis of over two thousand children's stories and pictures from the 1920s (the first revolutionary decade) and the 1970s. The stories are rated on the basis of over forty different gender-related variables. Despite the stated Soviet commitment to full female equality, the stories reflected the persistence of traditional patriarchal attitudes. No substantial differences were found between stories from the two decades in terms of gender images; strong sex-role stereotyping and a predominance of male characters were found in both.

592   RUESCHMEYER, MARILYN. *Professional Work and Marriage: An East-West Comparison*. New York: St. Martin's, 1981. 197 pp. Index.
Compares U.S. single- and dual-career families with dual-career families in the USSR and the German Democratic Republic. Uses both statistics and the results of in-depth personal interviews. Points up the differences between capitalist and socialist societies on issues of equality and job security, but also highlights problems common to dual-career families, including the ways in which the demands of professional work can undermine close human relationships. Raises important issues, but developments in Eastern Europe and the USSR are rapidly changing the conditions described here.

593   RYWKIN, MICHAEL. *Soviet Society Today*. Armonk, N.Y.: M. E. Sharpe, 1989. 242 pp. Index.
Contains a short and superficial section on women's roles under the heading "The Way of Life."

594   RZHANITSYNA, LUDMILA. *Soviet Family Budgets*. Translated by Galina Sdobnikova. Moscow: Progress, 1977. 181 pp. Bibliography.
A more detailed look at the Soviet wage system, with the pro-socialism gloss of the Brezhnev years. Some useful statistics; a few actual family budgets.

595   SACKS, MICHAEL PAUL. *Women's Work in Soviet Russia: Continuity in the Midst of Change*. New York: Praeger, 1976. 221 pp. Index.
An excellent survey of the topic, using a wide range of Soviet and English-language sources and some comparative data. Well-organized; matter-of-fact style. Covers the following topics: Theories of women's emancipation, conditions before the Revolution, the supply and demand for women workers in the Soviet period, women in the "non-agrarian labor force," time budgets of urban workers, female labor in the countryside. Covers the period to the early 1970s. An updated work on this topic is badly needed.

596   ST. GEORGE, GEORGE. *Our Soviet Sister*. New York: Robert B. Luce, Inc., 1973. 256 pp.
Written by a Russian-born free-lance writer. Generally favorable and written with an eye toward the demands of the then-burgeoning feminist movements in the West. Offers some good anecdotal evidence. Closes with an abridged version of Natalia Baranskaia's "Nedelya kak Nedelya."

597   SALOMAN, SAMUEL. *The Red War on the Family*. New York: J. Little & Ives, 1922. 178 pp.
Polemic against the 'Socialist plot' to destroy the family and substitute free love in its place.

598 SCHAPIRO, LEONARD, and JOSEPH GODSON. *The Soviet Worker: Illusions and Realities*. London: Macmillan, 1981. Reprint. New York: St. Martin's, 1981 and 1984. 291 pp. Index. Bibliography.
This book has no articles devoted specifically to women workers. Some useful anecdotal information in articles by Fyodor Turovsky and Murray Seeger, and information about maternity benefits and pensions in Alistair McAuley's article.

599 SCHILLING, GERHARD, and KATHLEEN M. HUNT. *Women in Science and Technology: US/USSR Comparisons*. Santa Monica, Calif.: Rand Corporation, 1974. 67 pp.
Notes greater participation of women in all parts of the USSR. In the United States, by contrast, "a large reservoir of female talent remains untapped or underdeveloped." In the USSR, however, the rate of female participation is not growing. Authors argue presciently that in the future, "the great necessity for participation of women will decline in many sectors of the Soviet economy whereas societal changes in the US will bring about considerable increases in the participation rates of women in professional life." Useful statistical tables and figures.

600 SCHLESINGER, RUDOLF, ed. *The Family in the USSR: Documents and Readings*. London: Routledge & Kegan Paul, 1949. 408 pp. Index.
A very important source. Key Soviet legislation and social commentary about women and the family for the period 1917–44, plus two 1915 letters from Lenin to Inessa Armand on the subject of marriage and free love. Unfortunately, the fate of Armand's letters to Lenin is not mentioned. Included are the December 1917 decree on divorce, the first Soviet laws on the family (1918–22), the 1926 Family Code, the 1936 law abolishing abortion, the 1943 law abolishing coeducation, and the Family Law of 1944. Selected writings include excerpts of Allexandra Kollontai from a critique of the feminists, a treatise on the transformation of women's roles, and from "Communism and the Family," "The New Morality and the Working Classes," and *Love of Three Generations*.

601 SCHWARZ, SOLOMON. *Labor in the Soviet Union*. New York: Praeger, 1951. 364 pp. Index. Chronological index.
Contains section entitled "Activation of Urban Labor Reserves: Female Labor."

602 SCOTT, HILDA. *Does Socialism Liberate Women?: Experiences from Eastern Europe*. Boston, Mass.: Beacon, 1974. 240 pp. Index.
This book is a case study of women in Czechoslovakia, but the observations about the successes and failures of a state policy in which laws promoting female equality conflict with strongly entrenched patriarchal traditions are applicable to the Soviet Union. Some useful comparative statistics, particularly about time budgets and the ideal spouse.

603   SEDUGIN, P. *New Soviet Legislation on Marriage and the Family*. Translated by Nicholas Bobrov. Edited by Jim Riordan. Moscow: Progress, 1973. 127 pp.

Summarizes the Fundamentals of Legislation of the USSR and the Union Republics on Marriage and the Family, adopted in 1968.

604   SEREBRENNIKOV, GEORGII N. *The Position of Women in the USSR*. London: Victor Gollancz, 1937. 288 pp. Index.

Positive survey of Soviet women's status. Discussion of women in the work force, on the collective farm, as professionals and administrators, as well as women's health and their social and cultural activities and conditions in the national republics. Little about family life; women's double burden considered eased by increase in communal childcare facilities. Contains reprint of extract from labor laws on work for women and minors and 1936 decree on prohibition of abortions, changes in divorce laws, state aid to large families, and broadening of child-care facilities.

605   SHREIR, SALLY, ed. *Women's Movements of the World: An International Directory and Reference Guide*. London: Longmans; Phoenix: Oryx, 1988. 384 pp. Bibliography.

Entry on Soviet women on pages 267–70. Mostly devoted to official organizations, such as the Soviet Women's Committee and the *Zhensovety* (Women's Councils). Brief mention of unofficial feminist activity in 1979.

606   SMITH, GREGORY MALLOY. "The Impact of World War II on Women, Family Life, and Mores in Moscow, 1941–1945." Ph.D. diss., Stanford University, 1990. 368 pp.

Images of women changed during the war—emphasizing independence in the early days, then motherhood and family life by 1944–45. Family life was deeply affected by evacuation, the massive mobilization of men, troubles in the schools, and changes in social and sexual mores. Some of these phenomena were permanent, others temporary.

607   SMITH, JESSICA. *Woman in Soviet Russia*. New York: Vanguard, 1928. 216 pp.

Firsthand account by a feminist, suffrage campaigner, member of Alice Paul's National Woman's Party, Birth Control League activist, and Communist sympathizer. Smith visited Russia several times, lived in Moscow for a year, and was involved in the Russian Reconstruction Farms project to introduce new farming techniques to the peasantry. Reveals her own prejudices about women's work ability ("as soon as skill is required [in farm work] women usually bungle the job pretty badly"). Good information on reaction of peasant women to emancipation. Eyewitness account of 1926 *Zhenotdel* Delegate conference. Revealing talks with *Zhenotdel* activists and descriptions of a "Red wedding," debates on the Marriage Law of 1926, Revolutionary morals in general, the work of building cooperatives, maternal and child care, and communal kitchens. Conveys the idealism of the immediate postrevolutionary period.

608   SOLOUKHIN, VLADIMIR. *A Walk in Rural Russia*. Translated by
      Stella Miskin. New York: E. P. Dutton, 1966. 254 pp.
The author describes a walking tour of the Vladimir region, taken with his wife in the summer of 1956. This rare translated eyewitness account of life in Russian villages of that period provides useful information about peasant women's lives.

609   *Soviet Women (Some Aspects of the Status of Women in the USSR)*.
      Moscow: Progress, 1975. 184 pp. Index. Bibliography.
A series of articles written for International Women's Year, including T. N. Sidorova on paid work and women's personality, Y. D. Yemelyanova on Soviet women's social and political activity, G. P. Sergeyeva on women's education and scientific/technological progress, E. Y. Novikova on women and trade unions, V. S. Yazykova on socialism and women's free time, Z. A. Yankova on women and the family, A. M. Fonarev on preschool education, and Y. Z. Danilova on new attitudes toward women.

610   STERN, MIKHAIL, and AUGUST STERN. *Sex in the Soviet Union*.
      Translated by Marc Heine. London: W. H. Allen, 1981. 221 pp. Index.
The only survey of its kind. Based on thirty years of medical practice, mostly in the Ukrainian town of Vinnitsa, and encounters with patients from all over the Soviet Union. The USSR did not have any Kinsey- or Hite-type surveys. The authors present an array of anecdotal evidence in discussing such subjects as sex within and outside of marriage; female sexual pleasure and the lack of it; forbidden sexual practices such as masturbation, prostitution, and sex crimes; and pornography. Lesbianism and homosexuality are discussed, but the authors, though they try, cannot overcome their bias on these subjects. Includes discussion of sex in the camps, in the republics, and among the masses and the privileged. A *Samizdat* pornography sample (drearily imitative, save for the Party slogans) is included at the end.

611   STITES, RICHARD. *The Women's Liberation Movement in Russia:
      Feminism, Nihilism, and Bolshevism, 1860–1930*. Princeton, N.J.:
      Princeton University Press, 1978. 464 pp. Index. Bibliography. 2d ed.
      with afterword. Princeton, N.J.: Princeton University Press, 1991. 476
      pp. Index. Bibliography.
A classic, pioneering account of the major paths to political activism taken by women. The product of prodigious research, this book is gracefully written, with due regard to the complexity of the topic. Stites excels at weaving into his narrative information from a dazzling array of sources ranging from literary figures to popular journals to street culture. Offers a balanced assessment of Bolshevik policies in relation to women in the 1920s.

612   STRAUS, KENNETH. "The Transformation of the Soviet Working
       Class, 1929–1935: The Regime in Search of a New Social Stability."
       Ph.D. diss., University of Pennsylvania, 1990. 729 pp.
Surveys the integration of peasants, women, and youth into the Soviet industrial work force. Argues that factory organization, the new workers, and regime
policies all aided in effecting the integration and changes evident by the time of
the second and third Five-Year Plans.

613   STRONG, ANNA. *This Soviet World*. New York: Henry Holt, 1936.
       301 pp. Index.
Glowing portrait of Soviet life. Chapter entitled "The Freeing of Women"
lauds dramatic changes and new opportunities for Soviet women and notes the
slow pace of change in the United States. (Strong later became disillusioned
with the Soviets, moved to China, and became a Maoist.)

614   SUNY, RONALD GRIGOR. *The Baku Commune, 1917–1918*.
       Princeton, N.J.: Princeton University Press, 1972. 412 pp. Index.
Several pages (64–65, 115) about *bab'ie bunty* (spontaneous demonstrations
and/or violent protests by women) and other unrest among women in Baku
and Georgia in 1916 and 1917. Otherwise, little else specifically about women.

615   SWERDLOW, AMY. "The Case of Women Strike for Peace and the
       Test Ban Treaty." Ph.D. diss., Rutgers University, 1984. 569 pp.
Contains some information about contacts between this U.S. women's peace
organization, the Soviet Women's Committee, and Soviet diplomats in their
efforts to end the cold war.

616   SYRKIN, MARIE. *Blessed Is the Match: The Story of Jewish Resistance*.
       Philadelphia: Jewish Publication Society of America, 1976. 366 pp.
Mentions women among the Jewish partisans, specifically around Vilna.

617   TATARINOVA, NADEZHDA. *Women in the USSR (at Home, at
       Work, in Society)*. Moscow: Novosti, 1969. 109 pp.
A propagandistic work on the life of emancipated women in the USSR.

618   THOMAS, JEAN McKAMY. "A Study of Day Care in the USSR and
       the USA." Ph.D. diss., University of Georgia. 209 pp.
Compares day-care centers in Moscow, Leningrad, and Tallinn with nine inner-
city centers in Atlanta, Georgia, in the following areas: qualifications of staff,
interaction between teachers and children, physical facilities and equipment,
teacher-child ratio, use of paraprofessionals, emotional climate, noise level and
kind of noise, relationships between children, and curricula.

619   THOMPSON, TERRY, and RICHARD SHELDON, eds. *Soviet
       Society and Culture: Essays in honor of Vera S. Dunham*. Boulder, Colo.:
       Westview, 1988. 290 pp. Index.

Contributions of most interest in terms of women and gender issues are Sheila Fitzpatrick's "Middle-Class Values" and "Soviet Life in the 1930s," Peter Juviler's "Cell Mutation in Soviet Society: The Family," Michael Paul Sacks's "Shifting Strata: Ethnicity, Gender, and Work in Soviet Central Asia," and John Bushnell's "Urban Leisure Culture in Post-Stalin Russia: Stability as a Social Problem?" The latter includes provocative data about the decline in the amount of housework done by men and comparative data on leisure time for men and women (mostly in the footnotes).

620 TROTSKY, LEON. *Women and the Family*. New York: Pathfinder Press, 1970. 78 pp.

Excerpts from Trotsky's writings, spanning from 1923 to 1936. Trotsky's views remain consistent throughout. He argues that women can be liberated within the family only if their household tasks—cooking, cleaning, child care—are socialized. Nowhere does he propose the far simpler, far less costly solution of men doing a share of domestic work.

621 *The USSR in Figures For 1979: Statistical Handbook*. Moscow: Statistika, 1980. 224 pp.

Population figures by sex from 1913 to 1980; educational levels of females and males from 1939 to 1979, birth, death, and natural increase rates from 1930, 1940, 1950, 1960, 1965, and all years from 1970 to 1979. Other statistics not broken down by sex.

622 *Woman and Russia: First Feminist Samizdat*. Translated, with an introduction, by the Women in Eastern Europe Group. London: Sheba Feminist Publishers, 1980. 103 pp.

Translation of the *Al'manakh: Zhenshchinam o Zhenshchinakh*, which first appeared in December 1979 in Leningrad and represented the first unofficial and overtly feminist publication since shortly after the October Revolution. Useful introduction provides some background information about the authors of the *Al'manakh* and a brief overview of the status of Soviet women. Reflecting the equating of Orthodoxy with dissent in some dissident circles, a piece by Tatiana Gorichena extolls Mary, "the Most Holy Queen [who] helped me to discover and resurrect my female self in all its purity and absoluteness." Rimma Batalova describes the horrors of her experience in a Soviet maternity hospital; Natasha Malakhovskaya argues that the Soviet family is matriarchal and that woman "is becoming everything." V. Golubeva critiques Soviet-style abortions; Julia Voznesenskaya's "Letter from Novosibirsk" recounts life in a Soviet women's prison; Zh. Ivina compares Marina Tsvetaeva and Walt Whitman as lesbian and gay poets, respectively (in the only major translation error, Ivina's name is given as Ivina Tallin, reflecting her Estonian home but not her name). Poetry by Tatiana Mamonova, short stories by I. Tishchenko and Sonia Sokolova, and Elena Shvartz's *Mahadevi* (the Hindu Great Goddess, mate, and counterpart to Siva the Great God) round out this first *Al'manakh*.

623   WOOD, ELIZABETH ANN. "Gender and Politics in Soviet Russia: Working Women under the New Economic Policy, 1918–1928." Ph.D. diss., University of Michigan, 1991. 691 pp.
A pioneering look at the New Economic Policy and its effect on women. Examines Bolshevik attempts to impose "feminism from above," focusing on the following: Bolshevik interpretations of the woman question; gender stereotypes during the Civil War; the effect of the New Economic Policy on women; and efforts, often conflicting, by the *Zhenotdely* and trade unions to organize women workers. Argues that Bolshevik policies often reinforced rather than eliminated gender stereotypes. Especially timely in light of the effects of *perestroika* (e.g., unemployment, diminished social services) on women workers. Useful statistical information about the New Economic Policy. Based on extensive archival and library research in the USSR.

624   YANOWITCH, MURRAY. *Social and Economic Inequality in the Soviet Union: Six Studies*. White Plains, N.Y.: M. E. Sharpe, 1977. 197 pp. Index. Bibliography.
Chapter 6 discusses the actual status of women in Soviet society, covering such topics as occupational status, earnings gap, the double burden, and power relations in the home.

625   ———. *Work in the Soviet Union: Attitudes and Issues*. Armonk, N.Y.: M. E. Sharpe, 1985. 196 pp. Index. Bibliography.
A thorough survey of the subject. See chapter 3 for a discussion of sex differences in work attitudes. Yanowitch presents evidence indicating that women's job satisifaction is increasingly connected with the content of their work and that women's "demands are now just as high as those of men."

626   ———, ed. *The Social Structure of the USSR: Recent Soviet Studies*. Armonk, N.Y.: M. E. Sharpe, 1986. 273 pp. Bibliography.
Contains a 1982 article by E. V. Gruzdeva and E. S. Chertikhina, entitled "Soviet Women: Problems of Work and Daily Life." Other articles provide additional information about women's place in the Soviet social structure in the early 1980s.

627   YAZYKOVA, V. *Socialist Life Style and the Family*. Translated by A. Lehto. Moscow: Progress, 1984. 212 pp.
Reflects transition period between Brezhnev and Gorbachev. Puts forth standard argument that Soviet socialism has benefited women. More space than usual is devoted to acknowledging the problems of high divorce rate and low birth rate; state strategies to combat these problems are described.

628   YEDLIN, TOVA, ed. *Women in Eastern Europe and the Soviet Union*. New York: Praeger, 1980. 302 pp. Index. Bibliography.
One of the spate of books about Soviet and Eastern European women that

appeared at the end of the 1970s but, regrettably, did not spawn more numerous efforts in the 1980s. Consists of papers that pertain to Soviet women, presented at the Conference on Women in Eastern Europe and the Soviet Union—many by U.S. scholarly pioneers in the study of Russian and Soviet women. Included are Alena Heitlinger on "Marxism, Feminism, and Sex Equality"; Richard Stites on "The Women's Liberation Issue in Nineteenth-Century Russia"; Barbara Alpern Engel on "Women Revolutionaries: The Personal and the Political"; Martha Bohachevsky-Chomiak on "Socialism and Feminism: The First Stages of Women's Organizations in the Eastern Part of the Austrian Empire"; Barbara Evans Clements on "Bolshevik Women: The First Generation"; Robert McNeal on "The Early Decrees of *Zhenotdel*"; Alix Holt on "Marxism and Women's Oppression: Bolshevik Theory and Practice in the 1920s"; K. Jean Cottam on "Soviet Women in Combat in World War II: The Ground/Air Defense Forces"; Bohdan Harasymiw on "Have Women's Chances for Political Recruitment in the USSR Really Improved?"; Janet Maher on "The Social Composition of Women Deputies in Soviet Elective Politics: A Preliminary Analysis of Official Biographies"; and Karol Krotki on "Some Demographic, Particularly Fertility, Correlates of Female Status in Eastern Europe and the Republics of the Soviet Union."

HISTORY AND SOCIAL SCIENCE ARTICLES AND PAMPHLETS

629 A. K. "A Demographic Problem: Female Employment and the Birth Rate." Translated in *Soviet Review* 11, no. 1 (Spring 1970): 76–81.
This is a translation of an article in *Voprosy ekonomiki* (1969, no. 4), signed only with the author's initials. Argues for allowing mothers to stay home or to work part-time or flex-time in order to take care of their children.

630 *American Women Behind the Iron Curtain*. Hudson, Wis.: Star-Observer Print, 1956. 56 pp.
A group of U.S. midwestern women professionals and journalists visited the Soviet Union in 1956 and wrote a series of newspaper articles about their journey. Naive and comical at times, but useful for information on early Soviet "thaw" overtures to the West and U.S. attitudes.

631 ANDERSON, BARBARA A. "The Life Course of Soviet Women Born 1905–1960." In *Politics, Work, and Daily Life in the USSR: A Survey of Former Soviet Citizens*, edited by James R. Millar, pp. 203–40. Cambridge: Cambridge University Press, 1986.
Data based on the Soviet Interview Project, conducted with recent Soviet émi-

grés, mostly in 1983. As Anderson notes, the data concern urban, largely Jewish, highly educated working women. Education is shown to be the key factor in determining female labor-force participation and earnings.

632   *A New Life for Women in the USSR*. Moscow: Novosti, 1975.
Pamphlet in honor of International Women's Year (1975). Extols Soviet achievements in emancipating women. Contains about thirty pictures.

633   ASHWIN, SARAH. "Development of Feminism in the *Perestroika* Era." *Report on the USSR*, 30 August, 1991: 21–25.
Rare coverage of women's political activity in this period, including the March 1991 independent women's forum in Dubna, outside Moscow.

634   BASKINA, ADA. *About Women Like Me: Public and Private Life in the USSR*. Moscow, Novosti, 1979. 75 pp.
Pamphlet extolling the advances made by Soviet women since the Revolution.

635   BIRYUKOVA, ALEXANDRA. *The Working Woman in the USSR*. Moscow: Profizdat, 1973. 53 pp.
Paean to the gains made by Soviet women, written when Biryukova was secretary of the All-Union Central Council of Trade Unions. She became the only female Politburo member appointed by Gorbachev.

636   BOBROFF, ANNE. "The Bolsheviks and Working Women, 1905–20." *Soviet Studies* 26, no. 4 (October 1974): 540–76.
Describes the evolution of Bolshevik strategy and tactics in relation to women workers. Bobroff argues that the militance of proletarian women compelled the Bolsheviks to pay more attention to them as an independent political force. Marred by factual inaccuracies; underplays Bolshevik writing about women before 1913 and overplays the strength of the feminist movement. Bobroff's argument has been criticized sharply by Rose Glickman in *Russian Factory Women* (entry 240).

637   BONNELL, VICTORIA E. "The Representation of Women in Early Soviet Political Art." *Russian Review* 50, no. 3 (July 1991): 267–88.
Notes "sparseness" of female symbols in political art of the early postrevolutionary period, in contrast to rich representation of women in such art during most of the tsarist era. Discusses the emergence of representations of women workers and peasants, arguing that these new icons symbolized Bolshevik ambivalence about gender issues.

638   BUCKLEY, MARY. "The 'Woman Question' in the Contemporary Soviet Union." In *Promissory Notes: Women in the Transition to Socialism*, edited by Sonia Kruks, Rayna Rapp, and Marilyn B. Young, pp. 251–81. New York: Monthly Review Press, 1989.

Buckley surveys Soviet ideology about women from 1930 to 1987, arguing that within the parameters of a set of common ideological goals about the emancipation of women, differences in approach can be identified for each successive Soviet leader. For example, under Stalin, women, a "great army of labor", were brought into the paid labor force in unprecedented numbers, and the women question was declared solved. In contrast, under Brezhnev, with women an integral part of the paid labor force, questions about sex roles and inequities in work and home responsibilities came to the fore, and the woman question was officially declared unsolved. Under Gorbachev, with women a steady 51 percent of the labor force, *glasnost* opened up the question of sex roles; the ultimate resolution of that debate remains to be seen.

639 BYSTYDZIENSKI, JILL. "Women and Socialism: A Comparative Study of Women in Poland and the USSR." *Signs* 14, no. 3 (Spring 1989): 668–84.
The author challenges the view that women's status in all socialist countries is essentially the same by comparing the position of women in Poland with that of women among the European Russian population of the USSR. She finds a higher percentage of Russian women in traditionally male occupations, greater income disparity between the sexes in Poland, and significant differences in attitudes toward women working outside the home. Bystydzienski notes also that closer family ties and the preeminent role of the Church in Poland are important in maintaining adherence to traditional family ties and concepts of role modeling.

640 CLEMENTS, BARBARA EVANS. "Working-Class and Peasant Women in the Russian Revolution, 1917–1923." *Signs* 8, no. 2 (Winter 1982): 215–35.
The attitudes of the majority of Great Russian women toward the Revolution. Argues that peasant women were essentially conservative in their response; proletarian women were more likely to join the Bolsheviks, but only a small minority did so. Ultimately, the masses and the leadership joined to form "the urban, nuclear, but still patriarchal family [that] became the foundation of Russia's modernized autocracy."

641 ———. "The Birth of the New Soviet Woman." In *Bolshevik Culture, Experiment and Order in the Russian Revolution*, edited by Abbott Gleason, Peter Kenez, and Richard Stites, pp. 220–37. Bloomington: Indiana University Press, 1985.
Changing conceptions of the ideal Soviet woman, from the "daughter of October" (the selfless revolutionary heroine of the 1920s) to the worker, wife, and mother of the 1930s. Concludes that the ultimate synthesis blended elements of feminist, socialist, and traditional Russian ideals.

642   ———. "The Utopianism of the Zhenotdel." *Slavic Review* 51, no. 2
       (Summer 1992): 485–96.
Clements argues that the women of the Zhenotdel had a vision of a socialist
future which differed significantly from that of the major male Party leaders,
who advocated a centralized economic transformation as the key to social transformation. The women's early radical ideas of the abolition of the family and
free love were soon replaced by an emphasis on gradual transformation at the
local, neighborhood level. The notion of women acting to help themselves
(*samodeiatel'nost*) was replaced under Stalin by the myth that the party had
achieved women's full emancipation.

643   DEMENT'EVA, I. "What Do We Know about the Family?" Soviet
       Education 32, no. 4 (April 1990): 83–91.
On improving parents' child-rearing skills. Discusses differences between mothers' and fathers' communication with children.

644   DODGE, NORTON T., and MURRAY FESHBACH. "The Role of
       Women in Soviet Agriculture." In *Soviet and East European Agriculture*,
       edited by J. F. Karcz, pp. 266–88. Berkeley, Calif.: University of
       California Press, 1967.
Comprehensive survey of female participation in the agricultural labor force.
Largely statistical and economic approach. Presents historical overview; covers
demographics, type of work performed (mostly unskilled heavy labor), condi-
tions on collective farms, and the preponderance of women in rural areas.
Conclusion: "Like the horse, women are likely to coexist with the tractor."

645   DUBROVINA, L. *Women's Right to Education in the Soviet Union*.
       Moscow: Foreign Languages Publishing House, 1956. 28 pp.
The official line on women and education, presented to the Commission on the
Status of Women of the United Nations Economic and Social Council.
Dubrovina was the deputy minister of education for the Russian Federation.

646   DUNHAM, VERA SANDOMIRSKY. "The Strong Woman Motif."
       In *The Transformation of Russian Society*, edited by Cyril E. Black, pp.
       459–83. Cambridge: Harvard University Press, 1960. 695 pp. Index.
See entry 274.

647   DUNN, ETHEL. "Post-Revolutionary Women in Soviet Central Asia,"
       Canadian-American Slavic Studies 9, no. 1 (Spring 1975): 93–100.
Generally favorable review of Gregory Massell's *The Surrogate Proletariat* (entry
577), but critical of the lack of comparative perspective, lack of statistics, and
the book's "verbose and repetitive" qualities.

648   DUNN, STEPHEN P., and ETHEL DUNN. "The Study of the Soviet
       Family in the USSR and in the West." Slavic Studies Working Paper

No. 1. Columbus, Ohio: American Association for the Advancement of Slavic Studies, 1977. 75 pp.

Another significant contribution from the Dunns. A comprehensive survey of the subject, including a historical overview and information about regional, class, and ethnic differences in family structure. Rich supporting material provided in 184 footnotes.

649 EASON, WARREN W. "Population Changes." In *The Transformation of Russian Society*, edited by Cyril E. Black, pp. 72–90. Cambridge: Harvard University Press, 1960.

An analysis of patterns of population change since 1861. Disputes the argument that the decline in birth rate after World War II was due primarily to war losses or rural-urban migration.

650 ENGEL, BARBARA ALPERN. "Women in Russia and the Soviet Union." *Signs* 12, no. 4 (Summer 1986): 781–96.

Bibliographical essay reviewing Rose Glickman's *Russian Factory Women* (entry 240; incorrectly cited here as *The Russian Factory Woman*), Linda Harriet Edmondson's *Feminism in Russia* (entry 231; incorrectly cited here as *The Feminist Movement in Russia*), the collection of essays in *Soviet Sisterhood* (entry 550), the Soviet feminist articles in Tatyana Mamonova's *Women and Russia* (entry 574), and the Soviet writings on women in Gail Lapidus's *Women, Work and Family* (entry 566). A very useful survey highlighting the key issues and debates in Western scholarship about women in Russia and the Soviet Union.

651 ———. "An Interview with Olga Lipovskaia." *Frontiers* 10, no. 3 (1989): 6–10.

Information about Olga Lipovskaia, the editor of the new femizdat entitled *Women's Reading* (*Zhenskoe chtenie*).

652 ENGELSTEIN, LAURA. "In a Female Voice." Review essay. *Slavic Review* 44, no. 1 (Spring 1985): 104–7.

Review of five Russian-language memoirs by women of the intelligentsia who confronted the moral dilemmas of the Stalin era—some in prisons and camps, some in their work and personal lives.

653 ESSIG, LAURIE, and MAMONOVA, TATIANA. "Perestroika for Women." In *Perestroika from Below: Social Movements in the Soviet Union*, edited by Judith Sedaitis and Jim Butterfield, pp. 97–112. Boulder: Westview Press, 1991.

Plusses and minuses for women in the changes brought about by perestroika. Authors argue that women have a long way to go both in the Soviet Union and the United States before they attain the power necessary to make real, structural changes in their lives.

654 EVANS, JANET. "The Communist Party of the Soviet Union and the Woman's Question: The Case of the 1936 Decree 'In Defense of Mother and Child.'" *Journal of Contemporary History* 16 (1981): 757–75.
Examines the Stalinist decrees of the mid-1930s and the climate of public opinion surrounding them. Argues that the tightening of controls on marriage and divorce—and even the outlawing of abortion, widely interpreted as a conservative backlash against female equality—had wide support, particularly among women who felt exploited by the Soviet sexual revolution and its encouragement of male promiscuity. With the tightening of sexual controls came a reaffirmation of women's equality in all spheres of life. Thus, in Evans's view, it is "simplistic" to view these decrees as a setback.

655 FARNSWORTH, BEATRICE BRODSKY. "Communist Feminism: Its Synthesis and Demise." In *Women, War, and Revolution*, edited by Carol R. Berkin and Clara Lovett, pp. 145–63. New York: Holmes & Meier, 1980.
Explores the ideology of "Communist feminism" by examining the role of early female Communists in the Party, their ideological debates, and the contradictions between theory and practice (particularly in relation to motherhood) in their own lives. Farnsworth argues that the goal of equality was soon superseded by the imperatives of modernization, thus sounding the death knell of Communist feminism. Huge numbers of women entered the labor force without adequate relief from their domestic responsibilities, and the government did little to ease their double burden. Useful bibliographic guide.

656 ———. "Village Women Experience the Revolution." In *Bolshevik Culture*, edited by Abbott Gleason, Peter Kenez, and Richard Stites, pp. 238–60. Bloomington: Indiana University Press, 1984.
How did peasant women, viewed by the Bolsheviks as the "darkest," most backward group in Russia, respond to the Revolution? Beatrice Farnsworth has been among the first of the current generation of scholars to do serious research about peasant women. In this essay she explores Bolshevik efforts at outreach to the villages of central Russia and peasant women's response to them. She emphasizes the persistence of traditional patriarchal culture and values after the Revolution. Arguing against any significant female solidarity within the family or the village as a whole, Farnsworth stresses the sources of tension between women, between mothers-in-law and daughters-in-law, and between women with children and childless women. Farnsworth elucidates gender differences in the holding of property, arguing that men's experience was more socialist (communal landholding and decision making) and women's more capitalist (their dowry and earnings were held as private property). Farnsworth concludes that peasant women responded selectively to the Revolution, welcoming laws that granted them equality in the family and freedom to divorce, but retaining their ties to traditional cultural symbols.

657 FISCHER, MARY ELLEN. "Women." In *The Soviet Union Today*, 2d ed., edited by James Cracraft, pp. 327–38. Chicago: University of Chicago Press, 1988. First Edition. Cambridge: Bulletin of Atomic Scientists, 1983. Index.

A brief survey (one of the thirty chapters in this book) of the status of Soviet women. Not significantly updated in the second edition to discuss changes under Gorbachev.

658 FITZPATRICK, SHEILA. "Sex and Revolution: An Examination of Literary and Statistical Data on the Mores of Soviet Students in the 1920s." *Journal of Modern History* 50 (June 1978): 252–78.

Discusses how students in the 1920s, the first to attend universities after the Revolution, dealt with the "sex problem." Relies heavily on a series of surveys of students in Moscow, Omsk, and Odessa. The surveys indicate that the students endorsed a far more liberated sexuality in theory than they did in practice.

659 FRANK, STEPHEN P. "Popular Justice, Community and Culture among the Russian Peasantry, 1870–1900." *Russian Review* 46, no. 3 (July 1987): 239–65.

Analysis of the peasant practice of *samosud* (taking justice into their own hands). Discussions of *samosud* as a means of perpetuating peasant women's subordinate status and of violence against women in the context of this practice. Takes issue with Farnsworth's conclusions in "The Litigious Daughter-in-Law" (entry 288).

660 GEIGER, KENT. "The Family and Social Change." In *The Transformation of Russian Society*, edited by Cyril E. Black, pp. 447–59. Cambridge: Harvard University Press, 1960.

General patterns in the transformation of the family in the past hundred years. Geiger argues that the Soviets succeeded to a great degree in their policy of "family homogenization." Short discussion of "the trend toward egalitarianism" within the family.

661 GIFFIN, FREDERICK, ed. *Woman as Revolutionary*. Introduction by Anne Fremantle. New York: New American Library, 1973. 256 pp.

Sections on Sofia Perovskaya from Vera Figner's *Memoirs of a Revolutionist*, on Alexandra Kollontai from her pamphlet "The Workers' Opposition in Russia," and on Isadora Duncan and Sergei Esenin.

662 GOLDBERG, MARILYN POWER. "Women in the Soviet Economy." *The Review of Radical Political Economics* 4, no. 3 (July 1972): 60–74.

Critical New-Left analysis. Pessimistic about future gains for Soviet women.

663   GOLDMAN, WENDY ZEVA. "Freedom and Its Consequences: The
      Debate on the Soviet Family Code of 1926." *Russian History* 11, no. 4
      (1984): 362–88.
Probably the freest and fullest debate about any issue in the Soviet period
occurred around the Family Code of 1926. An enlightening examination of the
various repercussions for women.

664   ———. "Women, the Family and the New Revolutionary Order in the
      Soviet Union." In *Promissory Notes: Women in the Transition to Socialism*,
      edited by Sonia Kruks, Rayna Rapp, and Marilyn B. Young, pp. 59–81.
      New York: Monthly Review Press, 1989.
Goldman argues that the "retreat" from women's liberation in the 1930s was
not chiefly the result of Marxist ideological shortcomings or "Bolshevik oppor-
tunism" but rather a "crushing material poverty." Soviet family policy is analyzed by examining homeless children (*bezprizorniki*), peasants, and urban
working-class women. As proof of Bolshevik good faith and ideals, Goldman
cites the 1918 Family Code. In her view, problems in its application stemmed
from the nature of Russia at the time ("largely rural, poverty-stricken") and
from the agricultural system, centered around the family as the chief economic
unit. The Code, stressing individual rights, conflicted with the communal and
patriarchal nature of peasant society.
    In reviewing the situation of the *bezprizorniki*, Goldman highlights the nega-
tive impact of the New Economic Policy on many women and children. For
example, the transition to this policy led to the closing of many children's
homes and the unemployment of their largely female staffs as the state philosophy shifted from outlawing adoption to relying heavily on it. In the cities the
notion of "free union" and easy divorce resulted in a skyrocketing unemployment rate, further impoverishing largely unskilled women workers. For
Goldman the 1920s represent a wholesale retreat from "the great potential of
the socialist experiment" as a result of the "terrible scarcity and underdevelop-
ment" of the decade, not because of lack of commitment to women's liberation.
Not discussed: the differences among Bolsheviks on the woman question, and
the policy debates of the 1920s.

665   GRUNFELD, JUDITH. "Women's Work in Russia's Planned
      Economy." *Social Research* 9, no. 1 (February 1942): 26–34.
A survey of the mobilization of female labor in the Soviet period and its impli-
cations for the war effort.

666   HAIGHT, AMANDA. *Anna Akhmatova: A Poetic Pilgrimage*. New
      York: Oxford University Press, 1976. Reprint. Oxford: Oxford
      University Press, 1990. 213 pp. Index.
See entry 353.

667 HAYDEN, CAROL EUBANKS. "The *Zhenotdel* and the Bolshevik
      Party." *Russian History* 3, pt. 2 (1976): 150–73.
Solid survey of the *Zhenotdel* (Women's Section) of the Soviet Communist
party, in existence from 1919–1930. Good material on the background of Party
work among women and attitudes of Party activists and leaders about the
notion of separate organizing among women. Describes Krupskaia's role in
publicly supporting the Zhenotdel's demise as the Party moved away from concern with emancipating women from household drudgery. See also the listing
for her dissertation (entry 554).

668 HELDT, BARBARA. "The Burden of Caring." *Nation* 243 (23 June
      1987): 820–24.
An excellent short survey of trends for women writers and poets under *glasnost*;
mentioned are Rimma Kazakova, Liudmila Petrushevskaia, Tatiana Tolstaia, I.
Grekova, Natalia Baranskaia, Elena Shvarts, and Irina Odoevtseva. Contains a
brief discussion of the sexism of male writers such as Victor Astaf'ev and Vasily
Belov.

669 ISPA, JEAN M. "Soviet Immigrant Mothers' Perceptions Regarding the
      First Childbearing Year: The 1950s and the 1970s." *Slavic Review* 47,
      no. 2 (Summer 1988): 291–306.
This article investigates Soviet women's attitudes towards pregnancy, childbirth, and postnatal care, as well as the women's support systems before and
after the birth of their children. The attitudes of recent Jewish immigrants from
the Soviet Union in the 1950s and 1970s are compared. Ultimately, Ispa finds
that "the degree of consistency has outweighed the degree of change."

670 JANCAR, BARBARA WOLFE. "Women and Soviet Politics." In *Soviet
      Politics and Society in the 1970s*, edited by Henry W. Morton and Rudolf
      L. Tokes, pp. 118–60. New York: Free Press, 1974.
Discusses the gap between the Soviet ideal of full emancipation for women and
the reality of women's continued low representation in the highest echelons of
political and economic power. Examines the causes of Soviet women's "passiv-
ity toward involvement." Useful survey bringing together contemporary
sources, incorporating some feminist scholarship, and including helpful tables
and a tellingly short appendix that lists all women in the Party leadership from
1912 to 1971.

671 ———. "Women in Communist Countries: Comparative Public
      Policy." In *Women and World Change: Equity Issues in Development*, edit-
      ed by Naomi Black and Ann Baker Cottrell, pp. 139–58. Beverly Hills:
      Sage Publications, 1988.
Comparison of women's status in Eastern Europe, the USSR, China, and
Cuba. Data up to 1980.

672 JUVILER, PETER. "The Soviet Family in Post-Stalin Perspective." In *The Soviet Union since Stalin*, edited by Stephen F. Cohen, Alexander Rabinowitch, and Robert Sharlet, pp. 227–51. Bloomington: Indiana University Press, 1980.

Survey of current trends including low birth rate, divorce rate, and the questions of authority in the family and of real equality for women. Tables of birth rates, marriages and divorces, and reasons for divorce.

673 "The Urban Family and the Soviet State." In *The Contemporary Soviet City*, edited by Henry Morton and Robert C. Stuart, pp. 84–112. Armonk, N.Y.: M. E. Sharpe, 1984.

Discusses trends such as declining birth rates, rising infant and adult mortality rates, rising divorce rates, the changing role of women in the family, and policy initiatives undertaken in the early 1930s to address these issues. Tables on divorce rates, birth rates, urbanization, consumer services, and Russian and Soviet vital statistics.

674 ———. "The Family in the Soviet Union." The Carl Beck Papers in Russian and East European Studies, no. 306. Pittsburgh, Pa.: University of Pittsburgh Center for Russian and East European Studies, n.d. 59 pp.

Juviler has written extensively on this subject. In his view, "family government relations have changed significantly since Stalin's day." The author reviews changes in laws on paternity and divorce among others, showing the evolution of a compromise between the "Bolshevik" ideology and principles of earlier times and "the demographic and political imperatives of today." In the case of paternity laws, for example, Juviler argues that the changes represent a compromise between women's and men's rights, in which men do better. Well-researched and comprehensive.

675 KAUSHIK, DEVENDRA. "The Soviet Women—The Dilemmas of the Dual Burden." In *Women of the World: Illusion and Reality*, edited by Urmila Phandis and Indira Malani, pp. 175–82. New Delhi: Vikas Publishing, 1978.

Brief survey of status of Soviet women, with attention to the double burden. Based exclusively on Soviet sources.

676 KONONENKO, YELENA. *Soviet Women: Their Role as Homemakers and Citizens*. Moscow: Novosti, 1976. 50 pp.

Another of the pamphlets extolling the advances of Soviet women, written for International Women's Year.

677 KRUTOGOROV, Y. *Women of the Village*. Moscow: Novosti, n.d. 72 pp.

Positive vignettes of rural women.

678   KUTSENKO, V. A. "The Socio-Occupational Self-Determination of School Students." *Soviet Education* 32, no. 4 (April 1990): 66–82.
Some information about gender differences in occupational choice. Expresses no perception of them as problematic.

679   LAPIDUS, GAIL WARSHOFSKY. "USSR Women at Work: Changing Patterns." *Industrial Relations* 14, no. 2 (1975): 178–95.
Compares patterns of female employment in the USSR, the United States and Western Europe. Similarities in occupational sex-segregation and wage differentials; differences in proportion of women performing heavy, unskilled labor and percentage of women in scientific and technical occupations. Argues here, as in other works, that "manpower [sic] needs have been more decisive than ideology in shaping women's roles in the economic sector."

680   ———. "The Female Industrial Labor Force." In *Industrial Labor in the USSR*, edited by Arcadius Kahan and Blair Ruble, pp. 232–79. New York: Pergamon, 1979.
An earlier, condensed version of *Women in Soviet Society* (entry 565), echoing its themes of the "interdependence of work and family roles." Argues that the large influx of Soviet women into the work force was primarily occasioned by the shortage of men. Useful charts on the distribution of women workers in the economy, the percentages of women in the labor force during different time periods, comparative birth rates, and time budgets.

681   ———. "The Soviet Union." In *Women Workers in Fifteen Countries: Essays in Honor of Alice Hanson Cook*, edited by Jennie Farley, pp. 13–32. Ithaca, N.Y.: Cornell University Press, 1984.
A conference paper adapted from *Women, Work, and Family in the Soviet Union* (entry 566). Includes text of the discussion that followed the presentation of the paper.

682   LEVIN, EVE, and ALLAN WILDMAN, eds. "Daughters and Stepdaughters of the Russian Revolution." *Russian Review* 51, no. 2 (April 1992): 155–203.
This collection of articles is derived from a panel of the same name presented at the Fourth World Congress for Soviet and East European Studies at Harrogate, England, in July 1990. In addition to the Introduction by Nina Perlina, the four entries are "Motherhood in a Cold Climate: The Poetry and Career of Maria Shkapskaia" by Barbara Heldt, "Larisa Reisner: Myth as Justification for Life" by Alla Zeide, "Primeval and Modern Mythologies in the life of Ol'ga Mikhailovna Freidenberg" by Nina Perlina, and "Voluntary Seclusion: The Life of a Lonely old Woman in a Deserted Village" by Bella Ulanovskaia. Heldt reviews Shkapskaia's poetry of the early 1920s as the closest "to inscribing the female, the maternal, body into Russian culture." Zeide discusses the life and mythology of

Reisner, the revolutionary activist. Perlina surveys the life of Ol'ga Mikhailovna Friedenberg, a brilliant classical scholar, victim of both anti-Semitism and sexism, who left a legacy of work that has outlived those of her tormentors and is finally getting the attention it deserves. Finally, Ulanovskaia describes a visit to Baba Niusha, a woman living by herself in an abandoned village, an "administrative gap" that personifies "contemporary Russian life in seclusion."

683   LUBIN, NANCY. "Women in Central Asia: Progress and Contradictions." *Soviet Studies* 33, no. 2 (April 1981): 182–203.
Survey of the Soviet record, its successes in improving women's status, and its shortcomings. Commentary on the continued strength of Islam and the old culture. Useful statistical tables.

684   LYANDRES, SEMION. "The 1918 Attempt on the Life of Lenin." *Slavic Review* 48, no. 3 (Fall, 1989): 432–48.
Argues convincingly that Fania Kaplan was falsely accused of the 1918 attempted assassination of Lenin. Marred by sexism—particularly in suggesting that "personal motives or emotional instability" were behind the deeds of female revolutionary terrorists such as Spiridonova and Brilliant, but not behind those of any male terrorists or revolutionaries discussed.

685   McAULEY, ALASTAIR. "The Woman Question in the USSR." *Slavic Review* 38, no. 2 (June 1979): 290–93.
Review of Atkinson et al., *Women in Russia* (entry 17). Critical of inadequate conceptual framework of discussions of Soviet policy.

686   MALACHOWSKAJA, NATALIA. "Terra Incognita on Women and Writing." *Trivia: A Journal of Ideas* 1, no. 1 (Fall 1982): 27–36.
First presented at the international feminist conference "Breaking the Sequence: Women, Literature, and the Future," held at Wellesley College, 30 April to 2 May 1981. Author one of the founders of the Maria group of Russian feminists. These women split from Tatyana Mamonova in 1980 after the publication of the first *Women's Almanac* to emphasize a Russian Orthodoxy-based spiritual feminism. This essay addresses the issues of women's creativity and of the female essence in literature and art.

687   MAMONOVA, TATYANA. "The USSR: It's Time We Began with Ourselves." Translated by Rebecca Park. In *Sisterhood is Global: The International Women's Movement Anthology*, edited by Robin Morgan, pp. 683–89. Garden City, N.Y.: Anchor/Doubleday, 1984.
General overview of problems for Soviet women, as well as a call to action.

688   MANDEL, WILLIAM. "Soviet Women and Their Self-Image." *Science and Society* 35, no. 3 (Fall 1971): 286–310.
Very positive presentation of the status of Soviet women, who "seem to feel no

resentment at the fact that men predominate overwhelmingly at the top level of all professions."

689 ———. "Soviet Women in the Work-Force and Professions." *American Behavioral Scientist* 15, no. 2 (November–December 1971): 255–80.
One of a number of articles by this pro-Soviet scholar, who argued—primarily on the basis of Soviet statistics and laws—that women made unprecedented strides toward equality in the USSR work force and professions.

690 MATTHEWS, MERVYN. "The Soviet Worker at Home." In *Industrial Labor in the USSR*, edited by Arcadius Kahan and Blair Ruble, pp. 209–23. New York: Pergamon, 1979.
Provides useful information about Soviet domestic life; includes comparative time budgets.

691 MOLOKHOV, A. N. "Abortions and Neuroses." *Soviet Review* 3, no. 6 (June 1962): 44–49.
In this author's view, "frequent abortions predispose toward prolonged hysteria." Suggests preventative measures to reduce the number of abortions and against "hysteria."

692 ———. "Youth Has Its Say on Love and Marriage." *Soviet Review* 3, no. 8 (August 1962): 21–40.
Answers to a 10 December 1961 *Komsomolskaya Pravda* questionnaire about the family, which included questions about eliminating women's double burden.

693 MOSKOFF, WILLIAM. "The Soviet Urban Labor Supply." In *The Contemporary Soviet City*, edited by Henry Morton and Robert Stuart, pp. 65–83. Armonk, N.Y.: M. E. Sharpe, 1984.
Discusses the role of women in the urban labor force and pressure to increase possibilities for part-time work.

694 NEHEMIAS, CAROL. "The Prospects for a Soviet Women's Movement: Opportunities and Obstacles." In *Perestroika from Below: Social Movements in the Soviet Union*, edited by Judith Sedaitis and Jim Butterfield, pp. 73–96. Boulder: Westview Press, 1991.
Reviewing the emergence of women's movements in general, Nehemias enumerates the factors militating for and against substantive improvements in the lives of Soviet women.

695 NOONAN, NORMA C. "Marxism and Feminism in the USSR: Irreconcilable Differences?" *Women and Politics* 8, no. 1 (1988): 31–49.
Useful article, arguing that despite official hostility toward the development of feminism in the USSR, a protofeminism, defined as "an early, or incomplete, man-

ifestation of feminism," has developed. Noonan cites works such as Baranskaya's story "A Week Like Any Other" (entry 815) and films such as *My Friend, Ivan Lapshin* as examples of this protofeminism, which she believes will aid in the attainment of many feminist goals. Accepts argument that Russian Social Democratic party has always been hostile to feminism. Helpful bibliography.

696   ———. "Two Solutions to the *Zhenskii Vopros* in Russia and the USSR-Kollontai and Krupskaia: A Comparison." *Women and Politics* 2, no. 3 (Fall 1991): 77–100.

Argues that Kollontai and Krupskaia represented two alternative views about the role of women in the new Soviet state. Kollontai advocated a radical restructuring of sex roles and the creation of a new Soviet woman. Krupskaia argued for women's dual role as "worker-mother." This latter view prevailed. In the post-Soviet period the debate has re-opened, with a range of viewpoints and no easy solutions on the horizon.

697   PAVLOVA, LUDMILA. *Women in My Country*. Moscow: Novosti, n.d.

Pamphlet lauding the advances made by Soviet women.

698   PETERSON, DEMOSTHENES. "The Number and Cost of Illegal Abortions in the USSR." Berkeley-Duke Occasional Papers on the Second Economy in the USSR, no. 9 (April 1987), pp. 3.0–3.12.

Peterson argues that private abortions in the USSR "constitute a significant share of all abortions performed, and when taken together, yield an abortion rate that is not only the highest in the world, but significantly higher than previous estimates by western scholars."

699   RAMER, SAMUEL C. "*Feldshers* and Rural Health Care in the Early Soviet Period." In *Health and Society in Revolutionary Russia*, edited by Susan Gross Solomon and John F. Hutchinson, pp. 121–45. Bloomington: Indiana University Press, 1990.

Information about women as *feldshers*, midwives, and nurses in the countryside. Feminization of the medical profession, recommitment to training *feldshers*, and recognition of their importance in rural areas.

700   ROEBUCK, C. M. "The Nationalization of Women: The Natural History of a Lie (Being a Study in Bourgeois Frightfulness)." London: British Socialist Party, n.d. 23 pp.

Background and refutation of persistent stories about Bolshevik nationalization and socialization of women. Probably published at the end of 1919.

701   ROSENTHAL, BERNICE GLATZER. "Love on the Tractor: Women in the Russian Revolution and After." In *Becoming Visible: Women in European History*, edited by Renate Bridenthal and Claudia Koonz, pp. 370–99. Boston: Houghton Mifflin, 1977.

Covers major points for the Revolutionary period, through the early seventies. Events and more current scholarship have overtaken this work, but it is still useful as an example of scholarly response to the second wave of feminism in the United States.

702 RUTHCHILD, ROCHELLE. "Sisterhood and Socialism: The Soviet Feminist Movement." *Frontiers* 7, no. 2 (1983): 3–12.
Survey of the women who published the first *samizdat* feminist journal and their work.

703 RYAN-HAYES, KAREN. "Marina Lebedeva's 'Mezhdu nami zhen-shchinami' Feuilletons." *Slavic and East European Journal* 36, no. 2 (Summer 1992): 172–88.
Analyzes the work of Marina Lebedeva (born 1950) in *Izvestia* during the period of glasnost, when feuilletonists became openly critical of the state and the party. Ryan-Hayes compares Lebedeva to the émigré writer Teffi. She writes for the 'little woman,' applauding women's solidarity but also insisting that women have a limited ability to understand the key issues affecting Soviet society. Ryan-Hayes observes that she writes in a "markedly feminine (though hardly feminist) voice."

704 SCHUSTER, ALICE. "Women's Role in the Soviet Union: Ideology and Reality." *Russian Review* 30, no. 3 (July 1971): 260–67.
Brief survey, with facts and figures about women's prominence in the work force. Concludes that "despite communist ideology the weight of Russian tradition still affects the status of women."

705 SEREBRENNIKOV, T. *Woman in the Soviet Union*. Moscow: Foreign Languages Publishing House, 1943. 63 pp.
Wartime pamphlet extolling Soviet gains for women. Pages 42 to 63 recount tales of the exceptional individual deeds of Soviet female workers, soldiers, and partisans in support of the war effort.

706 SHELLEY, LOUISE. "Female Criminality in the 1920s: A Consequence of Inadvertent and Deliberate Change." *Russian History* 9, pts. 2–3 (1982): 265–84.
Documents changes in the pattern of female crime, linking them to Soviet policies affecting the status of women. Examines growth in traditional and nontraditional female crime as women move more actively into the work force and traditional familial bonds loosen.

707 SOLOVEICHIK, S. *Soviet Children at School*. Moscow: Novosti, 1976. 25 pp.
Part of the series of pamphlets issued in honor of International Women's Year. Discusses women, children, and the school, as well as the typical school program.

708   SOVIET WOMEN'S COMMITTEE. *Lenin on the Role of Women in Society, and the Emancipation of Women in the USSR*. Moscow: 1975. 48 pp.
Lenin appears, of course, but this is actually a short history of women's achievements in the USSR, written for International Women's Year.

709   SPERLING, GERALD, and ELIZA ZURICK. "The Social Composition of the Communist Parties of Central Asia." *Studies on the Soviet Union*, n.s. 8, no. 1 (1968): 30–45.
Statistics on the number of women Party members and candidates for the 1944–62 period. Evidence for the special recruitment of women. Statistics apply to Kirghizia, Uzbekistan, and Tadzhikistan.

710   STERNHEIMER, STEPHEN. "The Vanishing Babushka: A Roleless Role for Older Soviet Women?" In *Quality of Life in the Soviet Union*, edited by Horst Herlemann, pp. 133–49. Boulder, Colo.: Westview, 1987. (First Printed in *Current Perspectives on Aging and the Life Cycle*, edited by Zena Smith Blau, pp. 315–34. Greenwich, Conn.: Jai Press, 1985.)
Challenges the "classic Western assumption" that older Soviet women relish, and are needed in, the role of caregiver. Argues that the vanishing of the *babushka* will adversely affect the status of Soviet female pensioners.

711   STITES, RICHARD. "Kollontai, Inessa, and Krupskaia: A Review of Recent Literature." *Canadian-American Slavic Studies* 9, no. 1 (Spring 1975): 84–92.
Reviews Kollontai's *Izbrannye Stat'l i Rechi*; Iring Fetscher's edition of *The Autobiography of a Sexually Emancipated Communist Woman* (entry 803); Alix Holt's translation of *Sexual Relations and the Class Struggle* and *Love and the New Morality*; Polina Vinogradskaia's *Pamiatnye Vstrechi*; and Robert McNeal's *Bride of the Revolution* (entry 370). Stites finds the latter most "disappointing" and criticizes McNeal for accepting as fact the hypothesis of Lenin's affair with Inessa Armand. Stites praises Holt; criticizes Fetscher.

712   ———. *"Zhenotdel*: Bolshevism and Russian Women, 1917–1930." *Russian History* 3, pt. 2 (1976): 174–93.
Critical of historians' lack of attention to the social-change aspects of Soviet policy and society in the 1920s. Background of women's organizing in the Party. Covers much the same ground as Hayden, but with more attention to *Zhenotdel* work out in the field, including the physically dangerous work of organizing among central Asian women.

713   ———. "Women and the Revolutionary Process in Russia." In *Becoming Visible: Women in European History*, edited by Renate Bridenthal, Claudia Koonz, and Susan Stuard, pp. 450–71. Boston: Houghton Mifflin, 1986.

Very good brief survey of topics covered in much more depth in Stites's book (entry 611). Useful for those who cannot get the book or who want the highlights on this topic. Helpful annotated bibliography. In the same volume, see also Temma Kaplan's brief essay on Russian women in 1917 (pages 432–38).

714   ———. "Women and the Revolutionary Process in Russia." In *Becoming Visible: Women in European History*, 2d ed., edited by Renate Bridenthal, Claudia Koonz, and Susan Stuard, pp. 451–71. Boston: Houghton Mifflin, 1987.
See entry 713.

715   ———. "Equality, Freedom and Justice: Women and Men in the Russian Revolution." Research Paper No. 67, The Marjorie Mayrock Center for Soviet and East European Research. Jerusalem: Hebrew University, 1988. 21 pp.
Seeks to take a "fresh look" at women and the Russian Revolution. By concentrating on "key concepts and ideas" as understood by women and men, workers, and the intelligentsia, seeks to understand how people in this period defined and constructed their reality. Maintains that in the creation of symbols, supposedly connoting a new order, inequalities such as those "between women and men, worker and peasant, city and country" were reinforced. Stites argues that concepts of freedom, equality, and justice had very different meanings for workers and peasants, and for women and men in these groups. Women in particular opted for family stability over free love and personal autonomy. Ultimately, they reacted to the turmoil of Revolution-induced change by accepting a version of the Stalinist "big deal" that roughly traded political autonomy (*zhenotdel*) and personal independence (free love) for family stability and financial security.

716   STRUMILIN, S. "Family and Community in the Society of the Future." *Soviet Review* 2, no. 2 (February 1961): 3–29.
The "dean of Soviet economists" presents his vision of the new Communist society. Envisions a network of self-governing communes "unencumbered with private property," an "economic democracy with centralized national economic planning, and growing democratization through self-government and self-rule in the localities."

717   TIRADO, ISABEL. "The Socialist Youth Movement in Revolutionary Petrograd." *Russian Review* 46, no. 2 (April 1987): 135–56.
Discusses the change in the composition of the Petrograd labor force, with its increasing numbers of women and youth, and the role of Krupskaia as "the symbol of Bolshevik support for the youth movement."

718 TROTSKY, LEON. *Women and the Family*. New York: Pathfinder, 1970. 78 pp.

This slim pamphlet shows Trotsky's views at different stages of his relationship to the Soviet government. Includes articles written in 1923 and 1925, a 1925 speech, a 1933 questionnaire response from a U.S. magazine, and an excerpt from *The Revolution Betrayed*. In his 1923 writings Trotsky argues for the building of model communities with communal dining and child-care facilities as the way to reconstruct the family. He subscribes to the concept of the "backwardness" of the masses of women. In 1925, writing about mothers and children, he favors an all-out fight against alcoholism. In his 1930s writings he condemns "Thermidor in the Family." The introduction by Caroline Lund seeks to answer Kate Millett's criticism of Soviet-style women's liberation by postulating a Trotskyist critique and alternative, and noting that at least in one aspect of his personal life, Trotsky was ahead of his times: he and his wife, Natalia Sedova, chose her name for their children.

719 "Union of Soviet Socialist Republics." In *Sisterhood is Global: The International Women's Movement Anthology*, edited by Robin Morgan, pp. 676–83. Garden City, N.Y.: Anchor/Doubleday, 1984.

Provides basic information about the USSR, as well as statistics about women in the USSR and an overview of their general status.

720 VIGDOROVA, FRIDA ABRAMOVNA. *Diary of a School Teacher*. Moscow: Foreign Languages Publishing House, 1954. 344 pp.

Published in the year after Stalin's death and based on the author's own experiences. A rare fictionalized presentation in English of the daily life of a schoolteacher. Conflicts between the privileged and less privileged are discussed, as well as the teacher's struggles with sexist attitudes. The gap between the ideals and the realities of Soviet school life is portrayed.

721 VIOLA, LYNNE. *"Bab'i bunty* and Peasant Women's Protest during Collectivization." *Russian Review* 45, no. 1 (January 1986): 23–42.

An examination of this widespread phenomenon during the period of collectivization. Viola argues that the Party responded differently to female and male protests against collectivization, viewing the former as reflecting women's backwardness and hysteria. Discusses ways in which women's protest was effective in forcing a retreat from the most-opposed aspects of collectivization, and how the Soviets manipulated the myth of the peasant for their own ends.

722 VORONINA, O. A. "Women in a 'Man's Society.'" *Soviet Sociology* 28, no. 2 (March–April 1989): 66–79.

A translation of an article that appeared in *Sotsiologicheskie issledovaniia* (1988), this essentially recapitulates discussions about problems in the "resolution of the woman question" in the USSR. Voronina discusses the labor force, emphasizing the persistence of traditional stereotypes about the sexes despite all the progressive legislation about women. Notes that work remains sex-segregated and that women continue to face the double burden of work outside the home and traditional roles within the family. The author notes that with the breakdown of the patriarchal family, the chief and often only parent is the mother. Criticizing the "essentially patriarchal approach of many sociologists and demographers," Voronina argues for policies that will offer women more choices as to how they combine paid work and motherhood.

723   WATERS, ELIZABETH. "In the Shadow of the Comintern: The Communist Women's Movement, 1920–43." In *Promissory Notes: Women in the Transition to Socialism*, edited by Sonia Kruks, Rayna Rapp, and Marilyn B. Young, pp. 29–56. New York: Monthly Review Press, 1989.

The author examines why the development of the Communist women's movement "served over a number of years to silence and exclude a feminist voice." She analyzes the *Theses of the Communist Women's Movement*, presented to the First Communist Women's Conference in Moscow in 1920, noting significant omissions, especially in relation to family and fertility issues. Reproductive rights issues were downplayed in the *Theses*, and women in the traditional work force and proletarian solidarity were emphasized. Radical and feminist issues challenging the nuclear family structure disappeared or were downplayed as the Communist movement confronted a very different set of social and political realities in the heady post-1917 days, when world revolution seemed imminent. Waters concludes that as the 1920s ended, "any special emphasis on women's social subordination in communist propaganda or campaigning came to be regarded as a capitulation to bourgeois feminism; the movement's aim was no longer the advancement of women but their mobilization for the advancement of the Comintern."

724   ———. "Restructuring the 'Woman Question': Perestroika and Prostitution." *Feminist Review* 33 (Autumn 1989): 3–19.

Another significant contribution to our understanding of contemporary changes in the USSR by an insightful and prolific feminist Sovietologist. Waters argues that *perestroika* has brought a change in Soviet attitudes toward prostitution and prostitutes. The socialist view of prostitutes as victims of an exploitative socioeconomic system has been replaced by "language brimful of moral fervour and righteousness." Waters views this as symbolic of the general indifference to the "woman question."

725   *Women in the Soviet Union: Statistical Returns*. Moscow: Progress, 1970. 54 pp.

Useful statistics. Twenty-seven statistical tables on subjects ranging from education, employment, and life expectancy to Hero-Mothers.

726   YANOWITCH, M. "Soviet Patterns of Time Use and Concepts of Leisure." *Soviet Studies* 15, no. 1 (July 1963): 17–37.

Surveys several time-use studies conducted in Siberia and Leningrad in 1958,

1959, and 1961. Discusses gender differences, showing, among other things, that women have far less free time than men.

727   ZIEMKE, EARL. "Composition and Morale of the Partisan Movement." In *Soviet Partisans in World War II*, edited by John Armstrong, pp. 141–96. Madison: University of Wisconsin Press, 1964.
Contains a short description (pages 146–48) of the role of women in the partisan units, primarily as the sexual partners of partisan leaders.

728   ZUZANEK, JIRI. "Time-Budget Trends in the USSR, 1922–70." *Soviet Studies* 31, no. 2 (April 1979): 188–213.
Comprehensive study with tables showing time-budgets for women and men from 1923–68. Unfortunately, the column for women in 1965–68 was cut off due to an error in printing.

AUTOBIOGRAPHIES AND BIOGRAPHIES

729   ABBE, JAMES E. *I Photograph Russia*. New York: R. M. McBride, 1934. 324 pp.
Describes his meeting with Vera Figner in the 1930s.

730   ALEXEYEVA, LUDMILA, and PAUL GOLDBERG. *The Thaw Generation: Coming of Age in the Post-Stalin Era*. Boston: Little, Brown, 1990. 339 pp. Index.
Memoirs by a dissident of her life and of the dissident movement of the 1970s. Stories of heroism, betrayal, and survival and about Larisa Bogoraz, Yuli Daniel, Anatoly Marchenko, Evgeniya Ginzburg, and others.

731   ALLILUYEVA, SVETLANA. *Twenty Letters to a Friend*. Translated by Priscilla Johnson McMillan. New York: Harper & Row, 1967. 246 pp. Notes.
Growing up with Stalin. Describes Alliluyeva's troubled relationship with her father; includes loving remembrances of her "cloudless childhood" until her mother's suicide in 1932. Rare glimpse into Stalin's personal life and his relations with the women closest to him.

732   ———. *Only One Year*. Translated by Paul Chavchavadze. New York: Harper & Row, 1969. 444 pp.
Sequel to *Twenty Letters* (entry 731). Chronicles Alliluyeva's December 1966 trip to India to bury her husband and her subsequent decision to defect to the West.

733 AMALRIK, GUZEL. *Memories of a Tatar Childhood*. Translated by
   Marc Heine. London: Hutchinson, 1979. 160 pp.
Memoirs of life in a Tatar family in Moscow from the early 1940s. Short sec-
tion at the end about the author's life in exile with her husband, dissident
Andrei Amalrik.

734 ANDREYEV, OLGA CHERNOV. *Cold Spring in Russia*. Translated
   by Michael Carlisle. Foreword by Arthur Miller. Ann Arbor, Mich.:
   Ardis, 1978. 283 pp.
Memoirs of the adopted daughter of Socialist Revolutionary party leader
Victor Chernov. Primarily covers the period 1917–21. Avoids detail about the
hardships of this period, especially for those designated political opponents of
the Bolsheviks.

735 ARMONAS, BARBARA. *Leave Your Tears in Moscow*. As told to A. L.
   Nasvytis. Philadelphia: J. B. Lippincott, 1961. 222 pp.
The author married a U.S. citizen in 1929 but was trapped in Lithuania at the
onset of World War II. Her efforts to rejoin her husband and daughter were
finally rewarded in 1960. Covers the German and Soviet occupations of
Lithuania and the author's years in a Siberian labor camp and final freedom.
Provides insights into life in the Lithuanian countryside.

736 BALABANOFF, ANGELICA. *Impressions of Lenin*. Translated by Isotta
   Cesari. Foreword by Bertram D. Wolfe. Ann Arbor: University of
   Michigan Press, 1964. 152 pp.
Balabanoff first met Lenin during the Conference of Socialist Women in Berne,
Switzerland, in March 1915. A gifted linguist, she translated for him and other
Socialists at various conferences. After the October Revolution, Lenin named
Balabanoff the first secretary of the Comintern. Horrified by the machinations
of Comintern members, particularly those of Chairman Zinoviev, she resigned
and left Russia. Describes Lenin's hostility to Kollontai after she joined the
Workers' Opposition, as well as Lenin's control of the women around him
(Armand and Krupskaia).

737 BERLIN, ISAIAH. *Personal Impressions*. Edited by Henry Hardy.
   Introduction by Noel Annan. London: Hogarth, 1980; New York:
   Viking, 1981. 219 pp. Index.
Describes meetings with Akhmatova in 1945 and in 1965 at Oxford.

738 BERBEROVA, NINA. *The Italics are Mine*. Translated by Philippe
   Radley. New York: Harcourt, Brace and World, 1969. 606 pp. Index.
   Biographical Notes.
The author's life from her pre-Revolutionary childhood in a liberal gentry fam-
ily in Tver province, her decision to leave Russia with her first husband, the

poet Vladislav Khodasevich, in 1922, through émigré life in Berlin and Paris to her emigration to the United States in 1950 and subsequent events to 1965.

739   BLUESTEIN, ABE, ed. *Fighters for Anarchism: Mollie Steimer and Senya Fleshin*. New York: Libertarian Publications Group, 1983. 84 pp.
Steimer, a Russian-born anarchist, was deported to the Soviet Union in 1921, where she met and participated in anarchist activities with her lifelong companion Fleshin. Account of their treatment and that of other anarchists by the Bolsheviks.

740   BRIK, LILI, and VLADIMIR MAYAKOVSKY. *Love is the Heart of Everything: Correspondence Between Vladimir Mayakovsky and Lili Brik, 1915–1930*. Edited by Bengt Jangfeldt. Translated by Julian Graffy. London: Polygon, 1986; New York: Grove, 1987. 294 pp. Index.
Introduction seeks to rehabilitate Brik from attacks by Soviet critics who have minimized her place in Mayakovsky's life. Letters and introduction give a good sense of this unconventional relationship. Many pictures.

741   BUCK, PEARL S. *Talk about Russia with Masha Scott*. New York: John Day, 1945. 128 pp.
The life story of a Russian peasant women, married to an American, as told to Pearl Buck. Discussion of the Revolution, collectivization, Stalin, and childbirth. Very positive about Soviet life.

742   CARLISLE, OLGA ANDREYEV. *Voices in the Snow: Encounters with Russian Writers*. New York: Random House, 1962. 224 pp.
Short childhood memoir of émigré life in France and account of a 1960 journey to Moscow commissioned by the *Paris Review*. Carlisle, granddaughter of the writer Leonid Andreyev and a noted translator, met Sholokhov, Yevtushenko, the sculptor Ernst Neizvestnyi, the painter Robert Falk, Ehrenburg, and Pasternak.

743   CAROTENUTO, ALDO. *A Secret Symmetry: Sabina Spielrein between Jung and Freud*. Translated by Arno Pomerans, John Shepley, and Krishna Winston. New York: Pantheon, 1982. 250 pp. Index. Bibliography.
Biography of this Russian-Jewish woman, first a patient of Jung's, then his adoring pupil while in medical school, and finally an established psychoanalyst and scholar in her own right. She influenced both Jung and Freud; the latter borrowed heavily from her in his *Beyond the Pleasure Principle*, and possibly in other works. Returning to Russia for good in 1923, Spielrein gained membership in the Russian Psychoanalytic Society, taught at the local university, founded a children's home, published a few articles in Western psychoanalytic journals, and completely disappeared in 1937, no doubt a purge victim.

744 CHARTERS, ANN, and SAMUEL CHARTERS. *I Love: The Story of Vladimir Mayakovsky and Lili Brik*. New York: Farrar, Straus & Giroux, 1979. 398 pp. Index. Bibliography.
Very informative. Based on interviews with Brik, Nora Polonskaia (Mayakovsky's last mistress), the translator Rita Rait, and Tatiana Yakovleva (the émigré Mayakovsky almost married). Offers more than Jangfeldt (entry 699) on Brik's life after Mayakovsky's suicide. Details about the Lili Brik-Mayakovsky-Osip Brik triangle. The authors generally refer to the women by their first names and the men by their last names.

745 CHUKOVSKAYA, LYDIA. *The Akhmatova Journals. 1938–1941*. Translated by Barry Rubin. London: Collins-Harvill, 1991. 220 pp.
Reminiscences about Akhmatova by a close friend during these troubled years.

746 COTTAM, KAZIMIRA JANINA. *Soviet Airwomen in Combat in World War II*. Manhattan, Kans.: Military Affairs/Aerospace Historian, 1983. 141 pp. Bibliography. Notes.
Consists of three sections: the author's survey of the ground and air crews of the women's air regiment, as well as other women pilots; a biography of fighter ace Lilya Litvak; and an abridged translation of the biography of dive-bomber pilot Klavdiia Fomicheva by her navigator-bombardier Galina Markova.

747 ——, ed. and trans. *In the Sky Above the Front: A Collection of Memoirs of Soviet Airwomen Participants in the Great Patriotic War*. Manhattan, Kans.: Military Affairs/Aerospace Historian, 1984. 270 pp.
Memoirs of Soviet women pilots of dive bombers, night bombers, and fighter planes, as well as support crews, during World War II.

748 DRABKINA, YELIZAVETA. "Mediation." In *The October Storm and After: Stories and Reminiscences*, pp. 339–45. Moscow: Progress, 1967.
Short reminiscence about Lenin by an old Bolshevik.

749 EBON, MARTIN. *Svetlana: The Story of Stalin's Daughter*. New York: New American Library, 1967. 216 pp. Index.
The only biography in English of Svetlana Stalin. Covers the period from her birth in 1925 to her defection in 1967.

750 FEINSTEIN, ELAINE. *A Captive Lion: The Life of Marina Tsvetayeva*. New York: E. P. Dutton, 1987. 289 pp. Index. Bibliography.
Popular biography by a translator of Tsvetaeva's verse. Relies on Karlinsky's earlier biography and works by other Tsvetaeva scholars.

751 FIELD, ALICE WITHROW. *Protection of Women and Children in Soviet Russia*. New York: E. P. Dutton, 1932. 241 pp.
Positive account of efforts to improve the status of women and quality of child care in the USSR. Most interesting for examples of Soviet propaganda aimed at women, pamphlets for women getting a divorce, forms for registration of marriage and divorce, signs and posters about pre- and postnatal care and proper child care and various medical forms for pregnant women and children.

752 GOLDMAN, EMMA. *Living My Life*. 2 vols. New York: Dover Publications, 1970. Vol.1, 503 pp.; vol. 2, 994 pp. Index.
Goldman intersperses some vignettes of her early life in Russia with tales of her move to New York City from Rochester and her early involvement in the U.S. anarchist movement. A good part of volume 2 (chapters 50 and 52) concerns Goldman's life in revolutionary Russia, to which she was deported on 21 December 1919. Her enthusiasm for the Bolsheviks quickly turned to disillusionment and then open criticism. In 1921 Goldman and her companion, Sasha Berkman, left Russia.

753 ———. *My Disillusionment in Russia*. Introduction by Rebecca West. Biographical sketch by Frank Harris. New York: Thomas Y. Crowell, 1970. 263 pp.
Reprint of 1925 "unexpurgated" edition. Encounters with the Left Socialist Revolutionary leader Spiridonova, anarchist leaders Kropotkin, Makhno, and Fanya Baron, as well as Comintern Secretary Balabanoff and Commissar Lunacharsky. Visits to factories, schools, and homes. Overall, a scathing indictment of the Bolsheviks for betraying the Revolution.

754 GURGANUS, JANE WOMBLE. "Nadezhda Krupskaia and Political Socialization, 1917–1930." Ph.D. diss., Emory University, 1973. 472 pp.
A study of Krupskaya's philosophy and its connection to Soviet political socialization. Attention devoted to the implementation of Krupskaya's policies in the period studied.

755 HINGLEY, RONALD. *Nightingale Fever: Russian Poets in Revolution*. New York: Knopf, 1981. 269 pp. Index. Bibliography.
Akhmatova, Mandelstam, Pasternak, Tsvetaeva, and the interweaving of their lives and work against the backdrop of the enormous changes of the period from 1889 to 1966.

756 HOOPER, GORDON R. *The Soviet Cosmonaut Team: A Comprehensive Guide to the Men and Women of the Soviet Manned Space Programme*. Woodbridge, England: Gordon R. Hooper, 1986. Rev. ed. Lowestoft, England: Gordon R. Hooper, 1990. 361 pp. Index.
Biographical information about all Soviet female cosmonauts, including Tereshkova and Savitskaia, and also those who, like Valentina Ponomaryova,

trained for but did not go on missions. Information about a five-woman cosmonaut team, together from 1962 to 1969.

757 INBER, VERA. *Leningrad Diary*. Translated by Serge M. Wolff and
       Rachel Grieve. London: Hutchinson, 1971. 207 pp.
The author, a well-known Soviet poet, remains in Leningrad with her husband, Director of the First Medical Institute, during the blockade, from August 1941 to January 1944. Her entries continue to June 7, 1944. Vivid portrait of daily life under the siege, some glimpses of a two-career marriage and the life of the Soviet elite.

758 KIRK, LYDIA. *Postmarked Moscow*. Chicago: People's Book Club,
       1952. 278 pp.
Memoirs of the wife of the U.S. ambassador to Moscow from 1949 to 1951.

759 KRUPSKAIA, N. K. *Soviet Woman, A Citizen with Equal Rights: A
       Collection of Articles and Speeches*. Moscow: Co-Operative Publishing
       Society of Foreign Workers in the USSR, 1937. 76 pp.
Speeches from 1935 and 1936, with titles like "A Strong Soviet Family," "Woman—Friend, Comrade and Mother," and "The Wife—Her Soldier Husband's Friend and Comrade," showing the new emphasis on the family and women's maternal role.

760 McCLELLAN, IRINA. *Of Love and Russia: The Eleven-Year Fight for
       My Husband and Freedom*. Translated by Woodford McClellan. New
       York: W. W. Norton, 1989. 320 pp.
Autobiography of a Soviet, married to an American professor in 1974, and her struggle to leave the USSR, finally fulfilled in 1986.

761 MANDELSTAM, NADEZHDA. *Hope Against Hope: A Memoir*.
       Translated by Max Hayward. Introduction by Clarence Brown. New
       York: Atheneum, 1970. 531 pp. Index. Explanatory notes.
The title is a play on words (*Nadezhda* means hope in Russian). A remarkable memoir of the period 1934–38, from the author's husband Osip Mandelstam's arrest to his death. Extensive discussions of earlier periods. Wonderful portraits, ranging from revolutionary activists such as Larisa Reisner and Bukharin to literary icons such as close friend Anna Akhmatova. This memoir is devoted to M. (Osip Mandelstam). Author reveals much indirectly, little directly, about herself.

762 ———. *Hope Abandoned*. Translated by Max Hayward. New York:
       Atheneum, 1974. 687 pp. Index. Explanatory notes. Chronology.
Complements *Hope Against Hope* (entry 761), adding more biographical information and describing the author's life after the death of her husband. Fuller

portrait of Anna Akhmatova. Wide-ranging, brilliant portrait of the life of the intelligentsia from the Revolution through the 1960s.

763   MARKOVNA, NINA. *Nina's Journey: A Memoir of Stalin's Russia and the Second World War*. Washington, D.C.: Regnery Gateway, 1989. 400 pp.
The life and experiences of the author and her family in Dulovo, a town near Moscow.

764   MAYNARD, JOHN. *The Russian Peasant and Other Studies*. London: Victor Gollancz. 1942. 512 pp. Index.
Peasant women and their response to collectivization. Available in numerous other editions.

765   MOSS, KEVIN MURPHY. "Olga Mikhailovna Friedenberg: Soviet Mythologist in a Soviet Context." Ph.D. diss., Cornell University, 1984. 303 pp.
Biography of the first woman to receive a doctorate in literature in the USSR (1935), founder and first chair of the Department of Classical Philology at Leningrad State University from 1932 to 1951, distinguished linguist, and cousin of Boris Pasternak, with whom she had a long correspondence. Moss seeks to make visible Friedenberg's scholarly work. In the Soviet Union little has been written about her as a scholar; in the West this aspect of her life has been completely ignored. Compares Friedenberg's work with that of Levi-Strauss and Bakhtin; supports the view that she was a forerunner of semiotics in the structuralist and formalist tradition.

766   MOSSMAN, ELLIOT, ed. *The Correspondence of Boris Pasternak and Olga Friedenberg, 1910–1954*. Compiled and edited by Elliot Mossman. New York: Harcourt Brace Jovanovich, 1982. 365 pp. Index.
A wonderful source book, containing the correspondence between Pasternak and his cousin, a classical scholar (entry 722). The letters span the period from 1910 to Friedenberg's period from 1910 to 1955. A number of journal entries vividly describe Friedenberg's moods and chronicle the Leningrad Blockade, which Olga and her mother survived. The diary in particular shows a strong mother-daughter bond, uncomplicated by Freudian angst, as Friedenberg and her mother endure the hardships of the purges and war together. Many family photos included.

767   MULLANEY, MARIE MARMO. "The Female Revolutionary, the Woman Question and European Socialism, 1871–1921." Ph.D. diss., Rutgers University, 1980. 645 pp.
Discusses the intersection of gender and revolutionary activity in the cases of five women—Louise Michel, Eleanor Marx, Alexandra Kollontai, Rosa Luxemburg, and Angelica Balabanoff. Each is examined in an analytical biog-

raphy as an example of a general type within the socialist movement. Significant similarities are elucidated. Traditional male-defined theories of the revolutionary personality are critiqued.

768 NAYMAN, ANATOLY. *Remembering Anna Akhmatova*. Translated by Wendy Rosslyn. New York: John Macrae/Holt, 1991. 240 pp. Index. Chronology. Notes.
Anatoly Nayman was Akhmatova's literary secretary for the last five years of her life, from 1960 to 1965. Vivid portrait, aided by the author's ability to place the poet and her work into the larger context of Soviet culture and politics.

769 NUDEL, IDA. *A Hand in the Darkness: The Autobiography of a Refusenik*. Translated by Stefani Hoffman. New York: Warner Books, 1990. 314 pp. Index.
The life of the famed refusenik. Mostly devoted to her trial, prison, and camp experiences and her Siberian exile.

770 PETROVA, NATALIA. *Twice Born in Russia: My Life Before and in the Revolution*. Translated by Baroness Mary Budberg. Introduction by Dorothy Thompson. New York: William Morrow, 1930. 194 pp.
Memoirs of a gentrywoman caught up in war and Revolution.

771 POHL-WANNENMACHER, HELGA. *Red Spy at Night: A True Story of Espionage and Seduction behind the Iron Curtain*. Translated by Rena Wilson. London: New English Library, 1977. 176 pp.
A German woman from Polish Galicia becomes a KGB spy after marriage to a Soviet army officer and several years in the camps.

772 RADER, INGE ANTONIE. "Krupskaya: Pioneer Soviet Educator of the Masses." Ph.D. diss., Southern Illinois University, 1974. 227 pp.
Studies all aspects of Krupskaya's life and work as an educational theorist. Devotes attention to her early political activities and writings, including a section on the first Russian Marxist pamphlet about women, *The Woman Worker*. Assesses her impact on contemporary Soviet education. Notes Western ignorance about aspects of her work separate from Lenin.

773 RATUSHINSKAYA, IRINA. *Grey is the Color of Hope*. Translated by Alyona Kojevnikov. New York: Alfred A. Knopf, 1988. 355 pp. Epilogue.
Prison memoir. Poet and writer Ratushinskaya was sentenced in 1983 to seven years of hard labor and five years of internal exile for "anti-Soviet agitation and propaganda." Released in 1986 on the eve of the Gorbachev-Reagan Reykjavík summit, she now lives in the United States. Stark description of women's lives in the "strict regime" labor camp to which she was sentenced.

774   ROSENBERG, SUZANNE. *A Soviet Odyssey*. New York: Oxford
       University Press, 1988. 222 pp. Index.
The daughter of militant revolutionaries, the author returned with her mother
to the Soviet Union in 1931, was arrested in 1950, and was released in 1953.
Her mother and husband perished in the camps.

775   ROSENBERG, WILLIAM G. *Liberals in the Russian Revolution: The
       Constitutional Democratic Party, 1917–1921*. Princeton, N.J.: Princeton
       University Press, 1974. 534 pp. Index.
Brief information about Kadet feminists Ariadna Tyrkova and Anna Miliukova
and their postrevolutionary activities.

776   SCOTT, MARK CHAPIN. "Her Brother's Keeper: The Evolution of
       Women Bolsheviks." Ph.D. diss., University of Kansas, 1980. 396 pp.
A study of eighty-three Bolshevik women. Analysis of their early backgrounds,
their family relations, the formation of their views, "the radical political influence of formal education," their work or professions, the influence of Tolstoyan
ideas, the "going to the people" movement and terrorism, the women's revolutionary activity, government action against them, the women's participation in
the October Revolution and Civil War, and their postrevolutionary activity.

777   SHULMAN, ALIX KATES, ed. *Red Emma Speaks: Selected Writings
       and Speeches by Emma Goldman*. New York: Vintage Books, 1972. 413
       pp. Index.
Part 4, entitled "Two Revolutions and a Summary," includes the afterword to
My Disillusionment in Russia (entry 753) and a short preface by Alix Kates
Shulman.

778   TAUBMAN, JANE. *A Life through Poetry: Marina Tsvetaeva's Lyric
       Diary*. Columbus, Ohio: Slavica, 1989. 295 pp. Bibliography. Notes.
Careful investigation of the poet's life, with emphasis on her place in the literary circles of her time, her relations with other poets, and the evolution of her
work. The only biography of Tsvetaeva that incorporates the growing literature
by Western feminist scholars about women's lives.

779   TAVIS, ANNA. "Lives and Myths of Marina Tsvetaeva." *Slavic Review*
       47, no. 3 (Fall 1988): 518–21.
Review of Karlinsky (entry 357) and Feinstein (entry 346) biographies of the
poet. Criticizes Feinstein for misstatements of fact and interpretation.

780   VISHNEVSKAYA, GALINA. *Galina: A Russian Story*. New York:
       Harcourt Brace Jovanovich, 1984. 510 pp. Index.
Childhood in the 1930s, adolescence in the Leningrad blockade, the politics of
Soviet music, marriage to Rostropovich, encounters with a drunken Minister
of Culture Furtseva (the only woman in the Politburo under Khrushchev), and
exile.

781 VOZNESENSKAYA, JULIA, ed. and comp. *Letters of Love*. Translated by Roger and Angela Keys. London and New York: Quartet Books, 1989. 119 pp.
Letters to friends, relatives and lovers, illustrating the details of camp and exile life. Moving vignettes illustrating the women's struggles. There have been many books about male political prisoners; this is one of the few about women.

782 WILLIAMS, MASHA. *White among the Reds*. London: Shepheard Walwyn, 1980. 216 pp. Index.
The author was three years old when her family fled Russia in 1917. In 1945–46 she became an interpreter for the British in Vienna. She describes the change in her attitudes toward the Soviet military representatives, from negative to positive, as she worked with them.

783 WINTER, ELLA. *I Saw the Russian People*. Boston: Little, Brown, 1945. 309 pp. Index.
Eyewitness account of the Soviet Union in the concluding days of the war. Discusses Nazi German concentration camps, women partisans and soldiers, collective farms run by women, hero mothers, new divorce laws, and women in the Leningrad blockade. Contains many individual stories.

784 ———. *And Not to Yield*. New York: Harcourt, Brace & World, 1963. 308 pp. Index.
The author, part of the U.S. radical circle that included her husband, Lincoln Steffens, took three trips to the Soviet Union, in 1930, 1931, and 1944, and wrote two books about them, sympathetic to the Soviets. Here she recounts some of the stories behind the books, including visits to newly liberated Minsk and a German death camp in Estonia, a meeting with Ivy Litvinov, and Eleanor and Franklin Roosevelt's changing attitudes toward Stalin and the Soviet Union.

785 *Woman under Fire: Six Months in the Red Army. A Woman's Diary and Experiences of Revolutionary Russia*. Foreword by Reginald Dingle. London: Hutchinson, [1930]. 286 pp.
Diary of "Miss X," a soldier in the "Women's Proletarian Battalion." Before the October Revolution she trained for three weeks with Bochkareva's Women's Battalion. She mentions almost being among the defenders of the Winter Palace against the Bolsheviks. Dated from 10 June 1918 to 4 February 1919. The anonymous author, of English descent, emigrated to England in 1923 and became a successful writer. The second part of the book is a severely critical analysis of the Bolsheviks and the situation in the Soviet Union.

786 YOUNG, CATHY (EKATERINA JUNG). *Growing Up in Moscow: Memories of a Soviet Girlhood*. New York: Ticknor & Fields, 1989. 334 pp.
Detailed memoirs of life in the 1960s and 1970s. Good anecdotal information about the Soviet educational system and the author's budding feminist consciousness.

787   ZEPPER, JOHN THOMAS. *A Study of N. K. Krupskaya's Educational Philosophy*. Ed.D. diss., University of Missouri, Columbia, 1960. 300 pp. Devoted primarily to an analysis of Krupskaya's educational philosophy, including the influence of U.S. progressive educators and the practices of vocational education on the development of her ideas. Emphasizes the importance of Krupskaya as the leading Soviet pedagogue from 1920 to 1932. Primarily a translation of Krupskaya's *Public Education and Democracy*.

788   ZETKIN, KLARA. *Reminiscences of Lenin: Dealing with Lenin's Views on the Position of Women and Other Questions*. London: Modern Books, 1929. 78 pp. Reprint. New York: International Publishers, 1934. 64 pp. Reprint. *My Recollections of Lenin*. Moscow, 1956.
Lenin's criticism of the advocates of a new sexual morality, specifically the theory that sexual desire should be as easily satisfied as thirst is by drinking a glass of water. A critique of Kollontai, although her name is never mentioned.

Alexandra Kollontai

789   ANDERSON, THORNTON. *Masters of Russian Marxism*. New York: Appleton-Century-Crofts, 1963. 296 pp. Index.
Pages 163–89 devoted to Kollontai; a brief biographical sketch is followed by selections from her writings ("The New Woman" from *Novaia Moral'i Rabochii Klass* [Moscow, 1919] and "The Workers Opposition" from the pamphlet *The Workers Opposition in Russia* [Chicago]). Short bibliography at end of section.

790   BOBROFF, ANNE. "Alexandra Kollontai: Feminism, Workers' Democracy and Internationalism." *Radical America* 11, no. 6 (November–December 1979): 51–75.
Alexandra Kollontai became a heroine of the second wave of feminism in the West for the way in which she sought to combine socialism and feminism (while attacking the feminist movement at every turn). Bobroff's article describes and analyzes Kollontai's ideas from a leftist feminist perspective.

791   CLEMENTS, BARBARA EVANS. "Emancipation through Communism: The Ideology of A. M. Kollontai." *Slavic Review* 32, no. 2 (June 1973): 323–38.
Argues for more attention to Kollontai's significant place in early Soviet history and for more serious attention to her personality and ideology. Links her personal and political struggles and contrasts her ideas with those of Lenin.

792 ———. "Kollontai's Contribution to the Workers' Opposition Movement." *Russian History* 2, pt. 2 (1975): 191–206.
Clements views Kollontai's role within the Workers' Opposition movement as clarifying its message, defending its cause at Party meetings and congresses, and pleading its case within the Communist International. Nevertheless, she views Kollontai as "not an integral member" of the Workers' Opposition. Kollontai paid dearly for her outspoken principles. She lost her job as head of the *Zhenotdel* and began a series of foreign assignments that essentially exiled and silenced her.

793 ———. *Bolshevik Feminist: The Life of Aleksandra Kollontai.* Bloomington: Indiana University Press, 1979. 352 pp. Index. Bibliography. Notes.
Thoroughly researched biography. Includes material from Western archives and from a series of interviews with Kollontai's Swedish friends. Not surprisingly, the bulk of the book concerns Kollontai's political activity from the late 1890s to 1924, when she was exiled to a series of diplomatic posts abroad. Straightforward presentation of Kollontai's political development, her battles with the feminists and with Bolshevik antifeminists, her stint as commissar of Social Welfare, the *Zhenotdel*, her involvement with the Workers' Opposition, and her 1920s literary works. Complements Farnsworth's biography of Kollontai (entry 796).

794 De PALENCIA, ISABEL. *Alexandra Kollontay, Ambassadress from Russia.* New York: Longmans Green, 1947. 309 pp.
The first biography in English of Kollontai. Written by the former Spanish Ambassador to Sweden, a close friend of Kollontai during their diplomatic stints together.

795 FARNSWORTH, BEATRICE BRODSKY. "Bolshevism, the Woman Question, and Aleksandra Kollontai." *American Historical Review* 81, no. 2 (April 1976): 292–316.
History of Kollontai's advocacy of the woman question, her relationship to the "bourgeois" feminists, and Bolshevik women's liberation debates in the 1920s. Argues that Kollontai abandoned her public struggle and submitted to Stalin, and thus contributed to creatng the myth of the liberation of Soviet women. See Farnsworth's biography of Kollontai (entry 796) for a fuller development of these ideas.

796 ———. *Aleksandra Kollontai: Socialism, Feminism and the Bolshevik Revolution.* Stanford, Calif.: Stanford University Press, 1980. 432 pp. Index. Bibliography. Notes.
Covers much the same ground as Clements (entry 793). Also well-researched and well-written. The two biographies complement each other and should be read together for the best available portrait of Kollontai to date.

797 HAUGE, KAARE. "Alexandra Mikhailova Kollontai: The Scandinavian Period, 1922–1945." Ph.D. diss., University of Minnesota, 1971.
The most extensive treatment of Kollontai's diplomatic career, not given much attention in the published biographies of her. Thorough research, with much information gathered in Scandinavia.

798 INGEMANSON, BIRGITTA. "The Political Function of Domestic Objects in the Fiction of Alexandra Kollontai." *Slavic Review* 48, no. 1 (Spring 1989): 71–82.
Seeks to focus more attention on Kollontai's stories, virtually ignored by her biographers. Views her stories as less about the struggle between the sexes than about the struggle between dying capitalism and emerging socialism. Explores the use of objects to symbolize the ongoing conflict between the haves (mostly male) and the have-nots (mostly female). Argues that Kollontai's fiction writing was her way of airing her opposition views without being purged.

799 KOLLONTAI, ALEXANDRA. *A Great Love*. Translated by Lily Lore. New York: Vanguard, 1929. 243 pp.
Contains the stories "Sisters" and "The Love of Three Generations."

800 ———. "The First Benefit." In *The October Storm and After: Stories and Reminiscences*, pp. 37–41. Moscow: Progress, 1967.
An excerpt from Kollontai's reminiscences about her first days as minister of Social Security. The first benefit went to a peasant for his horse, requisitioned by the tsarist government.

801 ———. *Sexual Relations and the Class Struggle. Love and the New Morality*. Translated and introduced by Alix Holt. Bristol, England: Falling Wall Press, 1972. 26 pp.
English translations of two of three essays published in 1919 as *The New Morality and the Working Class*. Helpful introduction by Alix Holt provides historical background for these works. First essay critical of bourgeois sexual morality; calls for its replacement by a proletarian morality. Second essay a review of *The Sexual Crisis* by Grete Meisel-Hess. Concludes by lauding the emergence of a new type of women, the "'bachelor-woman,' for whom love is not the only thing in life" (p. 26).

802 ———. *Women Workers Struggle For Their Rights*. Translated by Celia Britton. Introduction and notes by Sheila Rowbotham and Suzie Fleming. Bristol, England: Falling Wall Press, 1973. 35 pp.
Translation of Kollontai's 1918 pamphlet, discussing socialist women workers' movements in Europe and the United States, and the various forms that women workers' organizations have taken in the West. Introduction by Sheila Rowbotham provides biographical information and places Kollontai's work in

the general context of the development of women's liberation ideas in the twentieth century.

803   ———. *The Autobiography of a Sexually Emancipated Communist Woman*. Edited with an afterword by Iring Fetscher. Translated by Salvador Attanasio. Foreword by Germaine Greer. New York: Schocken Books, 1975. 137 pp.
The only English translation of Kollontai's autobiography. Includes (in italics) parts deleted before publication and omitted from Soviet versions of the autobiography.

804   ———. *Love of Worker Bees*. Translated and introduced by Cathy Porter. Afterword by Sheila Rowbotham. London: Virago, 1977; Chicago: Academy Chicago, 1978. 232 pp.
Also published under the titles *Red Love* and *Free Love*. This collection of a novel and two short stories places its characters in the revolutionary upheavals of 1917 and after. Vasilisa Malygina, the revolutionary idealist protagonist of the novel, falls in love with Vladimir, an anarchist who ultimately betrays her.

805   ———. *Selected Writings*. Translated with an introduction and commentaries by Alix Holt. London: Allison and Busby, 1977. 335 pp. Index. Chronology. Bibliography.
An excellent representative sample of Kollontai's political writing, with a very helpful biographical survey and introduction by Alix Holt (Elizabeth Waters). Sections cover such topics as social democracy and the woman question, exile and war, the Revolution, women and the Revolution, crisis in the Party, morality and the New Society, and diplomatic duties. Excerpts from Kollontai's novels and short stories are not included. Vivid portrayal of the personal and political conflicts between managers and workers under the New Economic Policy, as well as the difficulties of living as an independent, sexually active woman. Helpful chronology and bibliography.

806   ———. *A Great Love*. Translated and introduced by Cathy Porter. London: Virago, 1981. New York: Norton, 1981. 156 pp.
New translation of Kollontai's classic work, written in 1922 in Oslo. This collection consists of three stories: "A Great Love" (the longest and most important), "Thirty-Two Pages," and "Conversation Piece." In all three, the theme is the clash between the new sexual morality and the old. The stories are set in the post-1905 period of tsarist reaction among a group of revolutionaries in exile in France. In her introduction Cathy Porter notes the characters' similarity to Lenin, Krupskaia, Armand, and Maslov, a married Russian economist with whom Kollontai had a brief affair. Porter favors the view that Armand and Lenin were lovers and profers evidence to support that view in the introduction. She argues that Kollontai probably knew of the affair and modeled the characters Senya, Anyuta, and Natasha in the title story after Lenin, Krupskaia, and Armand, respectively.

807 ———. *Communism and the Family*. San Francisco: *Richmond Record*,
19__. 21 pp. Reprint. London: Socialist Workers Party, 1984. 16 pp.
A cogent statement of Kollontai's theory of the withering away of the old style
family as many of its functions, including the upbringing of children, are taken
over by the state, and as children become "the common possession of all the
workers."

808 ———. *Selected Articles and Speeches*. Translated by Cynthia Carlile.
Moscow: Progress; New York: International Publishers, 1984. 215 pp.
Collection includes the introduction to the book *The Social Basis of the Woman
Question* (1908),the pamphlet *On the History of the Movement of Women Workers
in Russia*, and various articles and speeches, almost entirely from the period
1908–19. Exceptions are an abridged version of the 1921 pamphlet *The
Woman Worker and Peasant in Soviet Russia*, the 1927 article "What Has the
October Revolution Done for Women in the West?", a 1946 paean to Soviet-
style women's emancipation, and a short reminiscence about Lenin. Six pages
of photographs.

809 PORTER, CATHY. *Alexandra Kollontai: The Lonely Struggle of the
Woman Who Defied Lenin*. New York: Dial, 1980. 553 pp. Index.
Bibliography. Notes.
Similar in scope to the Clements (entry 793) and Farnsworth (entry 796)
biographies. Reviewers have generally viewed Porter's effort as less successful.

810 STITES, RICHARD. "Alexandra Kollontai and the Russian
Revolution." In *European Women on the Left*, edited by Jane Slaughter
and Robert Kern, pp. 101–23. Westport, Conn.: Greenwood, 1981.
An excellent short survey of Kollontai's life and political activity through the
mid-1920s. Stites provides a clear explication of the major themes of
Kollontai's writings and activism.

FICTION, POETRY, AND LITERARY CRITICISM

811 AKHMATOVA, ANNA, MARINA TSVETAYEVA, and BELLA
AKHMADULINA. *Three Russian Women Poets: Anna Akhmatova,
Marina Tsvetayeva, Bella Akhmadulina*. Edited and translated by Mary
Maddock. Introduction by Edward J. Brown. Trumansburg, N.Y.:
Crossing Press, 1983. 109 pp. Notes.
Selected poems, with a two-page introduction by Brown. (Note: Additional
collections of Akhmatova's poetry are listed under Reform, Reaction, and
Revolutions: Fiction, Poetry, and Literary Criticism, entries 434–42.)

812 AKSYONOV, VASILY, VIKTOR YEROFEYEV, FAZIL ISKAN-
DER, ANDREI BITOV, and YEVGENY POPOV, eds. *Metropole,
Literary Almanac*. Foreword by Kevin Klose. New York: W. W.
Norton, 1982. 636 pp.
This celebrated pre-*glasnost* (1979) challenge to Soviet censorship contains the
short story "The Many Dogs and the Dog" by Bella Akhmadulina and poems
by Inna Lisnyanskaya ("On St. Vladimir's Day," "Of Fire and Wood," "Time
and I . . .," "Above the Sanitorium Section," "In Gegard," "The Blind Man,"
and one untitled poem).

813 AMERT, SUSAN. *In a Shattered Mirror: The Later Poetry of Anna
Akhmatova*. Stanford: Stanford University Press, 1992. 274 pp. Index.
Bibliography. Notes.
An analysis of Akhmatova's post-1935 poems, which, the author argues, have
been relatively ignored by critics. Focuses on "Requiem," "Poem without a
Hero," "The Sweetbrier Blooms," and the "Northern Elegies." Argues that for
Akhmatova poetry represented the sole refuge against twentieth-century "dis-
placement and homelessness." Extensive, helpful notes.

814 BALABANOFF, ANGELICA. *Tears*. New York: E. Laub, 1943. 157
pp. Index of Poems by Language.
Poems in French, Italian, German, English, and Russian by this prominent revolutionary, about human grief, but nevertheless optimistic in terms of the
Socialist vision of a new world.

815 BARANSKAYA, NATALYA. *A Week Like Any Other: Novellas and
Stories*. Translated by Pieta Monks. Seattle: Seal Press, 1990. 231 pp.
Baranskaya, born in 1908, first began writing after her retirement at age 58.
The title story in this collection is a classic description of the double burden: a
research scientist balances the demands of job, husband, and children, with little support from her mate, who suggests that she give up her paid work to stay
at home. First published in 1969, this story remains very timely. Other stories
in this collection focus mostly on women grappling with the particulars of
Soviet life (e.g., women on trial in a housing-complex comrades' court for
unruly behavior) or on universal problems (e.g., a girl torn between her
divorced mother and father). "The Petunin Affair" portrays a man caught in a
power struggle with an ambitious but blundering boss, a theme certainly not
unique to the Soviet work world.

816 BARKER, ADELE. "Irina Grekova's 'Na Ispytaniiakh': The History of
One Story." *Slavic Review* 48, no. 3 (Fall 1989): 399–412.
Compares the 1967 and 1986 published versions of this story by one of the
foremost contemporary Soviet female writers. The publication of the story,
about a Soviet army unit on manoeuvers in the summer of 1952, forced

Grekova's resignation as a mathematics professor at the war college where she worked. Although Grekova rejects the label "woman writer," her story was criticized after its first publication as typical *damskaia proza* (woman's prose). In fact, as she wrote in 1987 in *Moscow News*, her real sin was to be "honest in showing the daily life of the men on maneuvers without the usual varnish."

817   BERBEROVA, NINA. *Three Novels.* Translated by Marian Schwartz. 2 vols. London: Chatto and Windus, 1990 and 1991. Vol. 1., 215 pp.; vol. 2, 195 pp.
Volume one contains three short novels, *The Resurrection of Mozart, The Waiter and the Slut*, and *Astashev in Paris.* Volume two contains three more, *The Cloak, The Black Pestilence*, and *The Comb.*

818   BLAKE, PATRICIA, and MAX HAYWARD, eds. *Half-Way to the Moon: New Writing from Russia.* New York: Holt, Rinehart & Winston, 1964. 276 pp.
Patricia Blake helped lead the way in making post-Stalin poetry and writing known in the West. This volume contains a translation of Bella Akhmadulina's poem "Volcanoes" by W. H. Auden.

819   BLUM, JAKUB, and VERA RICH. *The Image of the Jew in Soviet Literature. Part I: Soviet Russian Literature. Part II: Jewish Themes and Characters in Belorussian Texts.* New York: Ktav, 1984. 276 pp. Index.
Attention devoted to such writers as Nadezhda Mandelshtam. Vera Rich has an interesting chapter on the portrayal of romances between Jewish women (*Emancipatki*) and Christian men in Soviet Belorussian novels

820   BOYM, SVETLANA. "Life and Death in Quotation Marks: Cultural Myth of the Modern Poet." Ph.D. diss., Harvard University, 1988. 451 pp.
Last chapter addresses "the myth of the poetess—a grotesque mask of literary femininity." Discusses Tsvetaeva, her suicide, and other female poets.

821   CHUDAKOVA, MARIETTA. "Life Space." In *World's Spring*, edited by Vladimir Gakov and translated by Roger Degaris, pp. 226–36. New York: Macmillan, 1981.
It is very rare to find Soviet women writing science fiction, and even rarer to find their stories translated into English.

822   CHUKOVSKAYA, LYDIA. *Sofia Petrovna.* Translated by Aline B. Werth. Revised and amended by Eliza Kellogg Klose. Evanston, Ill.: Northwestern University Press, 1988. 120 pp.
Olga Petrovna (in other versions Sofia Petrovna), a typist in a large Leningrad publishing house at the end of the 1930s, gets caught up in the purges. Her son is arrested, friends fired from their jobs, arrested or deported. She is

denounced and forced out of her job. Although written in the winter of 1939–40, with the memory of the 1937–38 purges still fresh, the Russian edition of this novel was first published in France in the 1960s. Originally published in English as *The Deserted House*.

823 CLOWES, EDITH W. "Characterization in Doktor Zivago: Lara and Tonja." *Slavic and East European Journal* 34, no. 3 (1990): 322–31.
Likens the two female characters to classical and Russian national epic heroines. Considers the application of New Testament archetypes as an added explanation of the author's character development.

824 DUNHAM, VERA. *In Stalin's Time: Middleclass Values in Soviet Fiction*. Introduction by Jerry Hough. Cambridge: Cambridge University Press, 1976. 283 pp. Index. Enlarged and updated edition, with new introduction by Richard Sheldon. Durham: Duke University Press, 1990. 288 pp. Index. Bibliography. Notes.
Postulates a "Big Deal" between the growing managerial class and the Stalinist regime, which provides a more convincing explanation for the survival, and even the popularity, of Stalin than coercion alone. In chapter 13 ("Women's Liberation Confused"), Dunham argues that after the war the Stalinist government retreated from full support for women's equality, and "it was women who had to make the adjustment." A key work in understanding the Stalinist period. Sheldon's introduction incorporates information about the period 1976–89; updated edition also includes a five-page postscript by Dunham.

825 FEINSTEIN, ELAINE, ed. and trans. *Three Russian Poets: Margarita Aliger, Yunna Moritz, Bella Akhmadulina*. Manchester, England: Carcanet, 1979. 80 pp.
Excerpts from the works of three prominent women poets of the late Soviet period.

826 GANINA, MAYA. *The Road to Nirvana*. Translated by Olga Shartse. Moscow: Progress, 1971. 344 pp.
Nine stories ("Nastya's Children," "Music," "I Wish I Had Not Met Him," "Stupid Fool," "Why Did They Chop Down the Chestnut Trees?," "All about Lyoshka," "The Love of a Great Man," "The Road to Nirvana," and "Islands") by a leading Soviet woman writer. Themes include a narcissistic father reassessing his priorities and choosing to keep his children after his wife dies, and an old man making a pilgrimage to the area where his son died.

827 GASIOROWSKA, XENIA. *Women in Soviet Fiction, 1917–1964*. Madison: University of Wisconsin Press, 1968. 288 pp. Index.
The only work of this scope to be attempted by a Western scholar. Excellent survey assessing the portrayal of peasants, workers, the intelligentsia, and "Amazons." Needs a sequel that covers literature after 1964.

828   GINZBURG, EUGENIA SEMYONOVNA. *Journey into the Whirlwind*. Translated by Paul Stevenson and Max Hayward. New York: Harcourt Brace Jovanovich, 1975. 418 pp.

One of the best memoirs of those who were swept up in the purges of the 1930s. Ginzburg, a teacher and ardent Communist, mother of two and wife of a high-ranking official, documents eloquently the events that took her from the classroom to the camps. Ginzburg provides a telling glimpse into the lives of the pre-purges Party elite, whose children judged their parents' status by their cars (Lincolns and Buicks highest, then Fords). She describes the various techniques of survival she learned at the bleakest of moments in the camps, and the people without whose help she would not have lived. (Ginzburg is the mother of the novelist Vasilii Aksyonov.)

829   GLADKOV, FEDOR. *Cement*. Translated by A. S. Arthur and C. Ashleigh. Afterword by Edward Vavra. New York: Frederick Ungar, 1980. 325 pp.

Classic 1920s novel about postrevolutionary social relations. While Gleb has been away fighting in the Civil War, his wife Dasha has been transformed by Bolshevik ideas of women's liberation. She abandons her former housewifely role, puts their daughter in a children's home (where she soon dies), and becomes head of the local *Zhenotdel* (Women's Section). The birth of the new woman is a key Soviet propaganda theme; this is one of the first works of fiction to address it.

830   GOSCILO, HELENA, ed. and trans. *Russian and Polish Women's Fiction*. Knoxville: University of Tennessee Press, 1985. 343 pp. Bibliography.

Selections by Russian writers include "Rank and Money" by Evdokia Rostopchina, "The Little Mermaid Rotozeyechka" and "Ham's Wife" by Olga Forsh, "Evdokia" by Vera Panova, and "A Ladle for Pure Water" by Inna Varlamova. Goscilo provides an introduction to the collection and a short literary-biographical background essay about each author and selection.

831   ———. "Tatiana Tolstaia's 'Dome of Many-Coloured Glass': The World Refracted through Multiple Perspectives." *Slavic Review* 47, no. 2 (Summer 1988): 280–90.

First of several articles to bring Tolstaia (the granddaughter of the writers Natal'ia Krandievskaia-Tolstaia and Aleksei Nikolaevich Tolstoi) to the attention of Western scholars and to discuss her work. Goscilo calls this Soviet writer "the most noteworthy prosaist of the young generation at large."

832   ———, ed. *Balancing Acts: Contemporary Stories by Russian Women*. Bloomington: Indiana University Press, 1989. 337 pp. Biographical notes.

Translations of work by sixteen contemporary Soviet women writers, with a preface and a very helpful introduction that places the writers in both historical and comparative Russian literary contexts. Goscilo considers women's literature to have produced "some of the most stimulating literary criticism and theory published in the last two decades." She criticizes Slavists, who as a whole "remain largely ignorant of or indifferent to both feminist criticism and fiction authored by Russian and other Slavic women." The translations are of high quality, and there are extensive explanatory footnotes. Writers included are Natalya Baranskaia, Tatiana Tolstaia, Elena Makarova, Anna Mass, Viktoria Tokareva, Liudmila Uvarova, Galina Shcherbakova, Liudmila Petrushevskaia, Irina Velembovskaia, Nina Katerli, Rimma Kazakova, Nadezhda Kozhernikova, Maia Ganina, and Inna Varlamova. A significant contribution to the field.

833   GRAY, FRANCINE DU PLESSIX. "The Russian Heroine: Gender, Sexuality and Freedom." In *Perestroika and Soviet Culture*, edited by Jane Burbank and William G. Rosenberg, pp. 699–718. *Michigan Quarterly Review* 28, no. 4 (Fall 1989).

This reprinted lecture is a pastiche of borrowed ideas and various inaccuracies that undermine any claim to expertise. One more demonstration that women's studies is still no more than an afterthought to many mainstream scholars.

834   GREENE, DIANA. "An Asteroid of One's Own: Women Soviet Science Fiction Writers." *Irish Slavonic Studies* 8 (1987): 127–39.

Comparisons between U.S. and Soviet versions of the genre. Analysis of the works of Ariadna Gromova, Valentina Zhuravlyova, and Ol'ga Larionova. Greene finds their work misogynistic and of poor quality. In contrast, she considers U.S. women science-fiction writers to be among the most innovative.

835   GREKOVA, I. *Russian Women: Two Stories*. Translated by Michel Petrov. New York: Harcourt Brace Jovanovich, 1983. 304 pp.

I. Grekova (literally translated, Ms. X) is the pseudonym of Elena Ventsel, a mathematician born in 1907 who began her writing career at age fifty, after having attained the rank of full professor. The two stories translated here are "Ladies' Hairdresser" (first published in *Novyi Mir* in 1963) and "The Hotel Manager" (1976). The first describes the budding friendship between the director of a Moscow computer institute and her hairdresser. Plavnikov, the hairdresser, is a genuine working-class hero whose life reflects some of the ravages and dislocations of the postwar generation. The character of the director, Kovaleva, reflects the dilemmas of many Soviet career women. A single parent, her time is "completely shredded" between the demands of work, her two spoiled sons, and her one passion, solving mathematical problems. "The Hotel Manager" chronicles the life of Vera Butova, from prerevolutionary poverty to life in the Soviet system as the doting wife of an officer to a successful career in widowhood as a hotel manager. Bonds between the women characters are vividly portrayed.

836   ———. *The Ship of Widows*. Translated and introduced by Cathy Porter. London: Virago, 1985. 179 pp.
Here Grekova tells the tale of five women living together in a communal apartment after World War II. They are typical of many women of that period—independent, often alone or struggling with men shattered by the war experience. Excellent for insight into Soviet women's experience during and after World War II. Helpful introduction by Cathy Porter. Wonderful portrait of Soviet women of this generation.

837   HELDT, BARBARA. "Men Who Give Birth: A Feminist Perspective on Russian Literature." In *Discontinuous Discourses in Modern Russian Literature*, edited by Catriona Kelly, Michael Makin, and David Sheperd, pp. 157–67. Houndmills, Basingstoke, Hampshire, England: Macmillan, 1989.
See entry 459.

838   HOLMGREN, BETH. *Women's Voices in Stalin's Time: The Works of Lydia Chukovskaia and Nadezhda Mandelstam*. Bloomington: Indiana University Press, 1993. Index. Bibliography. Notes.
Holmgren surveys the roles of women in developing and maintaining unofficial Russian literature during the Stalinist years by specific examination of the works of Lydia Chukovskaia and Nadezhda Mandelstam. Their works are seen as reflecting and facilitating significant roles for women in post-Stalin dissident circles.

839   INBER, VERA. "The Crime of Nor Bibi." In *The October Storm and After: Stories and Reminiscences*, pp. 139–68. Moscow: Progress, 1967.
Vivid story about the emancipation of one Uzbek woman.

840   KAPP, YVONNE, ed. *Short Stories of Russia Today*. Translated by Tatiana Shevunina. Boston: Houghton Mifflin; Cambridge: Riverside, 1959. 250 pp.
Includes two stories, "Nor-Bibi's Crime" and "Spring Cleaning," both by Vera Inber, the latter about life in Leningrad during the war. Also contains "Bondage" by Varvara Kartsovskaya. Short biographies of the authors.

841   KARLINSKY, SIMON, and ALFRED APPEL, JR. *The Bitter Air of Exile: Russian Writers in the West, 1922–1972*. Berkeley: University of California Press, 1977. 473 pp.
Includes Tsvetaeva's "Psyche" and "To Mayakovsky," an untitled poem, her essay "A Poet on Criticism," and a letter to Anna Teskova, as well as an essay by D. S. Mirsky on the poet. Also includes an excerpt from Galina Kuznetsova's *Grasse Diary*, including a short description of Gippius; Edythe Haber on Nadezhda Teffi and Teffi's "Time"; and Olga Hughes on Alla Ktorova and Ktorova's "The Face of Firebird."

842   KAY, SUSAN. "A Woman's Work." *Irish Slavonic Studies* 8 (1987): 115–26.
An analysis of the female characters in Natalya Baranskaya's works.

843   KWON, CHOL-KUN. "Siberian Mythology, Folklore, and Tradition in Valentin Rasputin's Novellas." Ph.D. diss., University of Kansas, 1986. 220 pp.
Focuses on the role of Siberian mythology, folklore, and tradition in Rasputin's longer works. Argues that this blending of traditional Russian and Asiatic elements cannot be understood by sole reference to the European context. Devotes chapters to the role of old women (*starukhi*) and to family relationships.

844   LANGLAND, JOSEPH, TAMAS ACZEL, and LASZLO TIKOS. *Poetry from the Russian Underground: A Bilingual Anthology.* New York: Harper & Row, 1973. 249 pp. Notes.
This anthology contains English and Russian versions of poems on facing pages. Includes poems by Bella Akhmadulina ("Conjuration," "I Swear," and "Bartholemew Night"), Muza Pavlova ("Friend"), Aida Yaskolka ("Variations about Myself"), and Anna Akhmatova ("Requiem: A Cycle of Poems").

845   LEDKOVSKY, MARINA, ed. *Russia According to Women. Literary Anthology.* Tenafly, N.J.: Hermitage, 1991. 175 pp. Biographical Notes.
Excerpts from writings by women during the Soviet period, save for Anna Akhmatova's "Memories of A. Blok," brief reminiscences mostly spanning the years 1913–1919. Also includes Marina Tsvetaeva, "My Jobs"; Evgenia Ginzburg, "Don't Cry in Front of Them"; I. Grekova, "Under the Street Lamp"; Natalia Baranskaia, "The Retirement Party"; Marina Rachko, "North of Russia"; Nadezhda Mandelshtam, "Memoirs"; Ruth Zernova, "Why Now?"; Lidia Chukovskaia, "Memories of Anna Akhmatova"; Ludmila Shtern, "Ineradicable"; Tatiana Nikolaeva, "Leningrad-Tbilisi"; Bella Akhmadulina, "The Many Dogs and the Dog"; and Irina Ratushinskaya, "The Little Gray Book" and "The Misunderstanding." Several different translators lent their talents to this evocative anthology primarily portraying the tragedies and triumphs of intelligentsia women.

846   LUKE, LOUISE. "Marxian Women: Soviet Variants." In *Through the Glass of Soviet Literature*, edited by Ernest J. Simmons, pp. 27–109. New York: Columbia University Press, 1953.
Examines the portrayal of women in Soviet literature as a barometer of changes in attitudes and official policy in relation to the woman question, beginning with Kollontai's "Love of Three Generations" and continuing in novels of the twenties and early thirties that were preoccupied with sex and attacked the old "bourgeois" morality of monogamous marriage and devotion to family. With the First Five-Year Plan, attention shifted to positive role models for women in the work force and to the "unity of the personal and social." In 1936 policy

shifts reemphasized woman's maternal role, and writers followed suit. Covers literature through end of Stalin's rule.

847   McLAUGHLIN, SIGRID. *The Image of Women in Contemporary Stories from the USSR*. Edited and translated by Sigrid McLaughlin. New York: St. Martin's, 1989. 247 pp. Glossary.
Stories from 1965 to 1986. Included in this anthology are I. Grekova's "A Summer in the City," Yury Trifonov's "Vera and Zoyka," Valentin Rasputin's "Vasily and Vasilissa," Lyudmila Petrushevskaya's "Nets and Traps," Natalya Baranskaya's "The Spell," Irina Raksha's "Lambushki," Vasily Belov's "Morning Meetings," Anatoly Kim's "Cage with a Color TV," Viktoriya Tokareva's "The Happiest Day of My Life" and "Between Heaven and Earth," Valentina Sidorenko's "Marka," Tatyana Tolstaya's "Dear Shura," and Sergei Zalygin's "Women and the NTR." Introduction puts the stories in context and provides McLaughlin's interpretations.

848   MAKIN, MICHAEL. "Text and Violence in Tsvetaeva's 'Molodets.'" In *Discontinuous Discourses in Modern Russian Literature*, edited by Catriona Kelly, Michael Makin, and David Sheperd, pp. 115–35. Houndmills, Basingstoke, Hampshire, England: Macmillan, 1989.
Examination of this poem (1922), relatively ignored by the critics.

849   MARSH, ROSALIND J. *Soviet Fiction since Stalin: Science, Politics and Literature*. London: Croom Helm, 1986. 338 pp. Index. Bibliography.
Very brief but suggestive treatment of the portrayal of Soviet women of science in the literature of the late 1960s and 1970s. Apparently, the only discussion of this subject in English.

850   MOROZOVA, VERA. *The Red Carnation: Stories*. Translated by Inna Medova. Moscow: Progress, 1981. 231 pp. Notes.
Translation of Morozova's *Zhenshchiny revoliutsii* (Women of the revolution)— stories about revolutionary activists Maria Golubeva, Klavdia Kirsanova, Ludmila Stahl, and Tatiana Liudvinskaia based on the author's archival research and interviews. Targeted for young as well as adult readers.

851   PACHMUSS, TEMIRA, ed. and trans. *A Russian Cultural Revival: A Critical Anthology of Émigré Literature Before 1939*. Knoxville: University of Tennessee Press, 1981. 454 pp. Index.
Contains the following works by émigré women writers: Zinaida Gippius's poems "Rain," "The Frog," "Moderation," "Never Read Poems Aloud," "Perhaps," and "The Ancient, the Old, and the Young," and her short stories "Outside of Time: An Etude" and "They Are Alike"; Marina Tsvetaeva's poems "My Regards to the Russian Rye," "The Taper," and "The Knight on the Bridge," and excerpts from her childhood reminiscence "My Pushkin";

excerpts from Nadezhda Teffi's "A Modest Talent" and "Diamond Dust," and her story "Talent"; Irina Saburova's short story, "Because of the Violets"; excerpts from Irina Odoevtseva's collections "Solitude," "The Golden Chain," and "My Portrait in a Rhymed Frame"; excerpts from Lidiya Chervinskaya's poems "Dawns," "Twelve Months," and several untitled poems; excerpts from Anna Prismanova's poems "Salt," "The Sisters," "Poison," and "The Smith"; and Tamara Velichkovskaya's poems "The White Staff" and "*Vozrozhdenie*." Biographical notes on each author, with a list of all their published works.

852   PANOVA, VERA. "Three Boys at the Gate." In *The October Storm and After: Stories and Reminiscences*, pp. 346–58. Moscow: Progress, 1967.
Socialist realist story in which three boys learn about their revolutionary heritage in Leningrad.

853   PARNOK, SOPHIA. "Eight Poems." Translated by Rima Shore. *Conditions* 6 (1980): 171–75.
See entry 477.

854   PEREVEDENTSEV, V. I. "Women in a Changing World." In *Soviet Studies in Literature* 25, no. 4 (Fall 1989): 48–86.
The title is a misnomer. In fact, Perevedentsev analyzes (from a distinctly male point of view) the women characters depicted by village prose writers Fedor Abramov and Sergei Zalygin, whose works encompass both peasants and urban dwellers. (In the sixties and seventies Perevedentsev proposed paying women to stay home and rear children to solve the demographic crisis.)

855   PETRUSHEVSKAYA, LYUDMILA. "Our Crowd." In *Glasnost: An Anthology of Literature Under Gorbachev*, edited by Helena Goscilo and Byron Lindsey, pp. 3–24. Ann Arbor, Mich.: Ardis, 1990.
Petrushevskaya, known for her plays, here writes a short story with a surprise ending, narrated by a woman, that shows a slice of Soviet domestic life. A leading Russian writer and playwright, Petrushevskaya has had very few of her works translated into English.

856   PROFFER, CARL R., and ELLENDEA PROFFER, eds. *The Barsukov Triangle, The Two-Toned Blond and Other Stories*. Ann Arbor, Mich.: Ardis, 1984. 370 pp.
This anthology of Soviet writing from the 1960s to the 1980s contains stories by Nina Katerli ("The Barsukov Triangle"), Inna Varlamova ("A Ladle for Pure Water"), Natalya Baranskaya ("The Retirement Party"), and I. Grekova ("One Summer in the City").

857	RATUSHINSKAYA, IRINA. *Beyond the Limit*. Translated by Frances Padorr Brent and Carol J. Avins. Evanston, Ill.: Northwestern University Press, 1987. 121 pp. Chronology. Notes.
English and Russian edition of forty-seven poems, mostly written in labor camps and prisons. Helpful chronology and notes.

858	———. *Pencil Letter*. London: Bloodaxe Books, 1988. 89 pp. Chronology.
Translations of eighty-nine poems by this dissident, imprisoned in 1983 for the crime of writing poetry and released in 1986 on the eve of the Reykjavík summit.

859	RICH, ELIZABETH TRACY. "Women in the Prose of Valentin Rasputin." Ph.D. diss., University of Michigan, 1985. 166 pp.
Analyzes the significance of the role of women, especially old women, in Rasputin's work. His female characters often symbolize the preservation of traditional peasant cultural and moral values. Examines the author's early characters, as well as Nastyona in *Zhivi i pomni*, Anna in *Poslednyi srok*, and Darya in *Proshchanie s materoi*.

860	RUTHCHILD, ROCHELLE. "Tatiana Shcherbina: A poet's life in the Soviet Union." Translated by Roberta Reeder and Raisa Shapira. *Women's Review of Books* 7, nos. 10–11 (July 1990): 8–9.
Interview with one of the most prominent and well-regarded of the glasnost generation of women poets. Views about women, feminists, and the role of poets by a member of the post-Stalin generation, born and educated in Moscow.

861	SANDLER, STEPHANIE, "Embodied Words: Gender in Cvetaeva's Reading of Puskin." *Slavic and East European Journal* 34, no. 2 (1990): 139–57.
Seeks to reclaim the importance of gender in Tsvetaeva's work in general, and specifically in her Pushkin texts, from 1929 to 1937. Argues that Tsvetaeva critiqued the cult of Pushkin but nevertheless identified with him. Striking sensitivity to the clash between Tsvetaeva's desire to write and the female social roles she had to fulfill. Helpful list of books.

862	———. "Sex, Death and Nation in the *Strolls with Pushkin* Controversy." *Slavic Review* 51, no. 2 (Summer 1992): 294–308.
An analysis of and defense of Andrei Siniavskii's 1975 essay, *Strolls with Pushkin*, against attacks by conservative critics, especially Solzhenitsyn. Sandler views Siniavskii as challenging traditional sexual imagery and gender roles, and Solzhenitsyn as part of that group which links "patriotic nationalism and conservative views about gender."

863   *Soviet Women Writing: Fifteen Short Stories*. Introduction by I. Grekova. New York: Abbeville Press, 1990. 351 pp. Biographical notes.
Stories published between 1972 and 1990, including Zoya Boguslavskaya, "What Are Women Made of?"; Lidia Ginzburg, "The Siege of Leningrad: Notes of a Survivor"; Tatyana Tolstaya, "Sleepwalker in a Fog"; I. Grekova, "Masters of Their Own Lives"; Nina Katerli, "The Monster"; Tatyana Nabatnikova, "In Memoriam"; Galina Kornilova, "The Ostrabramsky Gate"; Natalia Ilina, "Repairing Our Car"; Viktoria Tokareva, "Five Figures on a Pedestal"; Mari Saat, "The Cave"; Irina Polyanskaya, "Mitigating Circumstances"; Lyudmila Petrushevskaya, "The Overlook"; Inna Goff, "Infirmary at the Station"; Larisa Vaneeva, "Parade of the Planets"; and Vytaute Zilinskaite, "Sisyphus and the Woman."

864   SUMERKIN, ALEXANDER, ed. *Free Voices in Russian Literature, 1950s–1980s: A Bio-Bibliographical Guide*. New York: Russica, 1987. 510 pp. Index.
Very useful guide to dissident writers inside and outside the Soviet Union between 1957 and 1985.

865   TEFFI, NADEZHDA. *All about Love*. Translated by Darra Goldstein, introduction by Edward J. Brown. Ann Arbor, Mich.: Ardis, 1985. 201 pp.
Well-translated edition of this collection of stories by a leading émigré woman writer. Edward Brown's introduction is perfunctory. In general, this edition would have benefited from more introductory information about the author, her works, and this text in particular.

866   TOLSTAYA, TATYANA. *On the Golden Porch*. Translated by Antonina Bouis. New York: Alfred A. Knopf, 1989. 198 pp.
The following stories are included in this collection: "Loves Me, Loves Me Not," "Okkervil River," "Sweet Shura," "On the Golden Porch," "Hunting the Wooly Mammoth," "The Circle," "A Clean Sheet," "Fire and Dust," "Date with a Bird," "Sweet Dreams, Son," "Sonya," "The Fakir," and "Peters." Tolstaya is the most translated and, to many, the foremost contemporary woman prose writer in Russia.

867   ———. "Night." In *Glasnost: An Anthology of Literature Under Gorbachev*, edited by Helena Goscilo and Byron Lindsey, pp. 187–94. Ann Arbor, Mich.: Ardis, 1990.
Tatyana Tolstaya, the most well-known of contemporary Russian women writers, here repeats one of her major themes, the all-powerful mother and the infantilized male—in this case, eighty-year-old Mommy and her housebound son, Alexey Petrovich. Beautifully translated by Mary Fleming Zirin.

868 TSVETAEVA, MARINA. *The Demesne of the Swans*. Translated, with introduction, notes, and commentaries, by Robin Kemball. Ann Arbor, Mich.: Ardis, 1980. 211 pp.
"Definitive" version of the Russian text. Bilingual edition. Helpful introduction and extensive notes and commentaries.

869 VARLAMOVA, INNA. *A Counterfeit Life*. Translated by David A. Lowe. Ann Arbor, Mich.: Ardis, 1988. 189 pp.
Autobiographical novel about a Soviet woman's battle with breast cancer.

870 VASSILYEV, BORIS. *The Dawns are Quiet Here*. Translated by Hilda Perham and Natasha Johnstone. Edited by Robert Daglish. Moscow: Progress, 1975. 287 pp.
A gruff male sergeant commands a group of female soldiers, five of whom join him in a foray against a group of Germans parachuted behind the Soviet front-line in 1942. All the women die; only the sergeant survives.

871 VOZNESENSKAYA, JULIA. *The Women's Decameron*. Boston: Atlantic Monthly Press, 1986. 302 pp.
A fictionalized glimpse at Soviet women's lives, loosely based on Boccaccio's *Decameron*. Ten women, in a Leningrad maternity ward for the required ten-day isolation period after birth, while away the time swapping stories. Each day the women choose a different topic for their no-holds-barred tales. They begin with "First Love" and progress through "Seduced and Abandoned," "Sex in Farcical Situations," "Bitches," "Infidelity and Jealousy," "Rapists and Their Victims," "Money," and "Revenge" before ending with the more upbeat topics of "Noble Deeds and Happiness." The denizens of the *Decameron* maternity ward represent a cross-section of Russian society (except for one Jewish-Polish woman, no other nationalities are represented). Although frank about their sex lives, Voznesenskaya's characters generally express conventional values. All hold to the ideal of monogamous marriage, and deviance from the heterosexual norm is portrayed unflatteringly.

872 ———. *The Star Chernobyl*. Translated by Alan Myers. London: Quartet, 1987. 180 pp.
Realistic fiction about three sisters and Chernobyl's effects on them, weaving in actual documentary material about the Ukraine nuclear catastrophe.

873 WASILEWSKA, WANDA. *The Rainbow*. Translated by Edith Bone. Edited by Sonia Bleeker. New York: Simon & Schuster, 1944. 230 pp.
Stalin Prize-winning novel about a Ukrainian village occupied by the Germans. Role of women in the active and passive resistance to the Nazis emphasized. The author, a member of the Polish Socialist party, fled to the USSR in 1939 and became head of the Soviet-backed Union of Polish Patriots and a member of the Supreme Soviet.

874   ZALYGIN, SERGEI, comp. *The New Soviet Fiction: Sixteen Short Stories.*
      New York: Abbeville Press, 1989. 396 pp.
Contains translations of I. Grekova's "No Smiles," Lyudmila Petrushevskaya's
"Through the Fields," and Tatyana Tolstaya's "Fire and Dust."

875   ZERNOVA, RUTH. *Mute Phone Calls and Other Stories.* Selected and
      introduced by Helen Reeve. New Brunswick, N.J.: Rutgers University
      Press, 1991. 256 pp.
Nine stories from three decades of writing by this longtime activist and labor-
camp survivor, now living in Israel.

Author Index

171

Title Index

179

Subject Index

Abortion, 691, 698
Abramov, Fedor, 854
Activists. *See* Political activists; Women's movement
Actresses
Knipper, Olga, 385
Agriculture. *See* Farm workers
Akhmadulina, Bella, 490, 812
writings of, 811, 812, 818, 825, 844, 845
Akhmatova, Anna, 339, 353, 355, 465, 490, 664, 737, 745, 755, 761, 768
writings of, 434–43, 463, 481, 490, 811, 813, 845
Aksakov, Sergei Timofeevich, memoirs of, 88, 89
Alexander III, 320
Alexandra Feodorovna, letters to Nicholas II, 384
Aliger, Margarita, 825
Alliluyeva, Svetlana, 749
memoirs of, 731–32
Amalrik, Andrei, 733
Amalrik, Guzel, 733
Ancient period
Paleolithic images of women, 81
Andreyev, Olga Chernov, memoirs of, 734
Anna Ivanovna, 99, 103, 112
Anna Petrovna, 112
Anne. *See* Anna Ivanovna
Annenkova, Pauline Gueuble, 205
Armand, Inessa, 343, 399, 711, 736–37
Armonas, Barbara, memoirs of, 735
Artists, 400
Soviet, in exile, 538
Arts. *See also* Literature; Political art
Catherine the Great and, 165
medieval, portrayal of women in, 72
Asia, Central, 217
Soviet women in, 577, 619, 647, 683, 709
Authors. *See* Poets; Writers; names of individuals; and Author Index

Bakhtin, 383
Baku women, 614
Bakunin, Michael, 309
Balabanoff, Angelica, 271, 302, 310, 323, 345, 377, 736
writings of, 814
Baranskaya, Natalya, writings of, 815, 832, 842, 845, 847
Bariatinskaia, Anatole Marie, memoirs of, 324
Bashkirtseff, Marie, journals of, 325
Belorussia, women's monasteries in, 31
Belov, Vasily, story by, 847
Berberova, Nina
memoirs of, 738
novels of, 817
Bibliographies, general
on Russia and the Soviet Union, 5–9
of Slavic and East European studies, 1
on women in Russia and the Soviet Union, 10–12, 14–16
Birth rates, 672–73
and female employment, in USSR, 629
Bitt, Galina, 538
Bogdanovich, Ippolit, 143
Bogoraz, Larisa, 730
Boguslavskaya, Zoya, story by, 863
Boido, Eva, 330
Bolsheviks, 251, 323, 394, 395, 423, 511, 512
and feminism, 272, 544
Kollontai and, 793, 796, 809
and 1918 Family Code, 664
and peasant women, 656
Petrograd working women, 270
policies regarding women, 229, 611, 623, 636, 656, 700, 712
and sexual liberation, 295
women, study of, 389
and *Zhenotdel*, 667
Bonding, female, 222, 267
Botchkareva, Maria, 327, 328

193